Effective People Management in Africa

Edited by

Aloysius Newenham-Kahindi
University of Saskatchewan, Canada

Ken N. Kamoche
University of Nottingham, UK

Amon Chizema
Loughborough University, UK

and

Kamel Mellahi
Warwick University, UK

palgrave
macmillan

First published 2013 by
PALGRAVE MACMILLAN

Palgrave Macmillan in the UK is an imprint of Macmillan Publishers Limited, registered in England, company number 785998, of Houndmills, Basingstoke, Hampshire RG21 6XS.

Palgrave Macmillan in the US is a division of St Martin's Press LLC, 175 Fifth Avenue, New York, NY 10010.

Palgrave Macmillan is the global academic imprint of the above companies and has companies and representatives throughout the world.

Palgrave® and Macmillan® are registered trademarks in the United States, the United Kingdom, Europe and other countries.

ISBN 978–0–230–35491–3

This book is printed on paper suitable for recycling and made from fully managed and sustained forest sources. Logging, pulping and manufacturing processes are expected to conform to the environmental regulations of the country of origin.

A catalogue record for this book is available from the British Library.

A catalog record for this book is available from the Library of Congress.

100695748X

To my loving family, and late young brother Deonatus
Aloysius

To my loving family
Ken

To all the progressive people of Africa
Amon

To my mother, late father, wife and children: Ismail,
Hamza and Leyla
Kamel

Contents

List of Tables and Figures   ix

Preface   x

Acknowledgements   xiii

Notes on Contributors   xiv

List of Abbreviations   xviii

Introduction: New Directions in the Management of Human
Resources in Africa   1
Ken N. Kamoche, Amon Chizema, Kamel Mellahi and Aloysius
* Newenham-Kahindi*

Part I   People Management in African Countries

1   HRM Issues and Outcomes in Domestic Mergers and
    Acquisitions: A Study of the Nigerian Banking Sector   17
    Emanuel Gomes, Duncan Angwin, Emmanuel Peter and Kamel
    * Mellahi*

2   Factors Hindering the Adoption of HIV/AIDS Workplace
    Policies: Evidence from Private Sector Companies in Malawi   53
    Rhoda Bakuwa and Aminu Mamman

3   Privatization and Employment Relations in Africa: The Case
    of Mozambique   72
    Pauline Dibben and Geoffrey Wood

**Part II   Multinationals and People Management in
Africa**

4   Knowledge Appropriation and HRM: The MNC Experience
    in Tanzania   97
    Ken N. Kamoche and Aloysius Newenham-Kahindi

5 Human Resource Management in Southern African
   Multinational Firms: Considering an Afro-Asian Nexus   126
   Frank M. Horwitz

6 Managing Sustainable Development through
   Cross-Cultural Management: Implications for
   Multinational Enterprises in Developing Countries   152
   Aloysius Newenham-Kahindi

7 When Two African Cultures Collide: A Study of Interactions
   between Managers in a Strategic Alliance between Two
   African Organizations   180
   Emanuel Gomes, Marcel Cohen and Kamel Mellahi

8 Human Resource Strategies for Managing Back-Office
   Employees in Subsidiary Operations: The Case of Two
   Investment Multinational Banks in Tanzania   202
   Aloysius Newenham-Kahindi

Index   226

Tables and Figures

Tables

1.1 State of consolidated banks and acquisition group's
     capital base as on 31 December 2005   23
1.2 Interviewees   25
1.3 Integration approaches taken by merging Nigerian banks   32
1.4 Summary of HRM practices and merger outcome   41
2.1 Target populations of HIV/AIDS programmes   61
2.2 Descriptive statistics   63
2.3 Results of multiple regression analysis for factors
     hindering the adoption of formal HIV/AIDS workplace
     policy   64
3.1 Employment relations in the public and private sector in
     Mozambique   86
4.1 Citibank and Standard Bank   109
5.1 The six-factor Afro-Asian typology, following Jackson
     (2002)   131
5.2 South African MNC perceptions of key success factors in
     Chinese labour markets   138
5.3 Talent management factors in transitional economy
     contexts   141
5.4 Rankings 2010 (1–50)   142
6.1 Sample characteristics   162
6.2 Key features of institutionalization systems of selected
     South African MNEs' behaviour   165
8.1 Case study subjects and their banking activities in
     Tanzania   210
8.2 The two MNCs in Tanzania   212
8.3 Similarities in organizational systems   215
8.4 Differences in management practices   218

Figures

7.1 International market development of South African
     telecom companies in Africa   187
7.2 The new distribution of power   192

Preface

The compilation of this book began in 2010 following the First International Conference on HRM and the Management of Organizations in Africa held at the Nottingham Business School in the UK. The two-day conference, hosted by the Africa Research Group, was served by peer-reviewed and developmental papers, research workshops and roundtable discussions that addressed critical issues relating to people management, leadership and organizations in Africa. The conference was well attended by academic researchers, graduate students, keynote speakers and practitioners interested in management and leadership issues in Africa. Measured by the volume of papers presented and the quality of the delegate discussions, we feel confident in speaking of the conference as a success. Consequently, this could be taken to mean an increased interest in academic research on Africa. Such an interest could be a function of the recent changes on the continent. Indeed, Africa has recently witnessed significant transformation in the political, institutional and economic arenas. Moreover, it continues to attract an influx of foreign direct investment (FDI), mainly from emerging economies such as China, India and Brazil.

The challenge to manage people and organizations in the context of the changing economic and social landscape of Africa, and the strategic implications for organizations, is truly a fascinating topic for anyone interested in finding a sustainable and conducive way to do business in Africa. As we examine the subject in detail in this book, we observe that, for the last three decades, many FDIs, multinational companies (MNCs), multilateral agencies and consultants have developed concepts and practices to deal with management of people and organizations in Africa. However, such practices have often been transplanted from developed western markets or based on a few successful examples of experiences in emerging economies. The assumption has always been that what worked in these markets would work in Africa – the so-called one-size-fits-all approach. Of course, in the absence of local adaptation, this approach has not yielded results.

For many decades, the unheard indigenous business leaders and entrepreneurs in Africa, drawing from their ground-level experience, have intuitively felt that organizations and management of people in

Africa, in particular, need a different approach, one that must be deeply embedded in the African context. They have consistently advocated home-grown solutions, or have at least engaged in selective adaptation with foreign management practices, for a number of reasons. First, there has always been the sense that management that fails to embrace the dictates of the local context with deep-rooted knowledge and experience is bound to fail. Second, indigenous business leaders believe that local context knowledge and experience inspire and empower people to seek 'best practice' initiatives, which then work as a catalyst to generate local ideas and values crucial to effective people management, as well as organizational and national development-resilience. Such an approach also promotes self-reliance, confidence and social cohesion. This new strategic approach is both accepted and strongly reiterated by the editors and authors of this book as they seek to revisit and critique previous theories and practices, often derived from alternative economic systems. To a considerable extent, therefore, their contributions suggest approaches to managing people and organizations that reflect and satisfy the objectives and interests of multiple stakeholders in Africa (Mellahi and Collings, 2010).

Effective People Management in Africa aims at highlighting new realities, challenges and opportunities facing organizations and businesses in managing people in contemporary Africa. In particular, it seeks to propose alternative sustainable strategies or models that address critical realities ranging from managing knowledge and technology appropriation in organizations, navigating through institutional voids, the role of micro-financing in entrepreneurships, dealing with both formal and informal types of organizing, the role of informal and indigenous embedded knowledge and mode of production, to social problems of poverty and ecology.

Many of the chapters have previously appeared in the 2011 and 2012 special issues on HRM and Management of Organizations in Africa in the *Journal of World Business* and the *International Journal of Human Resource Management*, respectively. As emphasized earlier, a common theme is the realization that management of people and organizations in Africa should be informed and driven by locally identifiable practices. The book exemplifies these realities and offers insights and some practical solutions for dealing with issues of HRM.

We hope that the book serves as an invaluable source of knowledge on managing people and organizations in Africa. It is also our hope that it will promote an exciting and ongoing intellectual adventure, leading to further unearthing of the root causes of problems and solutions facing organizations and people management in Africa. Indeed, like other emerging markets in Asia and South America, Africa is currently of great continued interest to many scholars, MNC investors and multilateral organizations that seek to engage organizations and people to promote sustainable development.

While several themes are covered in the book, it is by no means exhaustive. There is still scope for exploring a multitude of issues that continue to be a challenge in managing people and organizations. For example, we still do not know much about comparative employment practices among African countries. Moreover, issues of industrial relations and corporate governance in the face of increasing foreign direct investment from Asia are – while important – understudied. Such issues allude to the salience of both formal and informal institutions in managing people in Africa.

Acknowledgements

We acknowledge Taylor & Francis (www.tandfonline.com) for allowing us to use the following articles originally published in the *International Journal of Human Resource Management* Special Issue on Management of HR in Africa (Volume 23 (14), 2012):

'Introduction: New Directions in the Management of Human Resources in Africa'

'Knowledge Appropriation and HRM: The MNC Experience in Tanzania'

'HRM Issues and Outcomes in Domestic Mergers and Acquisitions: A Study of the Nigerian Banking Sector'

'Factors Hindering the Adoption of HIV/AIDS Workplace Policies: Evidence from Private Sector Companies in Malawi'

'Evolving Human Resource Management in Southern African Multinational Firms: Towards an Afro-Asian Nexus'
In addition, we acknowledge Elsevier (www.journals.elsevier.com/journal-of-world-business/) for allowing us to republish two articles from the *Journal of World Business* Special Issue on Management of HR in Africa (Volume 46 (1), 2011):

'When Two African Cultures Collide: A Study of Interactions between Managers in a Strategic Alliance between Two African Organizations'. Licence number: 2891470572470

'Human Resource Strategies for Managing Back-office Employees in Subsidiary Operations: The Case of Two Investment Multinational Banks in Tanzania'. Licence number: 28914707334061

Contributors

Duncan Angwin is Professor of Strategy, Oxford Brookes University, UK. He researches strategic practice in Mergers and Acquisitions (M&A) and currently holds a major research award to study M&A communications practice at Said Business School, Oxford University. He sits on the Advisory Board of the M&A research centre, Cass Business School, London, and on the academic council of a Grand Ecole in Paris, France. He has published numerous journal articles; his books include, most recently, *Practicing Strategy* (2013).

Rhoda Bakuwa is Lecturer in General Management/Human Resource Management at the Malawi Polytechnic, a constituent college of the University of Malawi, Malawi. She holds a PhD in development policy and management obtained from the University of Manchester, UK. Her research interests focus on human resource management (HRM), training and development, HIV and AIDS in the workplace, and general organization management. Her articles have appeared in the *Journal of General Management, Journal of Social Aspects (SAHARA), International Journal of Human Resource Management* and *International Journal of the Academy of Organizational Behavior Management.*

Amon Chizema is Professor of International Business and Strategy at Loughborough University, UK. He holds a PhD from Loughborough University. His research interests lie in international corporate governance, boards of directors and executive compensation. His research has appeared in the *Journal of Management Studies, Journal of World Business, Corporate Governance: An International Review* and *International Business Review.*

Marcel Cohen is Integrity Manager of Millicom International Cellular in the DRC. He is an international specialist in ethics, integrity and good governance, and the implementation of codes of ethics. He has 25 years' experience in business management, particularly in African Francophone countries.

Pauline Dibben is Reader in Employment Relations at the University of Sheffield and has published widely on employment relations in emerging economies, with a particular focus on southern Africa. Articles have appeared in *Work, Employment & Society, Industrial Relations, Journal of World Business, Human Resource Management Journal* and *Industrial Relations Journal*. She is the co-author of *Employment Relations: A Critical and International Approach* and co-editor of *Modernising Work in Public Services* and *Contesting Public Sector Reforms*.

Emanuel Gomes is Lecturer in Strategy and International Business at the University of Sheffield, UK. His research interest is in the areas of M&A, strategic alliances and internationalization of the firm, particularly in the African context. He is the author of three books on M&A and strategic alliances and of several refereed articles. He is also the leading author of the Strategic Planning Software (www.planning-strategy.com), and serves as a reviewer to various international refereed journals.

Frank M. Horwitz is Director and Professor at Cranfield School of Management, Cranfield University, UK, since April 2009. He has lived and worked on four continents. He is a member of the British Academy of Management and the Association of Business Schools, is on the Strategy Council of the Sloan Centre on Aging & Work in Boston, USA, and is a Companion of the Chartered Management Institute and member of the Institute of Directors. He was previously Director of the Graduate School of Business, University of Cape Town, South Africa. He specializes in international human resources management, emerging market MNCs and employment relations. He has published numerous journal articles and book chapters and is the author of four books.

Ken N. Kamoche is Professor of HRM and Organization Studies at Nottingham University Business School, UK. He previously taught at Birmingham University, City University of Hong Kong and Nottingham Trent. His research interests include international HRM, Africa–China business relations, organizational improvisation and knowledge appropriation, with articles published in the *Journal of Management Studies, Organization Studies, Human Relations, Work, Employment and Society, British Journal of Management, Journal of World Business* and *International Journal of Human Resource Management*.

Aminu Mamman is currently Reader at the Institute for Development Policy and Management, University of Manchester, UK. He gained a master's and PhD from Cardiff Business School, UK. Research interests include managerial cognition, particularly with reference to globalization; organizational citizenship behaviour within the context of diversity; HRM in developing countries; comparative and international management; and diffusion and modification of management innovation. Articles have appeared in *Organization Studies, British Journal of Management* and *International Journal of Human Resource Management.*

Kamel Mellahi is Professor of Strategic Management and is Head of Group for Marketing and Strategic Management at Warwick Business School. His research focuses on organizational failure and renewal; business ethics and sustainability; and international business strategy, with particular emphasis on emerging economies and Middle East and North Africa region. He is the author of three books. Numerous papers have appeared in *Strategic Management Journal, Journal of International Business Studies* and *Journal of Management Studies.*

Aloysius Newenham-Kahindi is Associate Professor of Organizational Strategy and International Management, and a Hanlon Scholar for International Business at the Edwards Business School, University of Saskatchewan, Canada. His research focuses on organizational theory and strategy, sustainable development, comparative management within the context of international business and on the role of corporate languages and knowledge appropriation within multinational enterprises in subsidiaries' context. Articles have appeared in the *Harvard Business Publications, International Journal of Business Studies, Journal of World Business, Journal of Business Ethics, Global Strategy Journal* and the *International Journal of Human Resource Management.*

Emmanuel Peter is Head of Operations at FinBank, Abuja-Nigeria. He is experienced in M&A process management and was involved in two major Nigerian bank mergers in 2005 and 2010. His research has been published in the *International Journal of Human Resource Management.*

Geoffrey Wood is Professor of International Business at Warwick University, UK. He is also Honorary Professor at the University of Witwatersrand, Visiting Professor at Nelson Mandela University; South

Africa; and Adjunct Professor of Griffith University, Australia. He has published widely on the relationship between institutional context and work and employment relations outcomes. Recent co-edited and co-authored books include *Capitalist Diversity and Diversity within Capitalism* and *Handbook on Institutions and International Business*.

Abbreviations

ART	Antiretroviral therapy
BEE	Black economic empowerment
BRICS	Brazil, Russia, India, China and South Africa
CBN	Central Bank of Nigeria
CIVET	Colombia, Indonesia, Vietnam, Egypt, Turkey
CSR	Corporate social responsibility
CWN	Congolese Wireless Networks
DRC	Democratic Republic of Congo
EIU	Economist Intelligence Unit
ETB	Equatorial Trust Bank
FCMB	First City Monument Bank
FCS	Foundation Civil Society
FDI	Foreign direct investment
FSAs	Firm-specific advantages
GAAP	Generally Accepted Accounting Principles
GDP	Gross domestic product
HIV/AIDS	Human immunodeficiency virus/Acquired immunodeficiency syndrome
HR	Human resources
HRM	Human resource management
IBTC	Investment Bank Trust and Company
ICS	Industrial court system
ICT	Information and communication(s) technology
IFRS	International financial reporting standards
IHRM	International human resource management
ILO	International Labour Office
IMF	International Monetary Fund
ISA	International standards on auditing
LSE	London Stock Exchange
MBCA	Malawi Business Coalition against AIDS
MCCCI	Malawi Confederation of Chambers of Commerce and Industry
M&A	Mergers and acquisitions
MNC	Multinational company/corporation
MNE	Multinational enterprise

MTN	Mobile telephone network
NAC	National AIDS Commission
NEPAD	New Partnership for Africa's Development
NGO	Non-governmental organization
NYSE	New York Stock Exchange
OHS	Occupational health and safety
PHB	Platinum-Habib Bank
SADC	Southern African development community
SAPs	Structural adjustment programmes
SMEs	Small and medium enterprises
SOEs	State owned enterprises
ST	Standard trust
STI	Sexually transmitted infection
TQM	Total quality management
UBA	United Bank for Africa
UN	United Nations
UNAIDS	United Nations HIV/AIDS programme
UNDP	United Nations development programme
USAID	United States Agency for International Development
VCT	Voluntary counselling and testing
WHO	World Health Organization
WTO	World Trade Organization

Introduction: New Directions in the Management of Human Resources in Africa

Ken N. Kamoche, Amon Chizema, Kamel Mellahi and Aloysius Newenham-Kahindi

Introduction

The first named author edited a special issue on human resource management (HRM) in Africa in the *International Journal of Human Resource Management* a decade ago (Kamoche, 2002). At that time, it was fairly common to begin journal articles and doctoral literature reviews affirming that the literature on HRM and management in general in Africa was 'scarce/scanty/sketchy', and for authors to proceed as if they were in typically uncharted domain. We believe this affirmation to be largely untenable today. In proportion, of course, the amount of knowledge on the African management and organizational context, in high-impact publications, pales when compared with the West and Asia. The situation has changed considerably in the last decade or so, and the number of publications focused on African management, organizational and entrepreneurial issues grows every year. The relevant literature includes several books as well as articles in high-impact journals that characterize the diversity of HRM theory and practice, and how culture might be understood in highly complex societies (e.g. Jackson, 2004; Kamoche et al., 2004).

Our purpose in this edited volume is, therefore, not merely to add to the voices that call for more research *per se*, but to accomplish three major purposes. First, we attempted to determine the course that the literature on HRM in Africa has taken in the last decade. The research emphasis has shifted; while researchers previously lamented the unsuitability of western management practices, recent research indicates that various forms of hybridization, determined by both universal convergence factors (e.g. globalization and technology) and locally divergent factors (e.g. nepotism, bribery and corruption) (Azolukwam and Perkins, 2009) have appeared.

Second, we wanted to discover the new themes and debates researchers are tackling currently, and to provide these initiatives with a chance to participate in the mainstream international HRM debate. Researchers are starting to acknowledge that the predominance of research on multinational firms and large locally owned firms represents only a partial picture of the African organizational context. Although the emphasis is still on western multinationals in Africa, there is now a realization of the need to explore Asia–Africa relations. Some examples are Jackson et al.'s (2008) study of indigenous practices in Kenyan small and medium enterprises (SMEs), considering how managers adopt different cultural influences, instead of purely western approaches; and Horwitz et al.'s (2006) analysis of strategies for managing knowledge workers in Singapore and South Africa. Leadership is also a rising research paradigm, which has not been given much attention in the past. In a recent editorial to a special issue, Walumbwa et al. (2011) rightly point out the need to focus on the nature of leadership in the management of human resources, as well as the need to begin asking questions about the kind of leadership that is needed to drive African economies and organizations.

Third, we wanted to identify the topics that are expected to shape debate in the next decade and beyond. As we search for ways to develop more suitable theoretical lenses for understanding the management of people in Africa, Nkomo (2011) offers a post-colonial and anti-colonial analysis of 'African' management and leadership, an approach that has significant consequences for the way HRM and organization studies might be 'rewritten'.

In the 1990s, the Asian region became known as a major driving force of the world's economy, an occurrence that saw a concomitant attraction in academic research, with specific attention to China at the turn of the millennium (see the *IJHRM* special issue edited by Warner, 2000). China had lately opened its economy, joined the World Trade Organization (WTO) and established itself as the world's factory. What impact did that have on Africa, which still depended heavily on the largess of western governments and organizations like the International Monetary Fund (IMF) and World Bank? It is reasonable to say that, while Africa's influence on the world's economy remains modest in relative terms, the conception of Africa as a needy receiver of foreign aid has gradually given way to a more optimistic one of an attractive investment option. Horwitz et al. (2002) asked for more effective engagement between Africa and Asia, specifically regarding the dissem-ination of high-performance work practices, based on the notion of 'crossvergence'. Such an approach would accept that ideas and knowl-edge do not only flow in a single direction, challenging the presumed dominance of regions that have traditionally treated Africa as a recip-ient for foreign aid, technology, knowledge, expatriates and financial resources.

Africa has seen a substantial amount of investment by Indian, Malaysian and Singaporean organizations in the last decade, but the most significant development by far has been the unprecedented engagement with China. Chinese investments in Africa have increased from US$12 billion in 2002 to US$150 billion in 2010 and are pre-dicted to double to $350 billion by 2015 (depending on what reports one reads), though this still accounts for only a fraction of China's global trade. Much has been made of the lopsided nature of this engage-ment (Foster et al., 2008; Kamoche, 2011), and, without a doubt, there is a lot that both African and Chinese policy makers can do to level the playing field. African economies will need to encourage responsi-ble business and employment practices that protect workers' rights and safeguard jobs (Opondo, 2009), and place themselves as equally strong partners when dealing with players such as India and China (Broadman, 2007). This context produces exciting research possibilities on the broad range of topics pertaining to these relations, from the business strat-egy and policy levels to employment practices and labour relations. It also creates the chance to make an important contribution to the mainstream debate on foreign direct investments (FDIs), the role of multinational firms within the context of Africa, by investigating the extent to which African economies have formed and *can* form a partner-ship of true crossvergence with Asia, while restructuring their business and investment relations with the conventional partners in the West.

Researchers continually lament the challenges of doing business in Africa, pointing to problems that continue to pose a challenge to economic rejuvenation, employment creation, poverty reduction and improvements in living standards, such as deficient infrastructure, cor-ruption, ethnic chauvinism and so forth. However, it is clear that Africa is now creating enviable success stories across a wide range of fields. Examples include Safaricom in Kenya, which transformed mobile tele-phony, the Azalai hotel chain based in Mali, the Dangote conglomerate based in Nigeria, South African Airways and plenty of others. Some of these successes have been divulged widely in the media, including magazines such as *The Economist*. However, the jury is still out on why there has not been a corresponding academic interest in the form of exemplary case studies and journal articles in order that the important 'best practices' can be spread, taught and discussed, and brought into the mainstream as learning and research opportunities. This forum will hopefully stimulate further discussion on how problem-solving techniques or successful HR practices that have worked in one circumstance or specific region might be disseminated and adjusted to another, and how effective management and leadership styles developed in one sector might serve as a bellwether for sectors or regions riven with conflict and harmful labour relations.

Below we consider four themes that we expect will play a significant role in shaping the research agenda in Africa in the following years: corporate governance in an era increasingly defined by calls for greater transparency, the debate surrounding the role of FDI as African economies continue to rethink the viability of the foreign-aid model, the need for sustainable management in a dynamic context and the language as a critical tool to manage stakeholders' relationships.

Corporate governance and HRM practices in Africa

An under-researched subject, in the African background, is the issue of how multinational firms deal with corporate governance and corporate social responsibility in their HR strategies and practices (Amaeshi et al., 2006). Previous studies on corporate governance and corporate social responsibility, on the USA, Europe and lately Asia (Chizema and Shinozawa, 2012), have shown an evident distinction between the shareholder-oriented system of governance, which focuses on the supremacy of the shareholder, and stakeholder-oriented systems of governance, which include the interests of a wider constituency, including employees (Buck and Shahrim, 2005). Therefore, the relationship of different stakeholders, or the lack of it, has been well studied almost everywhere but Africa. In the context of the advocated homegrown management philosophies like *ubuntu*, an interesting question to consider is: what should be the shape of corporate governance in Africa? The governance of corporations is a derivative of national or political governance, since firms are guided by national institutions, including corporate law and governmental regulations (North, 1991). The notion of complementarity is central to this part of the story, referring to situations in which the functionality of an institutional form is conditioned by other institutions (Hopner, 2005). A weakness in one part of the system is likely to cause problems in the rest of the unit.

Particularly in the context of Africa, with weaker regulatory environments, multinational corporations may fail to institute and implement governance mechanisms that promote the interests of stakeholders, including employees.

With the arrival of a new set of investors from Asia (China, India, etc.), there is a potential shift in the corporate governance and management template, from an Africa–Europe model, informed by historical ties relating to the colonial era, to an Africa–Asia relationship, a manifestation of globalization. Therefore, we suggest that now is the time to seriously investigate the policies and mechanisms that influence the welfare of workers in Africa. However, with such multiple players involved, deriving from diverse institutional environments and equipped with a variety of norms that possibly diverge from their host environments, it is imperative that African countries (and, indeed, governments) improve their institutions. It is also important, therefore, that research in these areas takes an added dimension to inform policy. It is no coincidence that countries with organized industrial relations tend to have organized corporate governance as well (Hopner, 2005). Thus, to completely understand HR issues in Africa, it is crucial to examine governance at both the firm and national levels, at the same time.

Once we accept the idea and relevance of complementarity, we may find that it could be equivocal to search for 'one best way' of organizing industrial relations and corporate governance. Considering Africa as a unit of homogeneous components for purposes of research is also misguided, given the diversity of cultures, institutional environments and historical trajectories. In fact, previous studies have indicated that firms in a given national context adopt governance practices that suit their needs (Aguilera and Jackson, 2003) and that comply with local institutions. Therefore, an approach that is likely to provide practical and relevant results involves basing future studies on individual African countries with subsequent cross-country comparisons both within and outside Africa.

Multinationals, FDI and HRM in Africa

FDI plays an important role in encouraging new management systems and practices in host countries (Blomstrom and Kokko, 1988). Overall, FDI inflows into African countries are on the increase, but the large majority of these are resource-seeking investment going into natural resources exploitation (Anyanwu, 2006). Although the absence of systematic empirical research makes it very difficult to access the actual impact FDI has had on HRM practices in Africa, one could observe three opposite arguments regarding this matter. On the one hand, there are those who claim that multinational companies' (MNCs') managerial practices are sufficiently superior to those of local firms, and that FDI generates employment, brings much-needed capital, and raises skills of local African employees, resulting in the transfer of knowledge and modern management systems and practices (Dupasquier and Osakwe, 2006). The spillover of technical and managerial knowledge and skills to local firms is one of the most important benefits of FDI for African countries (Asiedu, 2004), according to the supporters of this argument. However, there are some major limitations to this line of research: to date there is no comprehensive evidence on the magnitude and exact nature of these spillovers, and, for the most part, this line of research has neglected local management practices and viewed local firms as passive recipients of western knowledge spillovers.

On the other hand, there is a body of research pointing to systematic differences between the ways in which western MNCs manage their human resources and African managerial values and practices (cf. Jackson, 2004). This line of argument undermines the importance of learning from western MNCs, and it describes western management practices as inconsistent with, and therefore inappropriate in, the African context. The discussion here is not centred around organizational performance but about the worry that western management practices may *substitute* local ones and erode long-cherished local norms and values. Asiedu (2004) noted that MNCs operating in Africa face the fraught challenge of lack of talent, effective work practices, and institutional and cultural differences. The main limitation of this line of research is its inability to express the precise institutional and/or cultural features that underlie the incompatibilities and inappropriateness of western practices.

Several scholars argue for a middle way; for MNCs to be effective in Africa, they must make adjustments to local practices and norms while seeking to implement standard global best practices, designing appropriate strategies of employment management by not just implementing well-established HRM practices but also shaping these practices to the specific context (Verburg, 1996). We argue that, instead of conducting more research for either side of the above convergence–divergence debate, scholars should reorient their research questions and focus on how MNCs balance the dual pressures of developing globally integrated management policies and practices while trying to adapt and respond to local cultural and institutional pressures. Hence, the notion of crossvergence discussed above.

MNCs operating in Africa have to figure out how to develop, recruit and retain talent, while facing the challenge of scarcity of skilled individuals. We propose that one way of developing local talents by MNCs is by drawing on their repository of knowledge embedded in their global network of subsidiaries (Mellahi and Collings, 2010). Gammelgaard et al. (2004, p. 195) noted that the success of MNCs 'is considered to be dependent on the ease and speed with which useful knowledge is spread throughout the organization'. One of the key means of acquiring and applying knowledge is learning from talented expatriates. The literature has not investigated how knowledge spillover happens in affiliates of MNCs in Africa, due to the fact that most of the prior work on knowledge spillover in Africa has focused on its importance and relevance to the African context. To address this issue, scholars need to identify and examine the elements that stifle or enhance knowledge transfer and sharing among expatriates and local African employees, and empirically verify/specify the conditions under which FDI can lead to knowledge spillovers in an African context. To do so, scholars need to consider the ability and willingness of local African employees to acquire and use knowledge and the willingness of expatriates to share knowledge with local workers. Similarly, there is a need for expatriates to appreciate not only how they can transfer knowledge, but also how they and their organizations can learn from the African experience and context. In this regard, Kamoche and Harvey (2006) have offered institutional theory as a conceptual lens to improve the process of knowledge diffusion whereby MNCs renounce the assumption that knowledge transfer to Africa is a one-way traffic. Also, research that compares the importance and impact of knowledge spillover from western, Asian and African MNCs is highly recommended.

Sustainable management practices within an African context

Some observers have proposed that African employees often behave as though they inhabit two parallel worlds – the world of work, built as a foreign industrial culture, and a broader African society, in which the worker carries on with his normal life (Anakwe, 2002). In this context, the African worker feels as though he is stepping out of his culture when he goes to work, and stepping back into it after work (Jackson, 2004). Though this supposed duality is difficult to sustain empirically, particularly among a highly urbanized workforce, it does, however, clarify the complexities of managing organizations effectively, and the need to go beyond improving employees' welfare to coping with critical relational issues that are primary to employees' everyday lives.

Recent research on the management of organizations in Africa has called attention to the need for substantial measures when handling employee issues (where employees are seen as internal stakeholders) and organizations. Still, there has been relatively little awareness of the broader context of local communities, those community stakeholders who are directly or indirectly affected by business activities in their environments (Kapelus, 2002; Jackson, 2004), and how they might influence the development of sustainable and effective management of organizations and employees within MNCs. It is important to contextualize, within the African institutional configuration, the term 'effective' management of HRM and organization, where human relations and leadership values are heavily influential on employees' and stakeholders' behaviour with regard to organizational success. The idea of 'human relations' within an African context indicates a thought system in which concepts and entities enjoy no final definition, but are constantly redefined in their context (Mbigi, 1997). It also designates a mode of logic or a way of ordering and making sense of what its people perceive to be appropriate and sustainable. 'Leadership' is thus understood as a socially constructed arrangement of handling and resolving any debate or conflict that may arise within a group or a society (Mbigi, 1997). It also implies that the leadership of knowledgeable, inspiring, responsible and caring leaders is used to encourage groups, communities or societies to collectively resolve problems that involve environmental, organizational, business or community subjects (Walumbwa et al., 2011). Since the term itself is established in dignity and respect, any form of discussion must be honoured and respected by all. We see the idea of 'making sense' as referring to the socially established organizational structures of meaning generated by organizations along with internal and external stakeholders to influence positive behaviour and attention in organizations and communities (Khayesi and George, 2011).

The nature of social organizations in Africa serves to highlight a culture of stakeholder orientation, humanistic values, harmonious teamwork and acceptance of responsibilities in managing business relations (Jackson, 2004; Newenham-Kahindi, 2011). However, to develop organizations and people (including employees) sustainably in an African context, the challenge has now resulted in pressure for MNCs to design new organizational strategies and capabilities that *'make sense'* within local contexts, which in turn creates an *inclusive* engagement platform for handling the inherent internal (e.g. organizational and HR practices) and external (e.g. local community stakeholders) issues.

To minimize the challenges of managing people and stakeholder issues in Africa, we propose that MNCs and other business organizations have to go beyond the transactional (e.g. where MNCs tend to control all forms of engagement with employees and other stakeholders) and transitional business behaviour (e.g. limited forms of cooperation with employees and other stakeholders) to a transformational approach (developing capability in dealing with the complexities of managing people, stakeholders and organization). Additionally, we suggest that MNCs must tackle finding out what is absent in the environment and within MNCs (both internally and externally) before designing their general business strategies. More importantly, they must utilize cross-relationship approaches that involve employees, community stakeholders, community social groups (e.g. public/private development groups) and government institutions, in order to obtain broader social licence and legitimacy to effectively operate in communities, and thus contribute to a positive organizational competitive advantage and better relationships with all relevant stakeholders, including employees (Newenham-Kahindi, 2011).

Language as a critical tool to manage (people) stakeholder relationships

Africa is the home of over 3,000 different ethnic languages broadly divided into six language families. Multilinguals are particularly common in Africa, where most children naturally grow up with more than two mother tongues, as several languages are spoken in their family or immediate neighbourhood. They are also part of societal and cultural identities and heritage. Thus, language could be used in two ways to develop dialogues leading to collaboration between MNCs and people (stakeholders): one, as a vehicle to understand and discover the counterparty's embedded identity, and, two, as a catalyst employed to overcome the challenges faced by the affected people (stakeholders) as a result of MNCs' business activities. These dialogues, so critical in the MNCs–stakeholder relationship-building process, embed meanings that are critical in promoting effective people management and organizations.

Though the topic of language in intercultural communication has not been discussed extensively in the mainstream management literature, we suggest that language is critical to effectively managing people and organizations in Africa. It not only impacts stakeholder relationship-building but also serves as a potential source of competitive advantage to overcome the liability of foreignness, risk and conflict resolution strategies, and enables actors to fully understand local tenets of leadership and management innovations, ability to build trust and managerial buy-in.

Structure of the book

The book is structured in two parts. The first part, People Management in African Countries, starts with a chapter by Gomes et al. The authors explore the issues of HRM practices throughout the pre- and post-merger and acquisition (M&A) process in recent domestic African M&A, with reference to Nigeria. The chapter shows that nearly all previous research on M&A has only focused on post-M&A. The authors argue that specific HRM issues, such as cultural due diligence, pre-merger communication, management and employee due diligence, and other important people management issues may influence subsequent post-acquisition management of people, and affect the overall outcome. The practical implications both pre- and post-M&A are that HRM matters throughout the merger process. Thus, the chapter highlights the need for acquirers to engage in rich, open and timely communications in order to achieve effective integration.

Chapter 2 deals with organizational response to HIV/AIDS in the workplace, the most crucial area for HRM in Africa. Bakuwa and Mamman observe that African firms have not, by and large, developed comprehensive strategies. Using a sample of private companies in Malawi, they explore managerial perspectives on the barriers to adopting a formal HIV/AIDS workplace strategy, and identify the difficulties associated with developing an HIV/AIDS strategy in an African context. The chapter reports that internal/organizational factors have a stronger impact on the adoption, or not, of formal HIV/AIDS strategy than external factors. This chapter contributes to this important debate and enhances our understanding of the role of Human Resources (HR) practitioners in Africa.

In Chapter 3 Dibben and Wood explore the impact of privatization on employment levels and the nature of employment relations in the public sector through exploratory in-depth research in Mozambique. The authors highlight the important role of the public sector in economic development, which is often discounted, and that the state has a vital role to play both in ensuring decent work and in addressing historical inequities.

The second part of the book addresses multinationals and people management in Africa. In Chapter 4, Kamoche and Newenham-Kahindi draw on Foucault's social theory to analyse the processes of knowledge appropriation through the management of human resources and culture in MNCs in Tanzania, comparing the approaches of two global banks, Citibank, an American bank, and Standard Bank, a South African bank. They examine how the two banks, deriving from diverse national environments, align their HR practices and policies with their conception of corporate culture in a manner that strengthens their ability to secure or appropriate knowledge and achieve the maximum contribution from human resources. The study finds that both banks developed their organizational and HRM practices and legitimized them through ethnocentric values. In the context of Africa, this study improves our understanding of the way MNCs appropriate knowledge and how such knowledge is rationalized at the level of the organization.

Africa is a significant component of the broader context of emerging economies, and it is in this regard that Chapter 5 is framed. Drawing on recent discussions of HR challenges for emerging market MNCs (and providing case examples from southern African countries), Horwitz claims that research on southern African HRM should adopt an integrative typology encompassing western instrumentalism, African humanism and east Asian attributes. Thus, while cultural and institutional components are pertinent in the study of southern African MNCs, there is a need to broaden the analysis away from the divergence–convergence between different countries and include within-countries variables. The author mentions that, due to the diversity in the workplace within southern African countries, MNCs face a 'double institutional challenge' – they need to tackle issues within host countries as well as issues between host and home countries.

In Chapter 6, Newenham-Kahindi examines the way multinational enterprises (MNEs) use internal stakeholders, employees, as intermediaries to influence local community stakeholder attitudes and behaviours during the implementation of sustainable development initiatives in a developing nation in East Africa. The author presents a case study of MNEs from an emerging market and a developed nation in the extractive mining sector with development ongoing in several poorer communities located in Lake Victoria Zone in Tanzania. This chapter illustrates how MNEs use various management strategies with stakeholders to address social issues of unemployment, poverty and ecology.

In Chapter 7, Gomes et al. examine the relations between managers in a strategic alliance between a South African MNC and a Congolese firm. The case study demonstrates the pitfalls of rushing to formalize a strategic alliance before acquiring sufficient knowledge of each partner's capabilities and culture. The chapter raises important questions about the little-explored problem of intra-African cultural conflict, and the effect of interactional injustices and perceived procedural injustices on working relations, resulting in mistrust and detachment between the two groupings. In the final chapter, Newenham-Kahindi compares the human resource practices of two multinational banks in Tanzania. The study sets out to examine how the organizational systems in the two banks, one American, the other South African, interact with and influence the host country's competitive and cultural environment and how these processes impact the human resource strategies. This chapter generates important insights into how MNC organizational systems interact with the host country contextual environment to influence the implementation of HR practices.

Taken together, these contributions offer a multifaceted perspective on the nature and challenges of managing people and organizations in an African continent that has undergone significant change from a time when structural adjustment programmes were all the rage. Organizations in Africa face multiple challenges, and, while topics like HR innovation, leadership, knowledge sharing, talent management, governance, sustainability and so forth are attracting attention, clearly, much work remains to be done. This book celebrates the achievements that scholars have made so far in enhancing our understanding of the nature of HR in Africa. It also accepts that researchers still have some way to go if we are to gain a more comprehensive picture of the advances that practitioners and entrepreneurs have made on the ground in designing structures and practices that strive to meet the needs of an increasingly demanding workforce. This forum, we believe, paves the way for further research that not only contributes to theory, but also demonstrates how new theory might be informed by developments in the practice of management in Africa.

References

Aguilera, R. and G. Jackson (2003) 'The Cross-national Diversity of Corporate Governance: Dimensions and Determinants', *Academy of Management Review*, 28 (3), 447–465.

Amaeshi, M. K., A. B. C. Adi, C. Ogbechie, and O. O. Amao (2006) 'Corporate Social Responsibility in Nigeria: Western Mimicry or Indigenous Influences?' *Journal of Corporate Citizenship*, 24, 83–99.

Anakwe, U. P. (2002) 'Human Resource Management Practices in Nigeria: Challenges and Insights', *International Journal of Human Resource Management*, 13 (7), 1042–1059.

Anyanwu, J. C. (2006) 'Promoting of Investment in Africa', *African Development Review*, 18 (1), 42–71.

Asiedu, E. (2004) 'The Determinants of Employment of Affiliates of US Multinational Enterprises in Africa', *Development Policy Review*, 22 (4), 371–379.

Azolukwam, V. A. and S. J. Perkins (2009) 'Managerial Perspectives on HRM in Nigeria: Evolving Hybridization?' *Cross Cultural Management: An International Journal*, 16 (1), 62–82.

Blomstrom, M. and A. Kokko (1988) 'Multinational Corporations and Spill Overs', *Journal of Economic Surveys*, 12 (3), 247–277.

Broadman, H. (2007) *Africa's Silk Road: China and India's New Economic Frontier* (Washington, DC: The World Bank).

Buck, T. and A. Shahrim (2005) 'The Translation of Corporate Governance Changes across National Cultures: The Case of Germany', *Journal of International Business Studies*, 36, 42–61.

Chizema, A. and Y. Shinozawa (2012) 'The "Company with Committees": Change or Continuity in Japanese Corporate Governance', *Journal of Management Studies*, 49 (1), 77–101.

Dupasquier, C. and P. N. Osakwe (2006) 'Foreign Direct Investment in Africa: Performance, Challenges, and Responsibilities', *Journal of Asian Economics*, 17 (2), 241–260.

Foster, V., W. Butterfield, C. Chen, and N. Pushak (2008) *Building Bridges: China's Growing Role as Infrastructure Financier for Sub-Saharan Africa* (Washington, DC: The World Bank).

Gammelgaard, J., U. Holm, and T. Pedersen (2004) 'The Dilemmas of MNC Subsidiary Knowledge Transfer', in V. Mahnke and T. Pedersen (eds) *Knowledge Flows, Governance and the Multinational Enterprise* (New York: Palgrave Macmillan), 195–210.

Hopner, M. (2005) 'What Connects Industrial Relations and Corporate Governance? Explaining Institutional Complementarity', *Socio-Economic Review*, 3 (2), 331–358.

Horwitz, F. M., C. T. Heng, H. A. Qiiazi, C. Nonkwelo, D. Roditi, and P. van Eck (2006) 'Human Resource Strategies for Managing Knowledge Workers: An Afro-Asian Comparative Analysis', *International Journal of Human Resource Management*, 17 (5), 775–811.

Horwitz, F. M., K. Kamoche, and I. K. H. Chew (2002) 'Looking East: Diffusing High Performance Work Practices in the Southern Afro-Asian Context.' *International Journal of Human Resource Management*, 13 (7), 1019–1041.

Jackson, T. (2004) *Management and Change in Africa: A Cross-Cultural Perspective* (London: Routledge).

Jackson, T., K. Amaeshi, and S. Yavuz (2008) 'Untangling African Indigenous Management: Multiple Influences on the Success of SMEs in Kenya', *Journal of World Business*, 43, 400–416.

Kamoche, K. (2002) 'Introduction: Human Resource Management in Africa', *International Journal of Human Resource Management*, 13, 993–997.

Kamoche, K. (2011) 'Contemporary Developments in the Management of Human Resources in Africa', *Journal of World Business*, 46 (1), 1–4.

Kamoche, K. and M. Harvey (2006) 'Knowledge Diffusion in the African Context: An Institutional Theory Perspective', *Thunderbird International Business Review*, 48, 157–181.

Kamoche, K., Y. A. Debra, F. M. Horwitz, and G. N. Muuka (eds) (2004) *Managing Human Resources in Africa* (London: Routledge).

Kapelus, P. (2002) 'Mining, Corporate Social Responsibility and the Community: The Case of Rio Tinto, Richard Bay Minerals and the Mbonambi', *Journal of Business Ethics*, 39, 275–296.

Khayesi, J. N. O. and G. George (2011) 'When does the Socio-cultural Context Matter? Communal Orientation and Entrepreneurs' Resource Accumulation Efforts in Africa', *Journal of Occupational and Organizational Psychology*, 84, 471–492.

Mbigi, L. (1997) *Ubuntu: The African Dream in Management* (Randburg, South Africa: Knowledge Resources).

Mellahi, K. and W. Collings (2010) 'The Barriers to Effective Global Talent Management: The Example of Corporate Elites in MNEs', *Journal of World Business*, 45, 143–149.

Newenham-Kahindi, A. (2011) 'A Global Mining Corporation and Local Communities in the Lake Victoria Zone: The Case of Barrick Gold Multinational in Tanzania', *Journal of Business Ethics*, 99, 253–282.

Nkomo, S. M. (2011) 'A Postcolonial and Anti-colonial Reading of "Africa" Leadership and Management in Organization Studies: Tensions, Contradictions and Possibilities', *Organization*, 18, 365–386.

North, D. C. (1991) 'Towards a Theory of Institutional Change', *Quarterly Review of Economics and Business*, 31, 3–11.

Opondo, M. (2009) 'The Impact of Chinese Firms on CSR in Kenya's Garment Sector', International Research Network Series Working Paper No. 7.

Verburg, R. (1996) 'Developing HRM in Foreign-Chinese Joint Ventures', *European Management Journal*, 14, 518–525.

Walumbwa, F. O., B. J. Avolio, and S. Aryee (2011) 'Leadership and Management Research in Africa: A Synthesis and Suggestions for Future Research', *Journal of Occupational and Organizational Psychology*, 84, 425–439.

Warner, M. (2000) 'Introduction: The Asia-Pacific HRM Model Revisited', *International Journal of Human Resource Management*, 11, 171–182.

Part I

People Management in African Countries

1
HRM Issues and Outcomes in Domestic Mergers and Acquisitions: A Study of the Nigerian Banking Sector

Emanuel Gomes, Duncan Angwin, Emmanuel Peter and Kamel Mellahi

Introduction

Considering how corporate mergers and acquisition (M&As) are becoming an important component of the African business landscape, with significant activity recently reported for South Africa (360 deals valued at $21.98 bn), Egypt (117 deals valued at $6.84 bn) and Nigeria (24 deals valued at $0.713 bn) (Zephyr, 2010), and with countries which have previously prohibited M&A, such as Libya, now beginning to embrace it, African M&A has not received much attention from academic researchers. The growing research on M&As has largely been limited to western developed countries (c.f. Larsson and Finkelstein, 1999; Weber and Camerer, 2003) and more recently fast-growing emerging economies, with China (c.f. Dong and Hu, 1995; Cooke, 2006; Lin et al., 2009); and India (c.f. Kumar and Bansal, 2008; Budhwar et al., 2009) receiving special attention. Consequently, there is scanty knowledge about the challenges from M&As among African firms. Even within the M&A process itself, there has been a ground swell of research signifying the relevance of the human aspect in successful organizational integration (c.f. Stahl and Mendenhall, 2005). Specifically, recent articles in this journal have emphasized the role which human resource management ('HRM') in particular may play in a successful M&A process (c.f. Antila, 2006). This chapter takes up these two themes by exploring issues in HRM practices throughout the M&A process in recent domestic African M&A. Based on semi-structured theme interviews with corporate-level managers involved in the recent waves of M&As in the Nigerian banking sector, this chapter seeks to identify HRM practices deployed during M&As and explore their association with M&A outcomes.

This study is important for two reasons. First, to the best of our knowledge, this is the first study on HRM practices during the M&A process in an African country. Previous work on M&As in Africa has looked at other aspects of M&A, including corporate governance in the Nigerian banking industry (Akintoye and Somoye, 2008), and financial performance of M&A in the Kenyan banking sector (Kithinji and Waweru, 2007). To date, no study in a refereed journal has specifically addressed HRM practices during the M&A process within African countries.

Second, this chapter impacts on the broader literature on HRM during M&As by studying these practices in the pre-merger alongside the post-merger phase. Although the study of HRM practices during the post-merger process has received attention in previous studies (Bastien, 1987; Buono and Bowditch, 1989; Schweiger and DeNisi, 1991; Chatterjee et al., 1992; Krug and Hegarty, 2001; Schuler, 2001; Schuler and Jackson, 2001; Faulkner et al., 2002; Aguilera and Denker, 2004; Papadakis, 2005; Antila, 2006), the existing body of knowledge on HRM during the pre-merger stage remains limited, with scholars continuing to call for more research into these important aspects (Schuler, 2001; Aguilera and Dencker, 2004; Budhwar et al., 2009). This is because HRM in the pre-deal stage of M&A may influence subsequent post-acquisition management of people (Aguilera and Dencker, 2004). HRM issues such as cultural due diligence, pre-merger communication, management and employee due diligence, future remuneration, and other key people management issues could play an important role in the M&A process and affect overall outcome.

The choice of the Nigerian banking industry was basically because the sector has been at the peak of the biggest M&A boom in its entire history. The 2005 wave of M&As in this sector was prompted by government regulation, as banks were asked to raise a minimum capital base within an 18-month period. This enforced industry consolidation was to improve the overall solvency and integrity of the banking system as a whole and had huge national implications for the strength and integrity of the country's economic system. The consolidation also had significant social impact, with an initial loss of 45,000 banking jobs in an already saturated labour market (Fanimo, 2006). Further monitoring of the banks by the Central Bank of Nigeria (CBN) has resulted in clearly defined outcomes, as the CBN test performed at the end of 2009 was to determine which banks were sound and which would go down or be nationalized. From this data, survival can be readily assessed.

Literature review and research framework

In this section, a framework is developed to guide our data collection and analysis. In line with past studies, we examine HRM issues at different stages of the M&A process. 'Analysing HRM issues throughout the M&A process, not just the outcomes, is essential since attention to the rationale behind the decision to merge or acquire, to integration planning and to due diligence takes place before integration and forms the basis of a successful deal' (Antila, 2006, p. 1000). Another reason for this study is the fact that management faces diverse challenges at different stages, and therefore HRM should not be studied in isolation (Charman, 1999; Habeck et al., 1999; Appelbaum et al., 2000; Schuler and Jackson, 2001).

Identifying M&A phases: The existing literature is not specific in terms of defining the phases of the M&A process. Some advocate seven phases (Buono and Bowditch, 1989), others four (Graves, 1981; Haspeslagh and Jemison, 1991), while others have categorized the process into three phases (Howell, 1970; Appelbaum et al., 2000; Bower, 2001; Schuler and Jackson, 2001; Aguilera and Denker, 2004; Antila, 2006; Budhwar et al., 2009). One major difficulty is defining each phase, and even those researchers who agree on the number of phases disagree on what those phases might be. Others also criticize the stage model, as some stages may run in parallel with others and the order of stages may, in some circumstances, be reversed (Mintzberg et al., 1976). However, there is one concrete moment in the M&A process which breaks the flow of the process and is not movable. The 'closing date' is the moment enshrined in legal procedure when ownership of the acquired company is formally transferred to the new owner, and at that point the owner has control over the acquired firm. In management language, the new owner can now make changes directly to the new subsidiary. The closing date bifurcates the M&A process into pre and post-acquisition phases of decision-making and implementation. This two-stage approach is adopted in this chapter.

Pre-M&A phase: While the origins of the pre-merger stage are difficult to discern, rather like night shading into day, the beginning of this phase can be predicted by when the deal is announced publicly (the 'announcement date') and the end is when the deal is closed (the 'closing date'). As Aguilera and Dencker (2004) explain, 'the premerger stage occurs between the announcement of the merger and its closing date'.

Although some seeds of success or failure of the M&A are planted in the pre-merger stage (Schuler and Jackson, 2001), and recent literature has begun to recognize the value of merger announcements increasing employee uncertainty (Hubbard, 2001; Risberg, 2001), 'the M&A literature has focused primarily on financial due diligence and strategic issues in the pre-merger process, with HRM being an afterthought that becomes relevant only in the integration stage of an M&A when the merger is implemented' (Aguilera and Dencker, 2004, p. 1356). Kidd, a partner at Egon Zehnder International, states that 'Many mergers do not create the shareholder value expected of them. The combination of cultural differences and an ill-conceived human resource integration strategy is one of the most common reasons for that failure' (Light et al., 2001).

The scanty research on HRM aspects of the pre-M&A stage (Schweiger and Webber, 1989; Mirvis and Marks, 1992; Schweiger et al., 1993; Appelbaum et al., 2000; Schuler and Jackson, 2001; Aguilera and Dencker, 2004) highlights these issues as important: methods of selecting, approaching and communicating with potential partners; ensuring legal compliance and equal opportunity (Mirvis and Marks, 1992); potential redundancies; retention agreements; reward and promotion procedures; leader selection; HRM due diligence; planning to coordinate the implementation through 'communicating expected roles in the newly formed entity' (Aguilera and Dencker, 2004); alignment of expectations and objectives (Barret, 1973; Schweiger and Weber, 1989; Weber et al., 1996; Angwin, 2001; Light et al., 2001; Vermeulen and Barkema, 2001; Peterhoff, 2004; McDonald et al., 2005; Papadakis, 2005; Mitleton-Kelly, 2006); setting expectations (Hubbard, 2001); and cultural assessments, that is, 'describing and evaluating the two companies' philosophies and values regarding such issues as: leadership styles; time horizons; relative value of stakeholders; risk tolerance; and the value of teamwork versus individual performance and recognition' (Schuler and Jackson, 2001, p. 244).

The post-M&A phase: This phase is triggered by the initiatives carried out at the pre-M&A stage. Schuler and Jackson (2001, p. 245) reported that 'lack of integration planning (in the first stage) is found in 80 per cent of the M&A's that underperform'. Research on the post-M&A stage have concentrated on the day-to-day management of the integration process (Birkinshaw et al., 2000); speed of integration (Ashkenas and Francis, 2000; Angwin, 2004; Homburg and Bucerius, 2006); allocation of resources to activities that help achieve the anticipated synergistic benefits (Birkinshaw et al., 2000; Schuler and Jackson, 2001; Vaara, 2003); and knowledge transfer between, and ability to learn from, the integrated companies (Buono and Bowditch, 1989; Haspeslagh and Jemison, 1991; Ingham et al., 1992; Gertsen et al., 1998; Birkinshaw et al., 2000; Schuler and Jackson, 2001; Vaara, 2003; Aguilera and Dencker, 2004).

During the post-M&A stage, researchers highlighted the importance of communication to support organizational realignment and help overcome resistance to changing the 'old way of doing things' (Schweiger and Weber, 1989; Weber et al., 1996; Angwin, 2001; Vermeulen and Barkema, 2001; Adebayo, 2005; McDonald et al., 2005; Mitleton-Kelly, 2006). Research evidence shows that, once the M&A is completed, integrating different organizational structures, management styles, processes and cultures poses immense challenges for managers of the new company, with the degree of persistence of old ways of doing things directly related to communication and integration strategies pursued by the new management team (Kitching, 1967; Ferracone, 1987; Vermeulen and Barkema, 2001; Budhwar et al., 2009; Gomes, 2009; Gomes et al., 2010).

Post-acquisition integration approach

The M&A process is believed to be influenced by pre- and post-M&A HRM practices. These are themselves strongly affected by different approaches to integration (Howell, 1970; Schweiger and Weber, 1989; Haspeslagh and Jemison, 1991; Weber and Schweiger, 1992; Schweiger et al., 1993). In order to capture the scope of integration approaches for the merging banks, this study uses Schweiger et al.'s (1993) framework to analyse the different integration strategy approaches. Their three integration categories are: (1) assimilation: when one of the combined firms decides to adopt (voluntarily or otherwise) the identity (e.g. HR, culture or management practices) of the other. When this is enforced, culture clash and resistance to change may occur; (2) novation: when combined units develop new working practices and culture, resulting in the creation of a new identity; (3) structural integration: when combined units retain their own identities, thus requiring less change.

Schweiger et al. (2003) argue that managers should be careful in chosing a particular integration approach, as this will require a higher or lower degree of change in working processes and procedure, such as reward policy, hours of employment, vacation policies and terminations. Each form of integration will require change decisions in terms of the distribution of decision-making power between the two firms. In order to examine HRM issues in the pre and post-M&A phases in Nigerian banks, we collected and analysed data using the above framework to answer the following questions: what pre and post-M&A HRM practices were employed by these banks? To what extent might these practices influence outcome?

Research method

An inductive multiple-case study involving the 19 merged banks was adopted. This approach enables a replication logic through systematic analysis of the various merger cases, each serving to confirm or disconfirm inferences drawn from the others (Eisenhardt, 1989; Graebner and Eisenhardt, 2004; Eisenhardt and Graebner, 2007; Yin, 2008). This generates better-grounded results than single case studies (Graebner and Eisenhardt, 2004). Given our research aim to analyse the HRM practices and their associations with merger outcomes during the 2005 merger activities in the Nigerian banking industry, a cross-sectional approach was followed and data were collected from newly merged bank employees.

This merger activity in the Nigerian banking was distinct and unusual compared with most previous M&A research studies. The CBN recognized that size had become critical for banks to be able to withstand the challenges of an increasingly globalized financial sector. They decreed that global banking groups should be created and that M&A was an appropriate method (Soludo, 2006). Before then, the Nigerian banking industry was composed of 89 banks, with 90 per cent classified as unhealthy and unsound, small in size and weak in terms of capital base (Nwosu, 2005). It was in the light of the above factors that the CBN, under the leadership of Prof. Charles Soludo, directed all banks in the country to raise their capital base from two billion Naira (N2 bn) (equivalent to £8 m) to 25 billion Naira (N25 bn) (equivalent to £100 m) within 18 months, effective from the date of pronouncement – 6 July 2004.

The resulting mega-merger activity proved to be a fertile terrain for our study, as, out of the 89 existing banks, 70 of them merged to form 19 banks, six remained independent as they did not need to merge to achieve the growth target imposed by the Central Bank, and 13 were liquidated (Chibuike, 2004) (see Table 1.1).

This study covers the 19 merged banks (see Table 1.1): five mergers involved two banks, another five mergers involved three banks, four mergers involved four banks, two mergers involved five banks, one

Table 1.1   State of consolidated banks and acquisition group's capital base as on 31 December 2005

Name of bank and acquisition group	Numbers of merged banks	Capital base (in billion)
Access Bank: –Access Bank; –Capital Bank Int'l; –Marina Bank	3	28
Afri Bank: –Afribank Int'l (Merchant) Bank; –Afribank of Nigeria	2	29
Diamond Bank: –Africa Int'l Bank; –Diamond Bank; –Lion Bank; –Prudent Bank; –Reliance Bank	5	33.25
Ecobank Nigeria: Did not merge and therefore was not included in this study	0	25+
Equatorial Trust Bank: –Devcom Bank; –Equatorial Trust Bank	2	26.5
Fidelity Bank: –Fidelity Bank; –FSB Int'l; –Manny Bank	3	29
First Bank of Nigeria plc: –FBN (Merchant Bankers) Ltd; –First Bank of Nigeria; –MBC Int'l Bank; –NBM Bank Ltd; –Trust Bank of Africa	5	44.67
First City Monument Bank: –Co–operative Development Bank; –MIDAS Merchant Bank; –Nigeria–America Merchant Bank; –First City Monument Bank	4	30
First Inland Bank plc: –First Atlantic Bank; –Int'l Merchant Bank(IMB); –Inland Bank; –NUB	4	30
Guaranty Trust Bank plc: Did not merge and therefore was not included in this study	0	34
Platinum– Habib Bank plc: –Habib Nigeria Bank; –Platinum Bank	2	25
IBTC–Chartered Bank plc: –Chartered Bank; –IBTC Ltd; –Regent Bank	3	35
Intercontinental Bank plc: –Equity Bank of Nigeria; –Gateway Bank of Nigeria; –Global Bank; –Intercontinental Bank	4	51
NIB Ltd (Citi Group): Did not merge and therefore was not included in this study	0	25
Oceanic Bank Int'l: –International Trust Bank; –Oceanic Bank	2	31

Table 1.1   (Continued)

Name of bank and acquisition group	Numbers of merged banks	Capital base (in billion)
Skye Bank: – Bond Bank; – Cooperative Bank; – EIB Int'l Bank	3	37.7
Spring Bank plc: – ACB Int'l Bank; –Citizen Bank Int'l; –Fountain Trust Bank; –Guardian Express Bank; –Omega Bank; –Trans Int'l Bank	6	27
Stanbic Bank Nigeria Ltd: Did not merge and therefore was not included in this study	0	25
Standard Chartered Bank: Did not merge and therefore was not included in this study	0	26
Sterling Bank plc: –Indo–Nigerian Bank; –Magnum Trust Bank; – Trust Bank of Africa; –NAL Bank	4	25
Union Bank: –Union Bank plc; –Union Merchant Bank; –Universal Trust Bank	3	58
United Bank of Africa: –Continental Trust Bank; –Standard Trust Bank; –United Bank of Africa	3	50
Unity Bank: –Bank of the North; –Centrepoint Bank; –First Interstate Bank; –Intercity Bank; –New Africa Bank; –NNB Int'l Bank; –Pacific Bank; –Societe Bancaire Nig. Bank; –Tropical Commerce Bank	9	30
Wema Bank: –National Bank of Nigeria; –Wema Bank	2	35
Zenith Bank: Did not merge and therefore was not included in this study	0	38

Source: Derived from Central Bank of Nigeria (2006).

merger involved six banks, and one very large merger involved nine banks.

We used semi-structured interviews to collect data for this study. Purposive and snowball techniques were used as a non-probability sampling method to minimize individual interest from overriding research purposes. Thirty-seven interviews were conducted with a range of interviewees including non-executive directors, former executive directors, principal managers, and other managers and staff from different departments, at both branch and head office level (see Table 1.2). Understandably, several interviewees requested anonymity. Interviews lasted between 30 and 60 minutes each, were tape-recorded

Table 1.2 Interviewees

Bank	Interviewee	Employment position	Date
FCMB	Interviewee 19	Head of retail banking	18 December 2009
	Interviewee 1	Branch staff	18 December 2009
	Interviewee 20	Branch head of operations	22 July 2010
ETB	Interviewee 21	Marketing officer	16 December 2009
			6 July 2010
	Interviewee 2		18 December 2009
UBA	Interviewee 3	Investment banker	14 December 2009
	Interviewee 22	Branch manager	14 December 2009
	Interviewee 23	Former general manager	27 May 2010
Bank PHB	Interviewee 24	Branch auditor	21 December 2009
	Interviewee 25	HR manager	09 July 2010
Diamond Bank	Interviewee 4	Branch staff	15 December 2009
	Interviewee 26	Former executive director	19 December 2009
	Interviewee 27	North east HR manager	09 July 2010
Access Bank	Interviewee 28	Branch manager	22 December 2009
	Interviewee 5	HR department	22 December 2009
	Interviewee 29	HR deputy manager, staff welfare unit	08 July 2010
Unity Bank	Interviewee 6	Head office staff	17 December 2009
	Interviewee 7	Financial control unit	17 December 2009
Union Bank	Interviewee 8	IT department	28 December 2009
	Interviewee 9	International operation	28 December 2009
Sterling Bank	Interviewee 30	Public sector department	27 December 2009
Skye Bank	Interviewee 31	Head customer service	27 December 2009
Spring Bank	Interviewee 10	Clearing staff	23 December 2009
IBTC–Chartered	Interviewee 11	Inspection department	23 December 2009

Table 1.2   (Continued)

Bank	Interviewee	Employment position	Date
Fidelity	Interviewee 32	Retail marketer	24 December 2009
FinBank[a]	Interviewee 33	Deputy operations manager	18 December 2009
	Interviewee 12	Operations staff	18 December 2009
	Interviewee 34	Regional manager north	18 December 2009
	Interviewee 35	Head office staff in HR department	09 July 2010
ICB	Interviewee 13	Branch staff	14 December 2009
First Bank	Interviewee 14	Auditor	22 December 2009
Afri Bank	Interviewee 36	Principal manager	16 December 2009
Wema Bank	Interviewee 15	Public sector	19 December 2009
	Interviewee 16	Head office	19 December 2009
Oceanic Bank	Interviewee 17	Branch staff	16 December 2009
	Interviewee 18	Clearing unit	16 December 2009

[a] First Atlantic Bank, Inland Bank, IMB Bank and NUB International Bank. The combination of these four names resulted in FinBank.

and transcribed. A subsequent interview with one of the respondents took place to clarify queries and obtain extra necessary data.

Further secondary data were collected from annual reports and other relevant official information pertaining to the mergers, newspapers, edited gazettes and magazines/media, online databases such as Econlit, Winecon and Science direct, and other internet sources. There were no previous indigenous research findings on this M&A activity, as this was the first of its kind. This makes this chapter foundational in its findings.

Following an inductive approach, data collected from various sources were analysed against key emerging themes related to HRM aspects associated with the various mergers. Cross-case comparisons were carried out in order to facilitate analysis of similarities and differences between cases, while preserving the independence of each merger case.

Data analysis

Merger rationale and expected resource redeployment

The main driver behind the 2005 Nigerian banking consolidation was the policy directive by the government through the CBN for all banks to strengthen their capital base to halt declining stakeholder confidence in the banks and to prevent distress. Mergers were regarded as the only alternative in order to have 'bigger and stronger' institutions.

Interviewees identified several additional reasons for mergers. Banks expected to use M&A as a means for acquiring other resources to enhance their R&D/technology, marketing and managerial capabilities. According to Onouha at Diamond Bank, there was a wish to spread geographically: 'regional differences was one of the factors considered by almost all banks during that era, as it was an opportunity to integrate and spread geographically'. In the Diamond Bank merger 'each partner was looking for a bank from another region different from theirs, Diamond Bank from the south and Lion Bank from the middle' (Interviewee 4). In the words of Abisi, an auditor with Platinum Habib Bank (PHB), the merger would achieve 'market complementarity as Platinum Bank was dominant in the south while Habib Bank dominated in the north'. By accessing new marketing capabilities, banks expected revenue growth from a large pool of customers by offering a broader service package from a single corporate structure.

Other motives included access to managerial resources to improve efficiencies of operations. As pointed out by Ibioma, a branch manager at Access Bank, 'it was the quality of Access bank management team that attracted other banks'. 'Access bank management was one of the best in the industry' (Interviewee 5).

In other banks there was no clear strategic rationale, apart from the general one imposed by the CBN directive. In the case of the FinBank merger, it 'was hastily packaged in order for the four banks to beat the CBN deadline. I don't think there was a clear cut objective for partnering among those banks. In the first place Inland Bank wanted to merge with GTBank but they could not agree on terms' (Habila).

Pre-merger phase

Partner selection

For Nigerian banks, informal relationships and family links between several banks seem to have superseded the more rigorous strategic and organizational fit selection criteria characteristic of M&A in the West.

As stated by Bamaiyi, Head of Retail Banking at First City Monument Bank Plc (FCMB), 'our former MD had some relationship on a personal level with the bank we merged with'. In the case of the Oceanic Bank merger 'the banks were controlled on the basis of family interest. There was a courtship as the banks were either founded or supported by the same family' (Interviewee 17). In the Equatorial Trust Bank (ETB) merger, the banks were owned by the same person. The importance of informal relationships seems to be of particular relevance in the African socio-cultural context (Anakwe, 2002).

HRM due diligence

Previous social networking between executives in the merging banks may have had crucial consequences for HRM due diligence. Apparent 'knowledge' of the merging partner might have created a 'familiarity illusion', which could have led to underestimating or even disregarding the need for HRM investigation and planning. In the case of ETB bank this may have contributed to a lack of formality in terms of pre-merger due diligence, as 'there was no difference in HR practices between these two banks. Remember the two banks were owned by one person (Mike Adenuga), even before the merger. The remuneration of the two banks was the same' (Goje – interviewee, 2010).

In the case of Wema Bank, three amalgamated banks from the same region, backgrounds were assumed to be similar and differences were underestimated: 'all the banks were from the west and having a similar background... but it was later discovered that we had a lot of differences operationally' (Interviewee 15).

HRM due diligence might also have been limited as most merging banks lacked previous experience, and hence did not have a sound understanding of merger process management. Lack of time also aggravated this situation. As Tifase, former general manager at United Bank for Africa (UBA), stated,

> There was not sufficient time for much planning. There was a government policy dictating that banks would have to merge to achieve the government requirements and banks simply had to find a partner. Between the announcement of the merger and the deal there were approximately six to nine months. Therefore, there was not much time... not enough planning. A lot was done as we went along... There was also very limited or no knowledge on M&A management.

However, in some cases a more formalized due diligence process took place. In the Sterling Bank merger 'the whole eighteen months were dedicated to understanding each other, as consultants took over the formal merger processes and legalities' (Marne). Similarly, in the Fidelity Bank merger 'joint seminars in the process of the merger were conducted to familiarize with each other' (Onouha). In the case of the FinBank merger, a HR manager reported 'there was some staff audit and analysis before the merger but it lacked defined criteria like age, minimum qualification' (Bitrus).

Cultural differences

Although the bank mergers were all within the same industry and the same country, there was evidence of significant cultural differences between different geographic regions, particularly, but not exclusively, between the north and south, which influenced the M&A process. At FinBank, 'two of the merged banks were from the north. They were behind in terms of western education. For example diploma holders were even managers, unlike in the south where BSc. degree was considered the minimum requirement to work in a bank' (Bitrus).

Communication management

Communications can play a key role in overcoming resistance to change. We categorized communication into 'open' and 'poor' types. In addition, we examined the intensity of communication between merging banks. Significant variances in communication were detected, with some banks demonstrating open and transparent communications with clear mechanisms for disseminating information down through the businesses. Uduka, Head of Customer Service at Skye Bank, said: 'there were concerns as to what comes next after the merger, due to industry wide panic, rumours of layoff, salary slash and so on; however the bank kept communicating to employees regularly'. Communication at Sterling Bank was effective as clear information was passed regularly through formal channels.

Information on progressive work of the consultants and management decisions were communicated on regular basis through the bank's formal channels for the whole period and even into the merger and post merger period...The bank had an intra-net through which it communicated to employees; staff can always drop in their inquiries which would receive response within 24 hours. Bank updates were also available every day.

(Marne)

Fidelity Bank used joint seminars as the main communication platform. 'We had joint seminars conducted before the merger; it was the major forum of communication among all levels of staff for all the banks in the group' (Onouha). The First Bank merger also communicated information frequently: 'a rule was made to bridge communication gap after the merger, every Monday morning staffs normally receive mail from the managing director circulated to all, which became a tradition' (Interviewee 14). In this case, email was the best medium, utilized directly by top management.

The case of the FCMB merger provides a good example of how communication was managed in a creative manner, taking into account the African context. In order to minimize fear, information was disseminated through an interactive communication mechanism called 'VILLAGE SQUARE' (Ogunsola). This mechanism proved effective as it was widely used and 'provided staff the opportunity to express their fears, concerns and opinions and have their questions answered'. Another interviewee attested to the fact that communication at FCMB was passed down through different media:

> In terms of communication media, this was done on a branch level as information was passed through to the Branch Managers who in turn met with their branch staff and passed information down to them. Emails were also sent out to staff informing of new developments...Information was passed across to all staff regarding the banks which we were merging with or acquiring.

(Ogunsola)

However, several merging banks did not seem to be able to manage communication effectively. In some cases, the main problem was associated with the fact that information was restricted to top management. At Wema Bank, 'general knowledge of the merger event was obvious but the process was kept secret at the top causing a lot of uncertainty and fear in the bank' (Interviewee 15). Similarly, at PHB, pre-merger communication 'was first restricted to the management and there was no assurance the merger would work or not' (Abisi).

Lack of time was an important factor limiting communication during the pre-merger phase. However, this was not the only constraining factor, as communication at Unity Bank was not equally disseminated across various regions: 'regionally people knew what was happening but bank wide there was little that employees knew' (Interviewee 6).

Furthermore, in the Spring Bank merger, poor communications resulted in lack of direction and understanding of what the merger rationale was, besides the objective to achieve the minimum financial threshold as directed by the CBN.

> Communication (at Spring Bank) was really poor as even senior managers could not tell what actually was going on at some point. Little attention was given to how the newly merged banks were to cooperate and succeed in the future; it was all about getting the N25 bn, soon after the merger, lack of communication left people in suspense.
>
> (Interviewee 10)

Similarly, at FinBank, 'there was no formal communication on the pre-merger development, most staff members waited to see if the bank would make it by appearing in the newspaper on 31st December 2005' (Habila).

Across the mergers, communications were targeted at a wide range of audiences ranging from a narrow range of recipients, such as board-level executives, to company-wide information dissemination. It is noteworthy that some banks used external advisors to help in the communication process, and in a limited number of cases there was recognition that a reflexive approach was effective in reassuring staff. A further important dimension is the timeliness of communications, with some banks continuing with a carefully thought-out communication programme instigated in the earlier pre-merger period, whereas other banks delayed until communication became essential.

In the few banks that had poor and restricted communication, such as Unity Bank, this was due to the large number of banks – nine – merging together. Managers were bogged down with sorting out administrative and regulative requirements to complete the merger. As pointed out by Interviewee 6, 'communication was not very effective due to nine banks merging at a time with so much to do'. Similarly, in the case of FinBank, a merger involving four banks, communication was difficult. According to Bitrus, 'there was no communication at all as everything was done in haste, no time to communicate among staff of the four banks. It was a kind of save our soul approach.'

The restriction of communications to top management level may be partly due to Nigerian culture being characterized by high levels of power distance; in such context certain types of information might be reserved to top leadership, who have the power to make decisions without much consultation with subordinates. Discrepancies in terms of communication at regional levels could also, arguably, be understood in terms of politico-socio-cultural differences between the northern and the southern parts of the country.

Post-merger phase

Post-merger integration approaches

For mergers within the same sector, appropriate integration approaches might be expected to be those in which maximum synergies are achieved through asset and capability redeployment to reduce duplications (assimilation) and to enable new forms of working practices to emerge (novation). Table 1.3 shows that nine out of the 19 bank mergers followed an assimilation approach, with four mergers using novation and three following a structual integration approach.

These different approaches to integration are likely to result in various degrees of HRM adjustment and organizational change. An assimilation approach will require high levels of transfer of tacit and socially complex knowledge-based resources as well as human resources to realize expected synergies, whereas a novation integration will likely witness less, and more incremental, change. The least adjustment is likely to be found in structural integration.

Table 1.3   Integration approaches taken by merging Nigerian banks

Integration approach		
Assimilation	Novation	Structural integration
FCMB	Unity	PHB
ETB	Sterling	IBTC–Chartered
UBA	Skye	FinBank
Diamond	Spring	
Access		
Union		
Fidelity		
Intercontinental		
First Bank		

Source: Adapted from Schweiger et al. (1993).

Structural integration: In these cases combined units retain their own identities, thus requiring less integration change (Schweiger et al., 1993).This occurred in three mergers (PHB, Investment Bank Trust & Company [IBTC]–Chartered and FinBank), with individual banks maintaining high levels of autonomy. The drivers for these mergers were government policy and market complementarity, for instance PHB (Platinum Bank, dominant in the south, and Habib Bank, dominant in the north) and FinBank (two banks from the south and two from the north). In both cases all pre-existing bank initials were kept in the new name to maintain each firm's identity. Significant regional cultural differences remained, primarily on a north–south divide, but the handling of these differences was quite different.

At PHB, keeping pre-existing banks separate meant 'there was no corporate culture clash; however the suspicion that has always existed between north and south was there for a long time' (Abisi, PHB). Potential north/south cultural issues were minimized by clear and regular communication of the new direction of PHB and through diligent training of all staff, which was carried out by a group of consultants 'from region to region at the same time'.

> All members of staff have undergone a new induction, everyone started from the same point. Nobody was given the chance to feel better than the other and no one was left behind. A clear cut vision of being one of the best Nigerian bank in the future was the target of the new bank. Staff were seen as stakeholders and treated as such.
>
> (Ishaya)

There were some redundancies, but these were small pockets and mostly voluntary.

The case of FinBank was much more problematic, as 'people were still keeping to their old way of doing things' (Bitrus). 'Cultural differences affected the merger greatly. To an extent people from first Atlantic and IMB (south), treated those from the north as unsound in banking practices. The northerners on the other hand felt those from the south were not trustworthy and that made the working environment tense' (Badamasi). A consequence of this situation was an adversarial quality, with each bank blaming the other: 'some of us from Inland Bank were sidelined in decision making' (Interviewee 12).

The difficulties with the FinBank merger were probably exarcerbated by more extensive downsizing of the workforce than happened at PHB.

Instead of the bank focusing on how to integrate people, the bank decided that people should go and that created panic. The reason for layoff was not communicated; employees kept thinking it could be anyone. The sacking was not once, not twice and not even thrice! Employees could not concentrate on the job – so much insecurity.

(Badamasi)

The only thing normally communicated to all staff was sack memos, thereby making the environment tense and affecting staff morale and performance... you could come to the office and before the end of the day you could have received a sack letter. Communication was always negative; staff did not expect anything different.

(Bitrus)

This contributed to raising stress levels at the bank and reduced staff morale.

The fear of job loss seems to have had the effect of emphasizing rather than reducing regional difference: the

constant sacking of staff... based on no clear criteria... with some legacy banks complaining of being marginalized because they were from one part of the country. Those sacked were promised compensation; however the bank did not deliver on its promise. Generally, lack of focus affected everything in FinBank. The integration approach was poor.

(Bitrus)

In seeking to explain the difficulties experienced in the post-acquisition phase, interviewees identified deficiencies in the pre-acquisition due diligence. The pre-merger HR due diligence 'lacked defined criteria, so what happened was each legacy bank forwarded staff lists on its payroll and that cannot be termed as a staff audit. Other banks had defined criteria like age, minimum qualification in their merger processes. Our merger did not have that' (Bitrus).

The IBTC–Chartered merger enjoyed a smoother merger process management. From its inception, the choice of the partners was made on the basis of operational similarities and involved banks that already enjoyed long-term banking relationships with each other. 'The merger was founded on cultural alignment of strict adherence to core banking practice which IBTC and Chartered Bank were known for and both banks were involved in key decision making... It was based on our operational similarities which made integration smooth and successful' (Interviewee 11).

Novation: Unity Bank, Spring Bank, Sterling Bank and Skye Bank are mergers which resulted in new working practices, culture and identity. Since this type of integration approach requires a high degree of reorganization and restructuring, as merging firms try to combine the best from all partners, HRM practices and policies assume a critical role for the success of the merger.

Each of these mergers resulted in the amalgamation of several partners: Unity Bank combining nine banks, Spring Bank involving six partners, and Sterling and Skye mergers involving five banks. As it would have been difficult for one bank to impose its identity, merging partners agreed that a new brand name reflecting all banks should be created. For instance, 'the name Unity Bank was new and is not connected to any of the nine legacy banks' (Interviewee 7).

Regional cultural differences were also important among novation mergers, but were handled with differing degrees of success. In the case of Unity Bank,

> because of the number of banks (nine) in the merger, the management became sensitive to people's culture. Corporate culture was not a problem; the regional executives selected were 'indigene' of those regions to avoid any culture conflict. Regional managers were selected from those regions. Considering the number of banks, we were careful in doing things. You can't send someone from Lagos to be in charge of Maiduguri (north) branch. It's ok now, but not when we started when we had more northerners.
>
> (Interviewee 6)

As the interviewee hints at the end of his statement, there were some early difficulties, and there seem to have been some discrepancies in the way information was disseminated across regions, as 'regionally people knew what was happening but bank wide there was little that employees knew' (Interviewee 6). The fact that HRM practices and policies were not equally realigned across all combining units and regions became a hindrance to integration and ultimately impaired the creation of a new organizational culture and identity.

The Spring Bank merger was a desperate attempt at survival. 'We were those banks considered by other banks too risky to merge with in 2005.' As a result, 'the bank emerged from a combination of weaker banks' (Interviewee 10). Although a 'novation' integration approach is intended to combine the best of both worlds, as all six merging banks were already in a weak position perhaps the merger resulted more in combining the 'worst of all worlds'. As argued by Interviewee 10,

> the old management was allowed to run it into more trouble... and little attention was given to how the newly merged banks were to cooperate and succeed in the future; it was all about getting the N25 bn. Soon after the merger, lack of communication left people in suspense. The absence of corporate culture was directly linked to the poor management in place after the merger. Supervision and monitoring was weak.

In contrast to the two cases above, the Sterling Bank 'novation' integration was successful. The involvement of external consultants seems to have played an important role. 'We had a team of consultants who handled the merger and integration processes. With the aid of consultants the banks became fully integrated by 1st January 2006... resulting in the creation of a new corporate culture' (Marne).

Similarly, the Skye Bank merger resulted in successful integration. In this case good communications and similar operations were seen as key reasons for success. Though there were initial concerns over 'what comes next after the merger, due to industry wide panic, rumours of layoff, salary slash and so on... the bank kept communicating to employees regularly' (Uduka). During the integration phase,

> there was a controversy in dress code and some were regarded as offensive culturally but corporate culture was not different due to similarities in operations which attracted the merger in the first place... There are two important features in any bank, one is the platform (software) and the other is the year end. All the banks in this group had the same, making integration simpler.
>
> (Uduka)

Assimilation: In this integration approach there is the potential for culture clash, as one or various of the combined firms adopt, voluntarily or otherwise, the identity of merging partners. HR executives need to be aware of the implications of choosing this integration approach, as it is likely to require a higher degree of change in working processes and procedure, reward policy, hours of employment, vacation policies, terminations and dress codes.

Tifase, former general manager at UBA, and responsible for coordinating the merger between UBA and Standard Trust (ST), asserts that, because UBA was a well-recognized brand nationally and internationally, the new entity adopted its name. However, in terms of integration approach, the new merged bank adopted the identity of the smaller partner, ST, which ended up with a stronger position in terms of the distribution of decision-making power between the two firms.

> ST despite being smaller and younger was perceived as the senior partner. Certain top positions and allocation of responsibilities were given to ST staff. It was perceived that ST staff were more forward looking, modern and up-to-date in their banking practices. UBA had a lot of luggage and was more out-dated and would not drive the merger. Even if UBA had a bigger name, a larger customer base, and a wider range of products, the younger bank ST took the commanding role.
>
> (Tifase)

It is unusual for a younger organization to take the leading role; the group MD came from ST and the Executive Directors 60 per cent were from ST and 40 per cent from UBA, with the same proportion taking place in the next level of management (Tifase). This gave rise to some HRM issues.

> The issue here was that the staff of ST were much younger than staff from UBA; the Director from ST was only 41 years old. I was 56. I was willing to obey but there was that inconvenience for an older person to obey the younger one. The younger manager would not find it comfortable to give orders to older manager. I personally had to make it clear that despite being older I was willing to follow orders. It was cultural. Because most ST Managers were 40-45-50 years old they find it difficult to work with managers from UBA who were older. A younger manager told me that he was finding it very difficult to give orders to the older manager because it was like disrespecting him. Age was something critical.
>
> (Tifase)

Age does seem important in terms of leadership positions in Nigeria, as 'authority is based largely on experience and wisdom, which are inferred from age' (Anakwe, 2002, p. 1045).

This high degree of combination had direct repercussions in terms of staff reduction, resulting in a cull, especially from UBA employees, with 3,000–4,000 staff being made redundant in the first few months after the merger. However, 'ST reduced staff, but in much smaller numbers because they were much smaller and already pretty focused. In contrast UBA was a big organization and it was easier to cut costs' (Tifase).

Staff who were let go were provided with a 'soft landing' so they could be retrained and the bank helped them find new job opportunities elsewhere. This finding seems to support the idea that the Nigerian and African system of work organization is characterized by a paternalistic approach in which the leader is regarded as the 'father of the group and is expected to cater to the members' livelihood' (Anakwe, 2002, p. 1044).

In the case of the Diamond Bank merger, access to new markets was the main driver for the deal. In their assimilation integration Lion Bank was absorbed into Diamond Bank. Ayuba, former executive director, stated: 'the immediate general approach implemented was that no branch manager or team leader in the defunct Lion Bank was allowed to be in charge in the new Diamond Bank. At the beginning they were only allowed to work as assistants to understudy the managers deployed by Diamond Bank.' In order to integrate the two banks, Diamond Bank used a specific HRM approach to enable cross-bank learning. According to Bello, north east HR manager,

> from the beginning it was agreed that Diamond had the best practice compared to Lion, thereby all effort pointed toward re-orienting Lion staff. This was done through job training to save time and cost. All Unit Heads in Lion Bank were asked to temporarily give up their position to Diamond staff in order to learn from them.

Initially staff coming from Lion Bank felt threatened. However, leadership addressed this by communicating the merger rationale and by informing staff about the expected changes. With 'adequate communication through regular meeting at zonal and regional level, confidence was restored and everybody started cooperating' (Bello). 'Communication was very effective between the two banks from the start of the merger processes' (Ayuba).

Later on, many Lion Bank staff were finally laid off as they were perceived to be unable to catch up with the speed of the post-merger process and were dragging the bank. 'With 85 per cent of the current staff, formally with Diamond, there was less need for new training and policy changes' (Bello). 'It cost the bank so much to have sound corporate culture after the merger as no fewer than 300 staff actually lost their jobs in the process after the merger' (Ayubo).

Access Bank was a merger between Marina Bank, Capital Bank and Access Banks in order to benefit from managerial resource redeployment, as 'Access Bank management was one of the best before the merger and is still is' (Interviewee 5). 'It was the quality of Access Bank management team that attracted other banks' (Ibioma). The perceived strength of Access Bank's management meant they were given full support to run the new bank after the merger. According to Kuti, HR deputy manager, leadership disseminated a very positive message, 'the better the bank, the better you are', to increase employee identification with the newly merged bank. 'Nobody was sacked but staff were positioned to work hard. In fact salaries were improved and other benefits were introduced, like performance benefits' (Kuti). 'Regular in house training was a strong avenue that promoted post-merger communication, information packs were normally distributed to participants to take back to branches' (Ibioma). In summary, Kuti remarks that

> the success of Access Bank today is tied to its staff. The bank has made a priority to have one of the best staff in the country through in-house regular training to whom a lot of time and attention were given by the management and shareholders to stage development over a long period and the dividend is what we have today ... We did not stop at N25 billion, we went further in training people on how to handle the 25 billion, we embraced change and challenges.

As a result of sound and consistent HRM practices and policies, this is one of the healthy banks emerging from the Nigerian merger activity.

The formation of FCMB involved several partners (First City Monument Bank, Cooperative Bank, Midas Bank, Nigerian American Bank) and the identity and name of the leading partner, FCMB, was adopted. Staff at all levels were clearly informed that the main merger resource redeployment objective was access to markets. 'Staff were made aware that the merger was an avenue for FCMB to expand into new areas like the South Eastern part of Nigeria.' According to Ogunsola, former Branch Head of Operations, 'FCMB made staff aware of the changes that would be required and this was passed ... through to the Branch Managers who in turn met with their branch staff and passed information down to them. Emails were also sent out to staff informing of new developments.' According to Ogunsola,

> a transition team was formed to enhance smooth implementation and to ensure that plans were made to integrate the software used by the different banks, the staff and top managers were also involved in the process ... Consultants were brought in from South Africa and everyone was trained and reminded about the mission statement, values, goals of the organization and their parts in making them achievable. Pension and retire plans were introduced and staff were

encouraged to be a part of this as this would help secure their retirement.

This retirement policy might have been adopted due to the influence of South African consultants, as Nigerian banks were known not to pay out gratuities to staff who retired. Equally, the new performance appraisal system introduced, whereby a certain percentage of the total package (variable pay) was based on performance, could also have resulted from the advice provided by foreign consultants, as, according to the normal practice until then, money earned from performance was a bonus. This new practice seem to have been received with some concerns, as stated by Ogunsola: 'staff received that with mixed feelings as staff felt cheated' (Ogunsola). This source adds that, in terms of training and development, line managers were encouraged to monitor their subordinates, identify areas of weakness and recommend for training where appropriate, as this would help improve productivity.

The handling of staff and redundancies was very arbitrary, and somewhat similar to the UBA merger, as 'the layoff did not really affect the staff of the original FCMB, but mainly affected the staff of the other merging partners who had older people in their work force'. Some staff of the original FCMB were relocated to other partners' branches (Ogunsola).

The Fidelity Bank merger consisted of three banks from different regions, and this gave rise to potential cultural problems. The bank acted cautiouslyhere was an allowance to accommodate all cultures. For instance, a branch in Kano can close the bank on Friday, during Muslim prayer, while the branch in Abuja can work on Saturday depending on the needs of the people of the locality and that is business culture' (Kelechi). 'Anytime the bank introduced a major change, it normally organizes a seminar to communicate to employees else other matters were communicated through line operations' (Onouha).

Discussion

These case findings provide considerable evidence that HRM issues are present and important during pre and post-merger phases in Nigerian M&A. There is some evidence that HRM issues are influenced by the strategic rationale for the deal, and there is also variation in post-merger integration approaches. Interestingly, there is less coherence between HRM practices, pre-merger strategy, integration approach and outcomes than might have been expected. Table 1.4 shows the results of the mergers and these HRM issues.

Table 1.4 Summary of HRM practices and merger outcome

Bank	Integration approach	Rationale/choice of partner (excluding CBN pressure)	Communications quality	Managing cultural differences	Performance: survival outcome
PHB	Structural integration	Mainly financial Market access north/south	Limited	Inadequate	Taken over by the government: failed merger
IBTC–Chartered	Structural integration	Operational similarities	Intensive	Effective	Cleared as a healthy bank by CBN. 2 October 2009
FinBank	Structural integration	Mainly financial Market access north/south	Limited	Inadequate	Taken over by government on 14 August 2009
Unity Bank	Novation	Similar sizes and ownership. Market access	Limited	Inadequate	Adjudged to have insufficient capital
Sterling Bank	Novation	Managerial quality	Intensive	Effective	Cleared as a healthy bank by CBN. 14 August 2009
Skye Bank	Novation	Operational similarities	Intensive	Similar culture	Cleared as a healthy bank by CBN. 2 October 2009
Spring	Novation	Purely financial	Limited	Inadequate	Taken over 2 October 2009
FCMB	Assimilation	Market access	Intensive	Effective	Cleared as a healthy bank by CBN. 2 October 2009
ETB	Assimilation	The two banks owned by the same individual	Intensive	Had similar culture	Taken over and later returned to original owner
UBA	Assimilation	Similarities in sizes and market share	Intensive	Effective	Cleared as a healthy bank by CBN. 14 August 2009
Diamond Bank	Assimilation	Access to new markets and customers	Intensive	Inadequate	Cleared as a healthy bank by CBN. 14 August 2009
Access Bank	Assimilation	Managerial quality and strategic clients	Intensive	Had similar culture	Cleared as a healthy bank by CBN. 2 October 2009

Table 1.4 (Continued)

Bank	Integration approach	Rationale/choice of partner (excluding CBN pressure)	Communications quality	Managing cultural differences	Performance: survival outcome
Union Bank	Assimilation	R&D capability and managerial quality	Limited	Inadequate	Taken over 14 October 2009
Fidelity Bank	Assimilation	Market access north/south	Intensive	Effective	Cleared as a healthy bank by CBN. 2 October 2009
Intercontinental	Assimilation	Ownership structure	Moderate	Had similar culture	Taken over by the government on 14 August 2009
First Bank	Assimilation	Parent subsidiary merger	Intensive	Had similar culture	Cleared as a healthy bank by CBN. 14 August 2009
Afri Bank	Assimilation	Parent subsidiary merger and strategic client in the other bank	Limited	Inadequate	Taken over by the government on 14 August 2009

Some of the merging bank groups probably failed due to the enormous complexity of the groups involved. For the largest and most complex groups, Unity and Spring Bank, involving nine and six banks respectively, this overall complexity may just have been too much for the banks to cope with. However, for mergers involving fewer banks, certain HRM themes emerge as being of particular importance to overall outcome. These are (i) the quality of HRM due diligence; (ii) the existence and handling of regional cultural differences; (iii) the extent and quality of communications and (iv) the use of integration advisors to facilitate the process.

(i) A number of the merging banks comment upon the importance of HRM due diligence, either in terms of explaining their success or bemoaning their integration difficulties. For instance, at FinBank, which experienced significant cultural difficulties and widespread dissatisfaction among personnel, the head office HR department blamed the lack of detailed pre-merger due diligence for not uncovering basic issues such as employee age and qualifications. At Sterling Bank, by contrast, 18 months were spent on fully understanding merging banks' HR issues. It is also noteworthy that, due to common family ownership, there may have been significant underestimation of the need for HRM due diligence as the banks were deemed to to be the same. This 'familiarity illusion' may have led to overconfidence in similarity and underexpectation of the needs of integration. Two of the three merged banks with common ownership (Oceanic and ETB) failed.

(ii) While there is significant literature which explores the effect of cultural differences upon M&A (Chatterjee et al., 1992; Datta and Puia, 1995; Weber et al., 1996; Very et al., 1997; Morosini et al., 1998; Lubatkin et al., 1999; Björkman et al., 2007; Stahl and Voight, 2008; Weber et al., 2009) and considerable evidence to support the claim that national cultural differences matter (Faulkner et al., 2002; Graebner, 2004; Graebner and Eisenhardt, 2004; Puranam et al., 2006; Puranam and Srikanth, 2007; Cording et al., 2008; Ellis et al., 2009; Puranam et al., 2009; Reus and Lamont, 2009), little attention has been paid to the importance of regional differences in culture potentially affecting M&A. There is an important cultural literature which points to significant variation in regional cultural variation within a country, to the extent that some researchers suggest that this variation is greater than that proposed for national differences (Zeldin, 1983). In the cases of merged Nigerian banks, many encountered significant difficulties in attempting to integrate banks from different geographic regions of the country, particularly, but not exclusively, between the north and the south. These differences reflect long-established divides in ethnic groups which do not consider themselves part of the same culture. Indeed, severe conflicts between ethnic groups persist today. Merging banks confronting these differences varied in their approaches to the challenge, from virtually ignoring the differences, such as at FinBank, to detailed and proactive engagement at Fidelity Bank. It is noticable that many of the banks experiencing cultural difficulties, such as PHB and FinBank, were later taken over by the government; however, some banks, such as FCMB, Diamond Bank and Fidelity Bank, were skilled at tackling the cultural issue through good communications practices.

(iii) A distinguishing characteristic of surviving Nigerian banks was good-quality communications throughout the merger process. In no instances where good pre and post-merger communications were deployed continuously and in depth through a variety of media was the bank subsequently found to be unhealthy. Even where there were significant cultural issues to tackle, those banks deploying detailed and continuous communications practices managed to remain as healthy institutions. In some instances, merging banks which started out with poor communications, such as PHB, subsequently improved their communications to employees but the bank still failed.

(iv) Mergers among Nigerian Banks were a new activity in 2005, and banks were having to learn how to set about these major changes. In all cases there was a lack of experience and many commented upon the perceived lack of time available for planning (although the time frame of 6–9 months would not be regarded as short by banks merging in other parts of the world). In many cases banks relied upon their own skills to tackle merging, but in some instances external consultants were brought in to facilitate integration. It is noticable that in those cases, such as Sterling Bank, the interviewees had much more detailed appreciation of what could be done in HRM terms and these integrations appeared to have progressed well, even though some of the recommendations were counter to local norms.

The merging banks made use of different post-acquisition integration approaches. Interestingly, these integration approaches do not fit particularly closely to stated strategies for the merger, with examples of merging for market access and operational similarity being present in all integration approaches. HRM issues are also not closely aligned with integration approaches, with examples of poor levels of communication as well as good practice in all integration styles. Similarly, the quality of cultural difference management seems independent of integration style, which is somewhat surprising where merging banks aimed to keep their units distinct. On this basis, the integration approach itself does not seem to indicate merger outcome.

The stated strategy of merging banks, apart from needing to react to the CBN directive, does seem to be linked to subsequent HRM practice. It is observable that, where banks did not really have a strategy except to merge in order to satisfy the Central Bank's financial criteria, subsequent communications were poor and there was little direction and attention to HRM issues. Two of these 'financial' mergers, FinBank and Spring Bank, were also in poor financial condition and subsequently failed. When mergers focused closely upon operational alignment, such as IBTC–Chartered, Skye Bank and UBA, there was good communication practice and good attention to cultural issues. These mergers were cleared as healthy.

The findings have implications for i) communications, ii) M&A experience and iii) strategic fit theories:

Communications theory argues that rich interactive open communications reduces negative individual employee attitudes between organizations through providing them with necessary information to justify inescapable changes during the merger process (Bastien, 1987; Schweiger and DeNisi, 1991; Ranft and Lord, 2002), to reduce uncertainty, develop shared understanding, perceived fairness (Ellis et al., 2009) and trust. Good communications establishes a favourable climate throughout the process and also facilitates interorganizational knowledge exchange, essential for synergies to be realized (Ranft and Lord, 2002). In the Nigerian cases the extent of communications usage is positively associated with interorganizational linkages and also mitigates the potential disruption of cultural differences. In this process of *enculturation* – the creation and maintenance of organizational cultures and the assimilation of members into the organization – rich and open communications among Nigerian banks can be seen to be central to reducing the potentially damaging effects of regional cultural differences. While the M&A literature has focused upon national cultural distance determining acquisition outcome, in this study the presence and nature of interorganizational communications can be seen to play an important role in determining the impact that regional cultural differences may have.

The Nigerian case is also interesting in terms of learning approaches to mergers. The acquisition literature has the longest history of studying learning in strategic contexts (Barkema and Schijven, 2008) and many studies, following a 'traditional learning curve perspective', have attempted to demonstrate that learning from prior mergers may lead to improved subsequent merger outcomes. This stream of enquiry, however, does not address the issue of those firms engaging in M&A for the first time and whether they can learn about mergers in other ways. In HRM terms the case evidence reported in this chapter suggests that the use of external consultants with significant prior experience does have a beneficial effect upon merger outcome. Learning theory in M&A to date has focused exclusively upon the firm's own experience and has disregarded the opportunities for merging firms to learn from other organizations such as management consultants. This influence is likely to be most pronounced in firms merging for the first time. The Nigerian cases show how South African experience has been largely beneficial in the Nigerian context and identifies other ways in which merging firms may learn about mergers. For a more complete learning theory of M&A the role of external influencers needs to be recognized. This insight is also interesting for engaging in the convergence/divergence thesis: whether all HRM practices are culturally determined or whether they will over time tend towards HRM universals present in industrial societies (Ralston et al., 2008), or, indeed, whether the mergers exhibit cross-vergence (Anakwe, 2002).

The observation that the Nigerian bank mergers do not show clear association between HRM practices and post-acquisition integration styles raises a question about the assumed fit of M&A strategy with HRM strategy (Aguilera and Dencker, 2004). This may be the result of lack of experience of M&A among Nigerian banks, which would suggest that future mergers may show much closer alignment between HRM and integration strategies as experience grows. However, it may also be indicative of other distinctive Nigerian factors at work, which may mean there is an indigenous approach to M&A that is not captured in generic M&A frameworks.

Conclusions

This chapter is distinctive in being the first to examine HRM issues in African M&A. Through focusing upon a major series of mergers among

Nigerian banks, this exploratory study has identified many HRM issues of importance to the integration process. Many of these have received significant attention at the generic level and are evident in these cases, such as the importance of timely, appropriate and continuous communications through multiple media. The study, however, has also identified other issues which are not so well recognized. Of great importance is the existence of significant regional differences in Nigerian culture. Without explicit planning and activity aimed at managing these differences, these regional variations caused substantial and enduring problems for some integrating banks. The importance of regional variation in culture is not fully recognized in the M&A literature. Another issue of importance in the Nigerian context was the lack of M&A experience, which meant that many banks were not really prepared for engaging in this activity. The comments on the lack of time are telling, as M&A in other contexts are transacted in an equally short time. The lack of experience may also be a reason why the Nigerian mergers do not fit easily into the post-acquisition integration framework used to classify them. The fact that there are a wide variety of HRM practices displayed within the same integration approach raises an interesting question about the extent to which HRM practices should be closely linked to overall integration approach in this context and in general. Nuances also emerged which are representative of Nigerian culture, namely, the importance of age in relation to seniority, and the assumed social role of the leader in these institutions. While other cultures have similar values, these need to be remembered in future deals. Also noteworthy was the use of international consultants to aid in the integration process. In the context of lack of experience, the use of these advisors appears to have been successful.

The practical implication for future Nigerian mergers is that HRM matters throughout the merger process. Many of the generic HRM practices identified earlier in the chapter are present, and several are critical to outcome. In particular, the role of communications cannot be overestimated, and it is particularly effective when it is rich, open and timely. Although merging within the same industrial sector and in the same country, there can be significant regional differences in culture which can cause significant harm to post-acquisition integration. Early recognition of these differences through thorough HRM due diligence can greatly aid subsequent integration efforts. For companies which have not merged before and so lack HRM merger experience, valuable assistance can be gained through the careful use of appropriate advisors, although detailed consideration should be given to the extent to which generic or context-specific advice should be tailored to local efforts.

The Nigerian banking context is novel for the extent of merger activity at one time. It also offers significant opportunity for further research in terms of the role of experience in subsequent M&A activity which is likely to occur. It may also allow a more precise picture to emerge about whether Nigerian mergers will converge towards generic prescriptions of HRM practices fitting with post-acquisition strategies or whether distinctive local differences will remain. A more micro focus upon specific communications activities over time may help inform the convergence, divergence, cross-vergence debate.

References

Adebayo, D. O. (2005), 'Perceived Workplace Fairness, Transformational Leadership and Motivation in the Nigeria Police: Implications for Change', *International Journal of Police Science & Management*, 7, 110–122.

Aguilera, R., and Dencker, J. (2004), 'The Role of Human Resource Management in Cross-Border Mergers and Acquisitions', *International Journal of Human Resource Management*, 15, 1355–1370.

Akintoye, I. R., and Somoye, R. (2008), 'Corporate Governance and Merger Activity in the Nigeria Banking Industry: Some Clarifying Comments', *International Research Journal of Finance and Economics*, 19, 126–138.

Anakwe, U. P. (2002), 'Human Resource Management Practices in Nigeria: Challenges and Insights', *International Journal of Human Resource Management*, 13(7), 1042–1056.

Angwin, D. (2001), 'Mergers and Acquisitions across European Borders: National Perspectives on Preacquisition Due Diligence and the Use of Professional Advisors', *Journal of World Business*, 36, 32–57.

Angwin, D. (2004), 'Speed in M&A Integration: The First 100 Days', *European Management Journal*, 22, 418–430.

Antila, E. (2006), 'The Role of HR Managers in International Mergers and Acquisitions: A Multiple Case Study', *International Journal of Human Resource Management*, 17, 999–1020.

Appelbaum, S., Gandell, J., Yortis, H., Proper, S., and Jobin, F. (2000), 'Anatomy of a Merger: Behavior of Organizational Factors and Processes throughout the Pre- during Post-Stages, Part 1', *Management Decision*, 38, 649–661.

Ashkenas, R. N., and Francis, S. C. (2000), 'Integration Managers: Special Leaders for Special Times', *Harvard Business Review*, 78, 108–116.

Barkema, H. G., and Schijven, M. (2008), 'How Do Firms Learn to Make Acquisitions? A Review of Past Research and an Agenda for the Future', *Journal of Management*, 34, 594–634.

Barret, P. (1973), *The Human Implications of Mergers and Takeovers*. London: Institute of Personnel Management.

Bastien, D. T. (1987), 'Common Patterns of Behavior and Communication in Corporate Mergers and Acquisitions', *Human Resource Management*, 26, 17–33.

Birkinshaw, J., Bresman, H., and Håkanson, L. (2000), 'Managing the Post-Acquisition Integration Process: How the Human Integration and the Task Integration Processes Interact to Foster Value Creation', *Journal of Management Studies*, 37, 395–425.

Björkman, I., Stahl, G., and Vaara, E. (2007), 'Cultural Differences and Capability Transfer in Cross – Border Acquisitions: The Mediating Roles of Capability Complementarity, Absorptive Capacity, and Social Integration', *Journal of International Business Studies*, 38, 658–672.

Bower, J. L. (2001), 'Not All M&A Are Alike – and That Matters', *Harvard Business Review*, 79, 92–101.

Budhwar, P. S., Varma, A., Katou, A. A., and Narayan, D. (2009), 'The Role of HR in Cross-Border Mergers and Acquisitions: The Case of Indian Pharmaceutical Firms', *Multinational Business Review*, 17, 89–110.

Buono, A. F., and Bowditch, J. L. (1989), *The Human Side of Mergers and Acquisitions. Managing Collisions between People, Cultures, and Organizations*. San Francisco, CA: Jossey-Bass.

Central Bank of Nigeria. Retrieved 2010-02-28, from http://www.cenbank.org/AboutCBN.

Charman, A. (1999), 'Global Mergers and Acquisitions: The Human Resource Challenge', *International Focus* (Society for Human Resource Management).

Chatterjee, S., Lubatkin, M. H., Schweiger, D. M., and Weber, Y. (1992), 'Cultural Differences and Shareholders Value: Explaining the Variability in the Performance of Related Mergers', *Strategic Management Journal*, 13, 319–334.

Chibuike, U. U. (2004), 'Ethics in Nigerian Banking', *Journal of Money Laundering Control*, 8, 66–74.

Cooke, F. L. (2006), 'Acquisitions of Chinese State-Owned Enterprises by Multinational Corporations: Driving Forces, Barriers and Implications for HRM', *British Journal of Management*, 17, S105–S121.

Cording, M., Christmann, P., and King, D. R. (2008) 'Reducing Casual Ambiguity in Acquisition Integration: Intermediate Goals as Mediators of Integration Decisions and Acquisition Performance', *Academy of Management Journal*, 51, 744–767.

Datta, D. K., and Puia, G. (1995), 'Cross – Border Acquisitions: An Examination of the Influence of Relatedness and Cultural Fit on Shareholder Value Creation in U.S. Acquiring Firms', *Management International Review*, 35(4), 337–359.

Dong, J. L., and Hu, J. (1995), 'Mergers and Acquisitions in China', *Economic Review*, 80(6), 15.

Eisenhardt, K. M. (1989), 'Building Theories from Case Study Research', *The Academy of Management Review*, 14, 532–550.

Eisenhardt, K. M., and Graebner, M. E. (2007), 'Theory Building from Cases: Opportunities and Challenges', *Academy of Management Journal*, 50, 25–32.

Ellis, K. M., Reus, T. H., and Lamont, B. T. (2009), 'The Effects of Procedural and Informational Justice in the Integration of Related Acquisitions', *Strategic Management Journal*, 30, 137–161.

Fanimo, D. (2006), 'Consolidation: Union Flays Sack of Bank Workers', *The Guardian*, 18 April, p. 51.

Faulkner, D., Pitkethly, R., and Child, J. (2002), 'International Mergers and Acquisitions in the UK 1985-94: A Comparison of National HRM Practices', *International Journal of Human Resource Management*, 13, 106–122.

Ferracone, R. (1987), 'Blending Compensation Plans of Combining Firms', *Mergers and Acquisitions*, September–October, 57–62.

Gertsen, M. C., Söderberg, A.-M., and Torp, J. E. (1998), *Cultural Dimensions of International Mergers and Acquisitions*. Berlin: Walter de Gruyter.

Gomes, E. (2009), *Acquisitions in the UK Car Industry: A Comprehensive Analysis of the Merger Processes*. KG, Saarbrucken: VDM Verlag Dr Muller Aktiengesellschaft & Co.

Gomes, E., Cohen, M., and Mellahi, K. (2010), 'When Two African Cultures Collide: A Study of Interactions between Managers in a Strategic Alliance between Two African Organizations. Special Issues: Managing People in Africa: Challenges for an Emergent Continent', *Journal of World Business*, 46(1), 5–12.

Graebner, M. E. (2004), 'Momentum and Serendipity: How Acquired Firm Leaders Create Value in the Integration of Technology Firms', *Strategic Management Journal*, 25, 751–777.

Graebner, M. E., and Eisenhardt, K. M. (2004), 'The Other Side of the Story: Acquisition as Courtship and Governance as Syndicate in Entrepreneurial Firms', *Administrative Science Quarterly*, 49, 366–403.

Graves, D. (1981), 'Individual Reactions to a Merger of Two Small Firms of Brokers in the Re-Insurance Industry: A Total Population Survey', *Journal of Management Studies*, 18, 89–113.

Habeck, M. H., Kroger, F., and Tram, M. R. (1999), *After the Merger*. London/New York: Financial Times/Prentice Hall.

Haspeslagh, P. C., and Jemison, D. B. (1991), *Managing Acquisitions: Creating Value through Corporate Renewal*. New York: The Free Press.

Homburg, C., and Bucerius, M. (2006), 'Is Speed of Integration Really a Success Factor in Mergers and Acquisitions? An Analysis of the Role of Internal and External Relatedness', *Strategic Management Journal*, 27, 347–367.

Howell, R. A. (1970), 'Plan to Integrate Your Acquisitions', *Harvard Business Review*, 48, 66–76.

Hubbard, N. (2001), *Acquisition Strategy and Implementation*, Revised edition. Basingstoke: Palgrave.

Ingham, H., Kran, I., and Lovestam, A. (1992), 'Mergers and Profitability: A Managerial Success Story?' *Journal of Management Studies*, 29, 195–208.

Kitching, J. (1967), 'Why Do Mergers Miscarry?' *Harvard Business Review*, 45, 84–101.

Kithinji, A. M., and Waweru, N. M. (2007), 'Merger Restructuring and Financial Performance of Commercial Banks in Kenya', *Economics, Management, and Financial Markets*, 2, 2.

Krug, J., and Hegarty, W. (2001), 'Predicting Who Stays and Leaves after an Acquisition: A Study of Top Managers in Multinational Firms', *Strategic Management Journal*, 22, 185–196.

Kumar, S., and Bansal, L. K. (2008), 'The Impact of Mergers and Acquisitions on Corporate Performance in India', *Management Decision*, 46, 1531–1543.

Larsson, R., and Finkelstein, S. (1999), 'Integrating Strategic, Organizational, and Human Resource Perspectives on Mergers and Acquisitions: A Case Survey of Synergy Realization', *Organization Science*, 10(1), 1–26.

Light, D., Kid, D., De Monaco, L., Freeland, G., and O'Sullivan, P. (2001), 'Who Goes, Who Stays?' *Harvard Business Review*, 79, 34–43.

Lin, Z., Peng, M. W., Yang, H., and Sun, S. L. (2009), 'How Do Networks and Learning Drive M&As? An Institutional Comparison between China and the United States', *Strategic Management Journal*, 30, 1113–1132.

Lubatkin, M., Schweiger, D., and Weber, Y. (1999), 'Top Management Turnover in Related M&A: An Additional Test of the Theory of Relative Standing', *Journal of Management*, 25, 55–73.

McDonald, J., Coulthard, M., and Lange, P. D. (2005), 'Planning for a Successful Merger or Acquisition: Lessons from an Australian Study', *Journal of Global Business and Technology*, 1(2), 1–11.

Mintzberg, H., Raisinghani, D., and Theoret, A. (1976), 'The Structure of Unstructured Decision Processes', *Administrative Science Quarterly*, 21, 246–275.

Mirvis, P. H., and Marks, M. L. (1992), 'The Human Side of Merger Planning: Assessing and Analyzing "Fit" ', *Human Resource Planning*, 15, 69–92.

Mitleton-Kelly, E. (2006), 'Coevolutionary Integration: The Co-creation of a New Organizational Form Following a Merger and Acquisition', *Emergence: Complexity & Organization*, 8, 36–47.

Morosini, P., Shane, S., and Singh, H. (1998), 'National Cultural Distance and Cross-Border Acquisition Performance', *Journal of International Business Studies*, 29, 137–158.

Nwosu, O. (2005), 'Reputation Management: Imperative of a New Order', *Financial Standard*, 20 June, p. 7.

Papadakis, V. M. (2005), 'The Role of Broader Context and the Communication Program in Merger and Acquisition Implementation Success', *Management Decision*, 43, 236–255.

Peterhoff, D. (2004), 'Designing HR Due Diligence in the Context of Mergers and Acquisitions', 7th IFSAM (International Federation of Scholarly Associations of Management) World Conference 2004.

Puranam, P., Singh, H., and Chaudhuri, S. (2009), 'Integrating Acquired Capabilities: When Structural Integration Is (Un)necessary', *Organization Science*, 20, 313–328.

Puranam, P., Singh, H., and Zollo, M. (2006), 'Organizing for Innovation: Managing the Coordination-Autonomy Dilemma in Technology Acquisitions', *Academy of Management Journal*, 49, 263–280.

Puranam, P., and Srikanth, K. (2007), 'What They Know vs. What They Do: How Acquirers Leverage Technology Acquisitions', *Strategic Management Journal*, 28, 805–825.

Ralston, D. A., Holt, D. H., Terpstra, R. H., and Yu, Kai-Cheng (2008), 'The Impact of National Culture and Economic Ideology on Managerial Work Values: A Study of the United States, Russia, Japan, and China', *Journal of International Business Studies*, 39, 8–26.

Ranft, A. L., and Lord, M. D. (2002), 'Acquiring New Technologies and Capabilities: A Grounded Model of Acquisition Implementation', *Organisation Science*, 13, 420–441.

Reus, T. H., and Lamont, B. T. (2009), 'The Double-Edged Sword of Cultural Distance in International Acquisitions', *Journal of International Business Studies*, 40, 1298–1316.

Risberg, A. (2001), 'Employee Experiences of Acquisition Processes', *Journal of World Business*, 36(1), 58.

Schuler, R. S. (2001), 'Human Resource Issues and Activities in International Joint Ventures', *International Journal of Human Resource Management*, 12, 1–52.

Schuler, R. S., and Jackson, S. E. (2001), 'HR Issues and Activities in Mergers and Acquisitions', *European Management Journal*, 19, 239–253.

Schweiger, D. M., Csiszar, E. N., and Napier, N. K. (1993), 'Implementing International Mergers and Acquisitions', *Human Resource Planning*, 16(1), 53–53.

Schweiger, D. M., and Denisi, A. S. (1991), 'Communication with Employees Following a Merger: A Longitudinal Field Experiment', *Academy of Management Journal*, 34, 110–135.

Schweiger, D. M., and Weber, Y. (1989), 'Strategies for Managing Human Resources During Mergers and Acquisitions: An Empirical Investigation', *Human Resource Planning*, 12, 69–86.

Soludo, C. (2006), 'Beyond Banking Sector Consolidation in Nigeria', 12th Annual Economic Summit Held at Abuja, Nigeria.

Stahl, G. K., and Mendenhall, M. E. (eds.) (2005), *Mergers and Acquisitions: Managing Culture and Human Resources*. Palo Alto, CA: Stanford University Press.

Stahl, K. G., and Voight, A. (2008), 'Do Cultural Differences Matter in Mergers and Acquisitions? A Tentative Model for Examination', *Organization Science*, 19, 160–176.

Vaara, E. (2003), 'Post-acquisition Integration as Sense Making: Glimpses of Ambiguity, Confusion, Hypocrisy, and Politicization', *Journal of Management Studies*, 40, 859–894.

Vermeulen, F., and Barkema, H. (2001), 'Learning through Acquisitions', *Academy of Management Journal*, 44, 457–476.

Very, P., Lubatkin, M., Calori, R., and Veiga, J. (1997), 'Relative Standing and the Performance of Recently Acquired European Firms', *Strategic Management Journal*, 18, 593–614.

Weber, R. A., and Camerer, C. F. (2003), 'Cultural Conflict and Merger Failure: An Experimental Approach', *Management Science*, 49, 400–415.

Weber, Y., and Schweiger, D. (1992), 'Top Management Culture in Mergers and Acquisitions: A Lesson in Anthropology', *The International Journal of Conflict Management*, 3, 285–302.

Weber, Y., Shenkar, O., and Raveh, A. (1996), 'National and Corporate Culture Fit in Mergers/Acquisitions: An Exploratory Study', *Management Science*, 42, 1215–1227.

Weber, Y., Tarba, S. Y., and Reichel, A. (2009), 'International Mergers and Acquisitions Performance Revisited – The Role of Cultural Distance and Post-acquisition Integration Approach', in C. Cooper and S. Finkelstein (Eds) *Advances in Mergers and Acquisitions*, Vol. 8. New York: JAI.

Yin, R. (2008), *Case Study Research Design and Methods*, Fourth edition. Thousand Oaks, CA: Sage.

Zeldin, T. (1983), *The French*. Flamingo: Fontana Paperbacks.

Zephyr, M&A report (2010), *South Africa Quarter 3, 2010*. Bureau Van Dijk.

2
Factors Hindering the Adoption of HIV/AIDS Workplace Policies: Evidence from Private Sector Companies in Malawi

Rhoda Bakuwa and Aminu Mamman

Introduction

HIV/AIDS has become a critical issue in the workplace. An early African contribution on the subject was made by Baruch and Clancy (2000), who acknowledge that 'although a sensitive issue, the subject of HIV/AIDS is relevant to many aspects and facets of management, such as Equal Employment Opportunity, effectiveness, industrial relations, family studies and career systems in organizations' (p. 789). The authors also acknowledge the dearth of literature on how organizations are managing AIDS in the African workplace. With the help of a national and international campaign, a lot has been done in setting up structures, systems and programmes for managing HIV/AIDS in the workplace and the wider society (ILO, 2001, 2006; Piot et al., 2001; Mahajan et al., 2007). There is also increasing research and knowledge of HIV/AIDS in the workplace, ranging from the academic to public policy (Dickinson and Innes, 2004; Arndt, 2006; Mahajan et al., 2007). In spite of the growing incidence of HIV/AIDS in the workplace, many organizations do not have an HIV/AIDS workplace policy. The primary aim of the chapter is to examine managerial perspective on the reasons why private sector companies in Malawi do not adopt formal HIV/AIDS workplace policy. Other related aims of the chapter are to analyse the relative significance of the factors hindering the adoption of the workplace policy, and, finally, to explore the implications of the findings for research in organizational innovation in general and African managers and HR practitioners in particular.

Literature on HIV/AIDS in the workplace

Impact of HIV/AIDS in the workplace

Researchers have identified several economic and social impacts of HIV/AIDS to the organization and employees. These include: loss of productivity, absenteeism, conflict, accidents, and misuse of tools and equipment (Fraser et al., 2002; Rosen et al., 2004a; Arndt, 2006; Mahajan et al., 2007). Simon et al. (2000) have provided an elaborate framework for analysing the economic impact of HIV/AIDS on African businesses. The framework is based on the progression of cases and their associated costs at both the employee and organizational levels. The costs include: sick leave and absenteeism; loss of productivity; and overtime. Indeed, the HR function has a role to play in enabling organizations to manage the cost impact effectively. For example, Baruch and Clancy (2000) have outlined several HRM implications, which include contingency planning by HR managers that takes into account the labour market characterized by the HIV/AIDS epidemic.

Organizational response

In a survey of 225 companies in Botswana, Namibia, Zimbabwe and South Africa, Mahajan et al. (2007) reported an increasing proliferation of workplace policies and programmes in large companies, which included safeguards against discriminatory practices, HIV education programmes, the growing provisions of voluntary counselling and testing (VCT) and enabling smaller companies to develop HIV programmes. In an investigation of the response of African business to HIV/AIDS, Simon et al. (2000) reported that African businesses adopted two strategies for dealing with HIV/AIDS in the workplace: prevention interventions, which include HIV/AIDS education among employees and their families, and cost avoidance. A key aspect of Malawi's response to HIV/AIDS in the workplace has been the number of organizations addressing HIV/AIDS and the participation of community-based organizations, civil society and the formal sectors (GoM/UNDP, 2005). The Department of Human Resource Management and Development (DHRMD) spearheads public sector planning and integration of HIV/AIDS, guided by a National Public Service HIV/AIDS Policy (GoM/UNDP, 2005). Within the private sector, the Malawi Business Coalition against AIDS (MBCA) was formed in 2003 following a World Bank mission that held consultative meetings with a stakeholder group of the private sector, the Malawi Confederation of Chambers of Commerce and Industry (MCCCI). The aim of MBCA is to coordinate the response of the private sector organizations, and serve as an umbrella organization providing grants and technical guidance to companies (GoM/UNDP, 2005).

Institutional frameworks and national structures

The management of HIV/AIDS in the workplace can be enabled or constrained by institutional frameworks. In countries like the USA, which has taken a lead, various legislative Acts provide protection for employees infected by the virus and require organizations to treat employees with dignity and equity (Franklin et al., 1992). Similarly, South Africa has the following legislation: Labour Relations Act 1995, which prohibits dismissal of employees with HIV/AIDS; Employment Equity Act 1998, which prohibits mandatory HIV/AIDS testing; Medical Schemes Act 1998, which prohibits medical schemes differentiating benefits based on HIV/AIDS status; Prescribed Minimum Benefit Amendment, which states that all medical aid scheme benefits must include HIV/AIDS testing, care and treatment (Mahajan et al., 2007). Across Africa more generally, extensive legislation remains uncommon.

Malawi's national structure for managing HIV/AIDS in the workplace was developed from an extensive stakeholder consultation. This led to a National HIV/AIDS Strategic Framework, which defined priorities for a national response adopted in 1999. This framework emphasized the need for an expanded and multisectoral response incorporating care, support and impact mitigation as integral parts of the national response (NAC, 2003, p. 2). Stakeholders also recognized that a more structured body was needed to strengthen leadership and coordination of Malawi's response to AIDS. This led to the creation of the National AIDS Commission (NAC), a stand-alone body located in the Office of the President and Cabinet, in order to signal a high level of political commitment and to encourage sectors other than health to become involved through the adoption of a multisectoral response to HIV/AIDS (World Bank, 2000; Barnett and Whiteside, 2002). According to the recent United States Agency for International Development report (USAID, 2010), the Malawi national framework has borne fruit. The report indicated that the country has had impressive success in antiretroviral therapy (ART). The report also indicated that 35 per cent of people in need of treatment were receiving ART. Similarly, the report indicated that ART has been provided free of charge in the public sector since 2004, through financial support provided by the Global Fund to Fight AIDS.

Theoretical perspectives and hypotheses

Theoretical perspectives

Adoption of HIV/AIDS workplace policy is an example of management innovation, because organizational innovation has been defined as the 'adoption of an internally generated or purchased devices, system, policy, program, process, product or service that is new to the adopting organisation' (Damanpour, 1991, p. 556). Similarly, Dewar and Dutton (1986, p. 1422) defined innovation as 'an idea, practice, or material artefact perceived to be new by the relevant unit of adoption'. Organizations' willingness to adopt a particular workplace policy would be constrained or enabled by key factors internal or external to the organization (DiMaggio and Powell, 1983; Weaver et al., 1999). A number of theoretical perspectives have been used implicitly or explicitly to explain the behaviour of organizations vis-à-vis their ability and willingness to adopt innovation (Thomas et al., 1993). These theoretical perspectives can be conveniently categorized into two: those that focus largely on external factors, and those that focus on internal factors.

External factors perspective

Prominent in this perspective are the open system theory and institutional theories which assume that, because the organization depends on the wide environment for its inputs, it would adopt working practices that fit the wider environment features (Jackson and Schuler, 1995). One of the most important inputs that an organization relies on from the environment is its people (Huselid et al., 1997). Therefore, organizations are expected to adopt policies and practices to fit the kinds of people in its labour market (Jackson and Schuler, 1995). For example, in a labour market characterized by specific social and economic features, organizations are expected to adopt the policies and practices that will enable the 'exploitation' of the talent of the 'people' with such a specific socio-economic background. Therefore, within the context of the open system school, obstacles to the adoption of an efficient working arrangement that fits the needs of the organization would come from internal forces such as organizational politics or ignorance of the efficacy of the innovation (Abrahamson, 1996). This is because, in an open system model, managers are appreciative of the importance of the external factors as well as the need to respond to them accordingly through the adoption of appropriate strategies and practices (Abrahamson, 1996; Weaver et al., 1999).

Institutional perspective

Institutional perspective is not necessarily a radical departure from the open system perspective, for it also assumes that the organizations rely on the external environment for their inputs and seek legitimacy for their behaviour (Goodstein, 1994; Teo et al., 2003). Therefore, an organization is subject to pressure to conform. Such conformity facilitates acceptance and legitimacy, which in turn contribute to organizational success and survival (DiMaggio and Powell, 1983). These pressures come from the state, through appropriate legislation, the business community to which the organization belongs, and professional associations within and outside its industry (DiMaggio and Powell, 1983). Given the integration of the world's economic and political systems, globalization also acts as another source of pressure to conform through international institutions and intergovernmental agencies. African organizations have been subjected to this pressure recently (Mamman et al., 2006, 2009).

Pressure from external factors coupled with the desire for external approval can lead to the adoption of workplace practices that would satisfy external stakeholders (Weaver et al., 1999). Conversely, external constituency can constrain organizations from adopting certain workplace practices that are deemed efficient or politically convenient (Abrahamson, 1996). Therefore, institutional theory is useful for examining the factors that lead organizations to adopt similar structures, strategies and processes – institutional isomorphism (Deephouse, 1996). However, we argue that organizations facing such pressure from external constituency would act differently where the internal pressure outweighs the external pressure (Weaver et al., 1999). For example, an organization is unlikely to succumb to external pressure to adopt HIV/AIDS workplace policy if the pressure is not backed up by strong legislation, or if the pressure from the national trade union movement and business associations is weak in comparison to the size and influence of the organization. This would be particularly the case in African countries, where there are weak formal national institutions and trade unions. Therefore, in such a context one would expect organizational size to be associated with managerial perception of the factors hindering the adoption of workplace policy.

Internal perspectives

For the purpose of this chapter, we adopt *resource dependence* and *resource-based* theories to explain why some organizations do not adopt certain workplace policy. While the former has some political angle, the latter is grounded in the notion of efficient rationalism (Greening and Gray, 1994). Resource dependence theory views organizations as political entities rather than purely as economic or social entities. Therefore, central to this theory is the notion of resource exchange among internal constituencies (Mintzberg et al., 1998). Also, the concept of power is central to such exchange among constituencies (Child, 1997). Therefore, to understand why some organizations adopt or do not adopt certain workplace policy, one needs to understand power and influence within organizations. Formal power normally resides with top management, while informal power can reside anywhere within the organization (Daft, 2004). For example, the power to command organizational resources can reside with a particular individual or department (Daft, 2004). Therefore, such departments or individuals can hinder the adoption or implementation of an innovation. In fact, there is an abundance of literature indicating the symbolic adoption of innovation because certain powerful people do not believe in it or perceive it as a threat to their power base (Pfeffer and Salancik, 1978; DiMaggio, 1988; Westphal and Zajac, 2001).

Resource-based theory adopts a view that organizations can use their rare, valued and inimitable resources to achieve competitive advantage (Barney, 1991). Implicitly, the organization will adopt a working practice that will ensure the exploitation of 'the resources' in order to achieve competitive advantage (Barney, 1991; Wright and Snell, 1998). In line with resource-based theory, one would expect the absence of certain resources to hinder the adoption of certain working practices. For example, the absence of HR and Occupational, Health and Safety (OHS) could hinder the adoption of HIV/AIDS workplace policy. It can also be argued that the use of resource-based theory like the open system and institutional theories can be a matter of efficiency choice. Thus, an organization would only use its resources and adopt appropriate working practice to exploit them if it believed that such action would lead to the achievement of competitive advantage or lead to the avoidance of the negative consequences of not doing so. Based on the literature reviewed, we advance the following hypotheses.

Hypothesis 1a: Internal factors will play a greater role in hindering the adoption of HIV/AIDS workplace policy because of the weakness in the institutional forces in the African business environment.

Hypothesis 1b: Given that organizational size is associated with resources and influence, we expect size to play a moderating role in the non-adoption of HIV/AIDS workplace policy.

Hypothesis 2: Based on the resource-dependence and resource-based theories, there will be a variation in the perception of the significance of the factors hindering the adoption of HIV/AIDS workplace policy across organizations.

Methodology

The present study is based on a survey of 152 private sector companies from the MCCCI directory. The instrument has high internal consistency (*Cronbach Alpha* = 0.89). In addition, company policies were also collected to determine the existence and types of workplace policies.

The questionnaire covered a wide range of issues pertaining to the non-adoption of HIV/AIDS workplace policies. To examine the relative significance of the selected factors, respondents were asked to respond to a list of statements pertaining to factors hindering the adoption of formal HIV/AIDS workplace policies in the organizations. The questions are based on a five-point *Likert* scale (one: strongly disagree to five: strongly agree). Nine possible factors derived from the literature were considered relevant to the organizational environment of the companies under investigation. The following five items were considered as internal factors: (1) HIV/AIDS not seen as a priority business issue; (2) lack of visible impact of HIV/AIDS; (3) lack of top management support; (4) lack of financial resources; (5) lack of OHS and HR expertise; (6) weak trade unionism. The external factors were measured using three items: (1) no participation of OHS and HR in the activities of HIV/AIDS institutions; (2) absence of HIV/AIDS legislation; (3) lack of awareness of other companies' responses. The dependent variable (degree of non-adoption) was measured as follows: 1: There is no HIV/AIDS policy; 2: A formal HIV/AIDS policy exists. Size was measured by the number of employees as categorized by MCCCI (1: small, 2: medium, 3: large).

Background statistics

From the 152 usable questionnaires, 31 per cent are from the service sector, 28 per cent from the trading sector, 24 per cent from manufacturing, 14 per cent from transport/communication/distribution and the rest from the construction industry. These figures on the company sector fairly reflect the representation of the sectors in the Malawi economy. However, agriculture, which is a significant sector of the economy, is not represented in our sample because it is not part of the population from which we drew our sample (i.e. MCCCI). It is worth pointing out also that 65 per cent of the respondents are from the HR department and 16 per cent from finance and marketing. Preliminary data analysis revealed that 50 per cent of the respondents are from large businesses, 34 per cent are from medium-sized business and the rest are from small-scale businesses. Although our sample is a fair representation of MCCCI membership in terms of company size, it does not reflect the composition of size of organizations in the Malawi economy, where micro and small-scale enterprises dominate the economy. However, investigating such an unorganized sector is beyond the scope of the current study. The descriptive data also revealed that 52 per cent of the respondents are HR staff in middle management positions while 44 per cent are in top management positions. Also, our preliminary analyses revealed that 62 per cent of the respondents have not adopted a formal HIV/AIDS workplace policy.

The study found that some companies have had formal HIV/AIDS workplace policies for a period of more than five years. However, in many of the companies, their HIV/AIDS workplace policies have only been in existence for a period of less than one to three years. The study found that, although the Malawi Business Coalition (MBC) against HIV/AIDS was established in 2003, this coalition started its full-fledged activities in 2005. It is worth noting also that, once companies have decided to join MBC, they are encouraged and assisted to come up with HIV/AIDS workplace programmes and also to develop a formal workplace policy on HIV/AIDS.

Companies that have adopted formal HIV/AIDS workplace policies used various channels to communicate the existence of such policies to their employees. The study found that 74 per cent of the companies that have adopted formal HIV/AIDS workplace policies communicated through internal notices or circulars and 53 per cent of the companies organized a formal launch, while only 37 per cent used unions or employee representatives to communicate the existence of such policies to their employees. We also found that all the companies (100 per cent) that have HIV/AIDS workplace programmes have adopted some form of HIV/AIDS prevention programmes. According to UNAIDS/WHO (2007), prevention remains the focus for companies addressing HIV/AIDS because this approach is consistent with the need for rapid and sustained expansion in HIV/AIDS prevention.

Regarding treatment of HIV/AIDS, the analyses revealed that relatively fewer companies have sexually transmitted infections (STI) programmes and VCT programmes in place. This could be due to the fact that these programmes might require staff with expertise such as in medical/occupational health in order to properly implement the programmes. We also examined whether there are significant variations in the adoption of STI management and VCT programmes among the surveyed companies because of the availability of staff with health and safety expertise. The results show that 72 per cent of the companies that do not have staff with health and safety expertise have not adopted STI management programmes, compared with 24 per cent of the companies that have staff with health and safety expertise that have not adopted STI management programmes. On the other hand, 28 per cent of the companies that do not have staff with health and safety expertise have STI management programmes in place, while 76 per cent of the companies that have staff with health and safety expertise have STI management programmes in place.

The study investigated the target population of the HIV/AIDS programmes that companies have adopted. As can be seen in Table 2.1, companies target their HIV/AIDS programmes to different groups. For example, all companies (100 per cent) that have HIV/AIDS prevention programmes focus on their employees, while only 13 per cent focus on their surrounding community. Similarly, all companies (100 per cent) that have treatment programmes focus on their employees, while only 6 per cent focus on the surrounding community. In a nutshell, although the companies extend some support to the community, they appear to be paying greater attention to their employees and the employees' families. What does this say about the companies' approach to corporate social responsibility (CSR)? The answer seems clear from the data. It seems that, although demonstration of CSR can be a significant factor in the adoption of the policy, the companies focus on what can have direct and immediate benefit to the company (Bloom et al., 2006). In other words, the companies are more utilitarian than altruistic in their approach to CSR.

Table 2.1 Target populations of HIV/AIDS programmes

		Target population (Valid per cent)				
		Company employees (%)	Families of employees (%)	Business partners (%)	Surrounding community (%)	Broader community (%)
HIV/AIDS programmes	Prevention programmes ($N = 87$)	100	66	23	13	10
	Treatment programmes ($N = 50$)	100	74	8	6	6

Results and discussion

Descriptive statistics and correlations

Descriptive statistics for all the variables are set out in Table 2.1. The data in Table 2.2 show that many of the variables correlate with non-adoption of HIV/AIDs workplace policy. This suggests some preliminary support for our propositions. For example, there is a significant relationship between organizational size and the non-adoption of formal HIV/AIDS workplace policy ($r = -0.318$; $P < 0.01$). Similarly, there is a significant relationship between non-adoption of formal HIV/AIDS workplace policy and lack of visible impact of HIV/AIDS ($r = -0.389$; $P < 0.01$); lack of participation of HR/OHS experts in interorganizational activities associated with HIV/AIDS ($r = -0.266$; $P < 0.01$); and lack of awareness of other businesses' response to HIV/AIDS ($r = -0.263$; $P < 0.01$).

The relative significance of factors hindering the adoption of HIV/AIDS workplace policy

One of the objectives of this study is to investigate the relative significance of the factors hindering the adoption of HIV/AIDS workplace policy. In our review of literature, we have identified nine relevant factors that can hinder the adoption of HIV/AIDS workplace policy in Africa. In order to determine the relative influence of the nine factors hindering the adoption of HIV/AIDS workplace policy, we need to look at the standardized beta value of each of the nine factors in Table 2.3. Each value will tell us how much of the factor contributed to the non-adoption of HIV/AIDS workplace policy. For example, the standardized beta coefficient for lack of HR/OHS participation in HIV/AIDS institutional activities has beta -0.208. This means that the factor contributed 20.8 per cent to the reasons for the non-adoption of HIV/AIDS workplace policy in our theoretical assumption. The standardized beta coefficient for No visible HIV/AIDS impact is beta 0.344; this means that the factor contributed 34.4 per cent to the reasons for the non-adoption. Similarly, because the lack of awareness of other businesses' response to HIV/AIDS has a beta coefficient of 0.203, it means that the factor contributed 20.3 per cent.

Using the same logic, organizational size accounted for 28.1 per cent and lack of top management support accounted for 18 per cent of the reasons for non-adoption of HIV/AIDS workplace policy. On the other hand, the smallest contributors are absence of legislation (3.2 per cent), HIV/AIDS not a business priority (5.4 per cent) and weak trade unions

Table 2.2 Descriptive statistics

Variable	Mean	s.d.	1	2	3	4	5	6	7	8	9	10	11
1. Non-adoption	1.60	0.40	1.0										
2. Size	2.34	0.74	-0.318	1									
3. Top management support	2.94	1.28	0.062	0.159	1								
4. Lack of legislation	2.75	1.23	0.017	0.147	0.185	1							
5. Lack of financial resources	2.34	1.08	-0.073	0.009	0.044	0.127	1						
6. HIV/AIDS not a priority	3.47	1.19	-0.132	-0.111	0.440	0.049	0.032	1					
7. Lack of visible impact	3.27	1.33	-0.389	-0.301	-0.053	-0.022	0.060	0.386	1				
8. Lack of HR and OHS expert	2.77	1.18	-0.179	0.019	0.016	0.048	0.209	-0.102	0.001	1			
9. Weak trade unions	2.40	1.18	-0.073	0.238	0.287	0.368	0.201	0.001	-0.003	0.158	1		
10. No business responses information	3.00	1.20	-0.263	0.118	-0.070	0.273	0.102	-0.127	0.017	0.234	0.133	1	
11. Lack of participation in HIV/AIDS activities	3.14	1.23	-0.266	0.135	0.086	0.265	0.093	-0.048	-0.021	0.162	0.094	0.459	1

$N = 152$.
Correlation = All the variables above $r = 0.170$ correlated at 0.05 level or above.

Table 2.3 Results of multiple regression analysis for factors hindering the adoption of formal HIV/AIDS workplace policy

Model		Unstandardized coefficients		Standardized coefficients		
		B	SE	Beta	t	Sig.
1	(Constant)	5.248	0.219		23.958	0.000
	Company size	-0.316	0.098	-0.318	-3.237	0.002
2	(Constant)	3.869	0.392		9.860	0.000
	Company size	-0.279	0.094	-0.281	-2.966	0.004
	No top management support	0.103	0.061	0.180	1.679	0.097
	Lack of legislation on HIV/AIDS	-0.019	0.058	0.032	-0.328	0.743
	Lack of financial resources	-0.103	0.061	-0.152	-1.684	0.096
	HIV/AIDS not a business priority	-0.034	0.069	-0.054	-0.490	0.626
	No visible HIV and AIDS impact	0.191	0.056	0.344	3.404	0.001
	Lack of HR and OHS experts	0.087	0.057	0.141	1.536	0.128
	Weak trade unions	-0.052	0.063	-0.084	-0.832	0.408
	Lack of awareness of other businesses' response	0.123	0.062	0.203	1.991	0.050
	Lack of participation in HIV/AIDS activities	0.116	0.055	0.208	2.091	0.040
R square	37%					
Adjusted R square	30%					
Regression F ($df = 10, 94$)	5.102					
P	0.000					

Note: Dependent variable: non-adoption of formal policy.

(8.4 per cent). We should point out that, as can be seen in Table 2.3, not all the contributions of the factors are statistically significant. The contributions that are statistically significant are: organizational size ($t = -2.969$; $P < 0.004$), no visible impact ($t = 3.404$; $P < 0.001$), lack of awareness of other businesses' response ($t = 1.991$; $P < 0.050$) and lack of participation in HIV/AIDS activities ($t = -2.091$; $P < 0.040$). However, based on beta coefficient of all the nine factors plus organizational size, we can safely say that, cumulatively, internal factors contributed more to our model for the non-adoption of HIV/AIDS workplace policy. Therefore, hypothesis 1a is supported.

It is clear from the analyses of the data that the most significant contributor to the non-adoption of HIV/AIDS workplace policy is the perception of lack of visible impact of the pandemic on the business. This is in line with research findings by Bloom et al. (2006), who found that companies tend to be more responsive to HIV/AIDS issues in the workplace when they see the impact on the company. Similarly, Backer and Rogers (1998, p. 17) reported that 'AIDS work-site programs were mainly initiated by the four study companies as a result of the efforts of a champion or the occurrence of a tragic event, such as a company employee contracting AIDS'. On the whole, our findings correspond with Dickinson and Stevens's (2005) findings of businesses' response to HIV/AIDS in the workplace. For example, Dickinson and Stevens (2005, p. 286) reported that the social pressure of other companies' responses has been of greater influence in determining South African businesses' responses to HIV/AIDS in the workplace. Dickinson also revealed that the visibility of the epidemic played a significant factor in explaining companies' responses to HIV/AIDS. Dickinson also highlighted the potential roles of individuals, which sometimes tend to be relatively weak. Ramachandran et al. (2007) also found that organizational size, availability of skilled workers and financial resources were related to firms' willingness to invest in HIV/AIDS prevention activities.

The present study also suggests that the less HR/OHS practitioners participate in interorganizational activities the less likely companies will be to adopt HIV/AIDS workplace policy. However, it is noteworthy that external factors cannot be ignored. For example, when companies are not aware of what their counterparts are doing to respond to HIV/AIDS in the workplace, they are less likely to do anything about it. Similarly, lack of HR/OHS participation in interorganizational activities associated with HIV/AIDS contributes significantly to the non-adoption of HIV/AIDS workplace policy.

Explanatory power of the factors influencing the non-adoption of HIV/AIDS workplace policy

The other dimension of the regression analysis tests the utility of our proposition that the nine factors plus organizational size can explain the non-adoption of HIV/AIDS workplace policy. This aspect of the analysis is vital, because without testing the efficacy of our theoretical model we cannot argue for the relevance of the variables explaining the non-adoption of HIV/AIDS workplace policy. The model as a whole is very effective in predicting the non-adoption of formal HIV/AIDS workplace policy. The regression F is significant (F (10, 94) = 5.102; $P < 0.000$), and the variance accounted for is substantial ($R^2 = 0.37$; adjusted $R^2 = 0.30$). This means that we are able to state with statistical confidence our theoretical proposition that the nine internal and external factors contribute to the non-adoption of HIV/AIDS workplace policy by the companies.

The first step in the analysis tested the moderating effect of organizational size (hypothesis 1b). As predicted, organizational size has a moderating effect, accounting for a significant variance in the theoretical model. The coefficient is significant ($t = -2.969$; $P < 0.004$). In other words, irrespective of the other nine factors, whether an organization ignores HIV/AIDS workplace policy or not would be partly be influenced by its size. This offers some support for hypothesis 1b, in which we expected size to play a moderating role in the non-adoption of workplace policy. We also found significant relationships between some internal factors (perceived impact of HIV/AIDS: $r = -0.389$, and weak trade unionism: $r = 0.238$) and organizational size (Table 2.3). This supports our expectation that internal factors will correlate significantly with organizational size. The reason for our expectation is simply because, in the absence of strong legislation mandating the adoption of HIV/AIDS workplace policy, non-adoption can be explained largely by internal factors. For example, in the case of Malawi, where there is no compulsion to adopt HIV/AIDS workplace policy, weak trade unions and perceived lack of impact of HIV/AIDS on the business will contribute to the non-adoption of HIV/AIDS workplace policy. This is supported by the data in Table 2.3.

A further three factors were significant in contributing to the efficacy of the model. These refer to lack of perceived visible impact of HIV/AIDS ($t = -3.404$; $P < 0.001$), lack of awareness of other businesses' response to HIV/AIDS ($t = -1.991$; $P < 0.05$) and lack of participation of HR and OHS experts in HIV/AIDS activities ($t = -2.091$; $P < 0.04$). The participation of HR/OHS practitioners or lack of it as a contributor to non-adoption has been highlighted in the literature. For example, Teo et al. (2003), maintain that participation in business associations that sanction the adoption of a particular innovation renders the adoption of such an innovation more proximate and salient.

There is some marginal support for the effect of lack of top management support ($t = -1.679$; $P < 0.09$) and lack of financial resources ($t = -1.681$; $P < 0.09$). Therefore, as stated earlier, cumulatively the internal variables (i.e. both significant support and marginal support) have more explanatory power in explaining the non-adoption of the policy. The relevance of top management support is consistent with the finding by Rosen et al. (2004a) which indicates that action on HIV/AIDS in the workplace significantly depends on the attitudes of senior managers. Indeed, in African culture, characterized by high centralization of decision-making and large power distance (Mamman et al., 2009), the role of top management support is crucial to the adoption or non-adoption of HIV/AIDS workplace policy. On the issue of lack of financial resources as a hindrance to the adoption of HIV/AIDS workplace policy, again the literature has something to say about it. However, action on occupational health and safety policy is dependent not merely on the availability of funding, but also on awareness and prioritization.

We tested hypothesis 2, which predicted that the existence of HR and OHS in organizations would lead to variation in the perception of the influence of lack of HR and OHS expertise in the non-adoption of HIV/AIDS workplace policy. The results of the t-test did not reveal any significant variation between the two groups across all the nine factors. Therefore, hypothesis 2 is rejected. This result opens up an opportunity for further investigation. For example, to be able to test the impact of the availability of resources, future research needs to ask specific questions on how lack of resources in a specific organization contributes to non-adoption of HIV/AIDS workplace policy in the organization.

Conclusion

This chapter sought to identify the factors that hinder companies from adopting HIV/AIDS workplace policy. Our investigation has found that factors such as organizational size, lack of perceived impact of HIV/AIDS on the business, lack of awareness of what other businesses are doing regarding HIV/AIDS in the workplace, and lack of involvement of HR and OHS personnel in boundary-spanning activities are the main contributors to the non-adoption of the policy. The chapter also sought to determine the relative significance of the factors. Again, the findings revealed that internal factors as opposed to external factors dominate the reasons for the non-adoption of HIV/AIDS workplace policy. Third, we set out to examine the degree to which resources (i.e. financial and human) play a role in hindering organizations from adopting the workplace policy. We found that lack of participation of HR and OHS staff in HIV/AIDS-related interorganizational activities is perceived as a significant factor hindering the adoption of HIV/AIDS workplace policy. However, lack of financial resources was not considered as a significant contributory factor.

Implications for managers and HR practitioners

From our discussion of these findings, there are also practical implications of campaigning against HIV/AIDS for HR departments and African HR practitioners. For example, for institutions campaigning against AIDS, they have potential allies in the form of HR professionals who can provide them with access to organizations and managerial expertise in policy implementation. For HR professionals, the issue provides them with the opportunity to improve their image by acting as a bridge between the community and the organization. To succeed, they have to acquire a new role as well as new skills in dealing with technical issues associated with HIV/AIDS as well as social skills, advocacy skills, conflict management, and so on.

The data indicate that, the larger the organization, the more likely it will be to adopt HIV/AIDS workplace policy. In other words, small organizations are less likely to adopt HIV/AIDS workplace policy, partly because they are less likely to have HR practitioners who participate in interorganizational activities associated with HIV/AIDS. This has implications for HIV/AIDS campaigning in the workplace in particular, and HIV/AIDS in the wider community. This is because micro, small and medium-size organizations account for the majority of employers of labour in Africa (Parker et al., 1995). Therefore, their involvement in HIV/AIDS campaigning is crucial to addressing the challenge. However, such organizations are either unable or unwilling to employ the services of HR and OHS experts. Given that HIV/AIDS affects both small and large organizations, managers need to consider training other categories of employees to take on extra responsibilities related to HIV/AIDS in the workplace if they cannot afford dedicated HR/OHS staff.

Finally, the foregoing discussion has highlighted the potential role of HR departments and HR practitioners in managing the HIV/AIDS epidemic on the continent. For example, experts recommended that companies should stay well informed about the epidemic and its implications, formulate and practise appropriate policies, engage health insurance providers and negotiate appropriate policies, provide employees with opportunities to attend company-sponsored AIDS education seminars, explore the opportunity for multi-employee insurance coverage, and stay abreast of legislation. Experts also raised important questions regarding HIV/AIDS in sub-Saharan Africa which have significant implications for HR departments and HR practitioners. These include: HR capacity to deal with the crisis, policies for dealing with absenteeism, sickness and care of dependents, stress among employees, exposure of health personnel to HIV/AIDS, the psycho-social impact of the epidemic on the rest of the employees, and risk profiles of employees in terms of gender, age, and other demographic backgrounds. All these issues have generated roles for HR practitioners both within and outside the organization.

References

Abrahamson, E. (1996). Management Fashion. *Academy of Management Review*, 21(1), 254–285.

Mahajan, A. P., Colvin, M., Rudatsikira, J.-B., and Ettl, D. (2007). An Overview of HIV/AIDS Workplace Policies and Programmes in Southern Africa. *AIDS*, 21(Suppl. 3), S31–S39.

Arndt, C. (2006). HIV/AIDS, Human Capital, and Economic Growth Prospects for Mozambique. *Journal of Policy Modeling*, 28, 477–489.

Backer, T. E. and Rogers, E. M. (1998). *Final Report – Diffusion of Innovations and the Business Responds to AIDS Program*. Los Angeles: Human Interaction Research Institute (H-92).

Barnett, T. and Whiteside, A. (2002). *AIDS in the Twenty-First Century: Disease and Globalization*. Basingstoke: Palgrave Macmillan.

Barney, J. B. (1991). Firms Resources and Sustained Competitive Advantage. *Journal of Management*, 17, 99–120.

Baruch, Y. and Clancy, P. (2000). Managing AIDS in Africa: HRM Challenges in Tanzania. *International Journal of Human Resource Management*, 11(4), 789–806.

Bloom, D., Bloom, L., Steven, D., and Weston, M. (2006). *Business and HIV/AIDS: A Healthier Partnership? A Global Review of the Business Response to HIV/AIDS 2005–2006*. Davos, Switzerland: World Economic Forum.

Child, J. (1997). Strategic Choice in the Analysis of Action, Structure, Organizations and Environment: Retrospect and Prospect. *Organization Studies*, 18, 43–76.

Daft, R. (2004). *Organization Theory and Design*. Mason, Ohio: Thomson South-Western.

Damanpour, F. (1991). Organizational Innovation: A Meta-Analysis of Effects of Determinants and Moderators. *Academy of Management Journal*, 34(3), 555–590.

Deephouse, D. L. (1996). Does Isomorphism Legitimate? *Academy of Management Journal*, 39(4), 1024–1039.

DiMaggio, P. J. (1988). Interest and Agency in Institutional Theory. In L. G. Zucker (ed.) *Institutional Patterns and Organizations: Culture and Environment*, 3–22. Cambridge, MA: Ballinger.

Dewar, R. D. and Dutton, J. E. (1986). The Adoption of Radical and Incremental Innovations: An Empirical Analysis. *Management Science*, 32, 1422–1433.

Dickinson, D. and Innes, D. (2004). Fronts or Front-Lines? HIV/AIDS and Big Business in South Africa. *Transformation*, 55, 28–54.

Dickinson, D. and Stevens, M. (2005). Understanding the Response of Large South African Companies to HIV/AIDS. *Journal of Social Aspects of HIV/AIDS*, 2(2), 286–295.

DiMaggio, P. and Powell, W. W. (1983). The Iron Cage Revisited: Institutional Isomorphism and Collective Rationality in Organizational Fields. *American Sociological Review*, 48(2), 147–160.

Franklin, G. M., Gresham, A. B., and Fontenot, G. F. (1992). AIDS in the Workplace: Current Practice and Critical Issues. *Journal of Small Business Management*, 30(2), 61–73.

Fraser, F. K., Grant, W. J., Mwanza, P., and Naidoo, V. (2002). The Impact of HIV/AIDS on Small and Medium Enterprises in South Africa. *The South African Journal of Economics*, 70(7), 1216–1234.

GoM/UNDP (2005). *Malawi Human Development Report 2005: Reversing HIV/AIDS in Malawi*. Lilongwe: UNDP, accessed on 26 February 2007 from: http://www.systemdynamics.org/conferences/2008/proceed/papers/HEADL449 .pdf, accessed October 16th, 2013.

Goodstein, J. D. (1994). Institutional Pressures and Strategic Responsiveness: Employer Involvement in Work-Family Issues. *Academy of Management Journal*, 37(2), 350–382.

Greening, D. W. and Gray, B. (1994). Testing a Model of Organizational Response to Social and Political Issue. *Academy of Management Journal*, 37, 467–498.

Huselid, M. A., Jackson, S. E., and Schuler, R. S. (1997). Technical and Strategic Human Resource Management Effectiveness as Determinants of Firm Performance. *Academy of Management Journal*, 40, 171–188.

ILO (2001). *An ILO Code of Practice on HIV/AIDS and the World of Work*. Geneva: International Labour Office.

ILO (2006). *HIV/AIDS and Work: Global Estimates, Impact on Children and Youth, and Response*. Geneva: International Labour Office.

Jackson, S. E. and Schuler, R. S. (1995). Understanding Human Resource Management in the Context of the Organizations and Their Environments. In M. R. Rosenzweig and L. W. Porter (eds) *Annual Review of Psychology*, Vol. 46, 237–264. Palo Alto, CA: Annual Reviews.

Mahajan, A. P., Colvin, M., Rudatsikira, J., and Ettl, D. (2007). An Overview of HIV/AIDS Workplace Policies and Programmes in Southern Africa. *AIDS*, 21(3), 31–39.

Mamman, A., Akuratiyagamage, V., and Rees, C. (2006). Managerial Perceptions of the Role of Human Resource Function in Sri-Lanka: A Comparative Study of Local, Foreign-owned and Joint-Venture Companies. *International Journal of Human Resource Management*, 17(10), 1–12.

Mamman, A., Baydoun, N., and Liu, K. (2009). Exploring the Meanings of Globalization in Beijing. *Global Business Review*, 10(1), 67–86.

Mintzberg, H., Ahlstrand, B., and Lampel, J. (1998). *Strategy Safari: The Complete Guide through the Wilds of Strategic Management.* London: Prentice-Hall.

NAC (2003). *National HIV/AIDS Policy: A Call to Renewed Action.* Lilongwe: Government of Malawi.

Pfeffer, J. and Salancik, G. (1978). *The External Control of Organizations: A Resource Dependence Perspective.* New York: Harper and Row.

Piot, P., Bartos, M., Ghys, P. D., Walker, N., and Schwartlander, B. (2001). The Global Impact of HIV/AIDS. *Nature*, 410, 968–973.

Ramachandran, V., Shah, M. K., and Turner, G. L. (2007). Does the Private Sector Care about AIDS? Evidence from Firm Surveys in East Africa. *AIDS*, 21(Suppl. 3), S61–72.

Rosen, S., MacLeod, W., Vincent, J., Thea, D., and Simon, J. (2004). Why Do Firms Take Action on HIV/AIDS? Evidence from Nigeria. *The Journal of Business in Developing Nations*, 8, 1–38.

Simon, J., Rosen, S., Whiteside, A., Vincent, J., and Thea, D. (2000). The Response of African Businesses to HIV/AIDS. In *HIV/AIDS in the Commonwealth 2000/01.* London: Kensington Publications.

Teo, H. H., Wei, K. K., and Benbasat, I. (2003). Predicting Intention to Adopt Inter-Organizational Linkages: An Institutional Perspective. *MIS Quarterly*, 27(1), 19–49.

Thomas, J. B., Clark, S. M., and Gioia, D. A. (1993). Strategic Sense Making and Organizational Performance: Linkages among Scanning, Interpretation, Action, and Outcomes. *Academy of Management Journal*, 36, 239–270.

Parker, R., Riopelle, R., and Steel, W. (1995). Small Enterprises Adjusting to Liberalisation in Five African Countries. World Bank Discussion Paper, No. 271, African Technical Department Series. Washington, DC: The World Bank.

UNAIDS/WHO (2007). Modelling the Expected Distribution of New HIV Infections by Exposure Group, Geneva: UNAIDS/WHO.

USAID Report (2010). Accessed on 12 March 2012 from: www.usaid.gov.

Weaver. G. R., Trevino, L. K., and Cochran, P. L. (1999). Corporate Ethics Programs as Control Systems: Managerial and Institutional Influences. *Academy of Management Journal*, 42, 41–57.

Westphal, J. D. and Zajac, E. J. (2001). Decoupling Policy from Practice: The Case of Stock Repurchase Programs. *Administrative Science Quarterly*, 46, 202–228.

World Bank (2000). *Intensifying Action against HIV/AIDS in Africa: Responding to a Development Crisis.* Washington, DC: World Bank publication.

Wright, P. M. and Snell, S. A. (1998). Towards a Unifying Framework for Exploring Fit and Flexibility in Strategic Human Resource Management. *Academy of Management Review*, 23, 756–772.

3
Privatization and Employment Relations in Africa: The Case of Mozambique

Pauline Dibben and Geoffrey Wood

The impact of privatization on the public sector has generated much discussion over recent years, in both advanced and emerging economies. Across much of Africa, the imposition of structural adjustment policies by international financial institutions has led to wholesale privatizations since the 1980s. Given that the state was the major employer in many African countries, this has had far-reaching implications for much of the workforce, and has contributed towards a large informal sector and residual, yet still important, public sector. This chapter seeks to explore the impact of privatization on employment levels and the nature of employment relations in the public sector through exploratory in-depth research in Mozambique. The job cuts resulting from privatization in Mozambique had major implications for employment levels. Moreover, the residual public sector is characterized by a lack of union power and low pay, yet relative job security and equity. It is concluded that the important role of the public sector in economic development is often discounted, and that the state has a vital role to play both in ensuring decent work (and, indeed, acting as a role model in this regard) and in addressing historical inequities.

The privatization of state assets and public services has been widely applied across Africa, and the employment and social outcomes of this policy remain controversial (Bayliss and McKinley, 2007; Nellis, 2008; Josiah et al., 2010, Van Johnston and Seidenstat, 2007). Privatization in Africa occurred relatively later than in developed states, often being introduced at a rapid pace as part of a structural adjustment programme required by international institutions such as the International Monetary Fund (IMF) and the World Bank (Pollert and Hradecka, 1994). However, such programmes have arguably been enforced without adequate attention to country context (Stiglitz, 2002).

An area that has received relatively little attention in the academic literature is the impact of privatization on work and employment (Appiah-Kubi, 2001; Josiah et al., 2010). Moreover, since the great swathes of privatization, there has been a general lack of analysis of the current status of public sector employment relations. To some extent, this is not surprising, given the decreased numbers now employed within the formal economy. Indeed, in many countries, over 75 per cent of the workforce is now in the informal economy. Yet, consideration of public sector work is necessary, given its broader potential to act as a role model (Dibben and James, 2007; Tangri and Mwenda, 2001) and its possible value in addressing the historical inequities present in ex-colonial emerging economies.

The study of employment relations in Africa could potentially cover many aspects. A central feature of employment relations in both advanced and emerging economies is the level of unionization and union strength (Brewster and Wood, 2007). Other essential features include recruitment, retention and remuneration (Debrah and Mmieh, 2009). Furthermore, given the history of colonial rule in much of Africa, an additional aspect of employment relations that has attracted attention is the contentious issue of equity (O'Laughlin, 2000; Horwitz et al., 2002).

This chapter engages with the impact of privatization on employment, and the current status of public sector employment relations, and does so through examining the case study of Mozambique. This country is of particular interest due to its rapid privatization, and its reputation of economic success in recent years, which have led to comparisons with the fast-growing Asian economies of Malaysia, India and China (Clement and Peiris, 2008). Yet it shares with other countries within Africa a history of colonial rule, civil war and high levels of poverty. Privatization was an integral part of its transition from a socialist to a capitalist economy, and so it also shares some commonality with transitional economies in Eastern Europe (Pitcher, 2002; see Woldu and Budhwar, 2011 for discussion of culture and employment in Eastern European countries).

The chapter proceeds as follows. The first sections examine existing evidence on the impacts of privatization on work and employment relations within Africa, and then detail the political and economic context in Mozambique (CTA, 2005). This sets the scene for examining two key research questions: what has been the impact of privatization on levels and conditions of employment in Mozambique? And what is the current status of public sector employment relations? In examining the second of these questions, attention is paid to unionization; recruitment; job security; pay and equity. The concluding sections discuss the more general implications of the further contracting out of public services, and the potential contribution of the public sector as a model employer within emerging economies.

The implications of privatization for levels and conditions of employment

Privatization in developed countries has been a key strategy of governments since the 1980s, with Britain, Australia and New Zealand commonly regarded as the front runners of privatization reforms (Bortolotti et al., 2003). Here, it has been applied in different forms, including: the sale of state owned enterprises to the private sector; the sale and contracting out of publicly financed services (O'Flynn and Alford, 2008); the part-ownership or leasing of public sector infrastructure to the private sector, often underpinned by private finance agreements frequently referred to as concessioning; and the 'marketization' of public services, through outsourcing to the private or voluntary sectors and/or the introduction of private sector practices into the public sector (Teicher et al., 2006). Generally, privatization is taken to imply private sector involvement, although outsourcing to the third sector, which is not addressed in depth here due to the potentially different aims and restrictions of non-profit organizations, is also an area that is ripe for further in-depth research.

The assumption that privatization leads to improved efficiency implies that there will be improved economic growth and hence a rise in the levels of employment based on the more efficient utilization of the relevant organization's physical and human assets (Przeworski et al., 2000; Pamacheche and Koma, 2007). However, empirical evidence from advanced economies has cast doubt on any overall increase (Sachdev, 2001; Conley, 2002), and has pointed, instead, to the intensifying of work for those remaining (Marsden, 2007) and employment that is often insecure and/or short-term (Beaumont et al., 2007).

In emerging economies similar trends have been apparent. Evidence has indicated a range of impacts as a result of privatization and contracting out, including: a reduction in employment levels; lower job security; wage freezes or reductions; and an increasingly hostile stance towards unions (Moody, 1997; Kamoche, 2002; Birdsall and Nellis, 2003). For example, in Zambia, privatization led to the loss of 61,000 jobs, and in countries such as Zambia, Zimbabwe and Namibia permanent, formal sector jobs were replaced by contract work and casual jobs without job security (ALRN, 2002).

It could be argued that a reduction in the numbers employed within the public sector is positive, given that state enterprises have been over-staffed. This is reflected by the reduction in numbers of employees often found both before and after privatization (Birdsall and Nellis, 2003). Moreover, there has been evidence of benefits from privatization for some workers. For example, in Ghana, between 1989 and 1999 the pri-vatization of over 70 per cent of Ghana's public enterprises benefited the managerial elite. However, this should be weighed against the bulk of indigenous Ghanaians losing jobs, and wages for those in privatized organizations declining to about 28 per cent below average civil ser-vice pay. Those who suffered most were immobile, unskilled and older workers (Appiah-Kubi, 2001). Meanwhile, in the case of Kenya, market reforms led to a deterioration of bargaining, greater confrontation, and a general reduction in employment rights (Fashoyin, 2007; Budwhar and Debrah, 2001). However, HR outcomes from the privatization process are by no means uniform; there is some evidence to suggest that, when privatized organizations have been purchased by foreign multinationals, there has been a diffusion of HR practices from the country of origin (Horwitz, 2007).

The changes associated with privatization have signalled, for many, the end of secure employment and a model of career planning predi-cated on seniority, although, in most cases, the importance of personal connections has persisted or has even been accentuated (c.f. Hyden, 1987). In terms of reward, there is evidence of a greater widening of the pay gap between a managerial elite and unskilled or poorly skilled workers or those in a poorer bargaining position (Klerck, 2007; Van Slyke, 2003). Finally, pressures from the World Bank and the IMF have encouraged more hardline approaches towards collective organization, with countries being coerced into cutting back on labour rights (Cooney et al., 2011). In practical terms, this has meant that unions have had to contend not only with the inevitable job losses that have accom-panied privatization, but also with a reduced ability to seek recourse from the law for their remaining constituents, as well as access to basic organizational rights (Brewster and Wood, 2007; Cooney et al., 2011).

The political and economic context of Mozambique

In common with other countries in the region, Mozambique experi-enced extensive privatization in the 1990s, against the background of colonial rule, civil war, and high levels of poverty. Portuguese colonial rule ended in 1975 following ten years of anticolonial war. After independence, the country was ruled by Frelimo; after initial experiments at direct worker control of enterprises, it reverted to a state socialist economy (Hanlon, 1991; Haines and Wood, 1995). Poorly planned agricultural policies, the deposal of traditional rulers and wilful destabilization by the former Rhodesia and apartheid South Africa led to 16 years of civil war, during which the rebel movement, Renamo, challenged the Frelimo government (Hanlon, 1991; Haines and Wood, 1995). Much of Mozambique's infrastructure was destroyed, and many people lost their lives. Large numbers of skilled Portuguese colonists had already fled the country (Hanlon, 1991). The early 1990s arguably marked the beginning of a new era for Mozambique. In late 1992 the war ended, and in 1994 the first democratic elections were held. In these, as in subsequent elections, Frelimo remained in government, and Renamo was institutionalized as the non-violent opposition. For over 15 years, there has been relative political stability, although some tension has arisen in recent years over increased prices of food and fuel (AIM, 2010a).

Mozambique has faced many challenges in striving for development, but has been praised by the IMF for its success in building infrastructure, reducing poverty and increasing GDP by around 8 per cent each year since 2002 (IMF, 2006; Mangwiro, 2008; AIM, 2011). However, it should be noted that the economic growth is fuelled by a small number of companies; the exports of the aluminium smelter Mozal accounted for almost 60 per cent of total export earnings in the first quarter of 2010 (AIM, 2010e). The country has also benefited from debt cancellation, and is now seeking to develop both rural and urban areas and encourage tourism in its areas of natural beauty. Nevertheless, the country still faces many challenges, including the effects of civil war on its limited transport system across northern parts of the country, the wholesale collapse of industry and regular cycles of drought and floods. At the same time, although levels have decreased, there is extreme poverty among around 45 per cent of the population (IMF and IDA, 2006), around 16 per cent of the population are HIV positive (Clement and Peiris, 2008) and only a small percentage (around 8 per cent) of the employable population is in formal sector work (EIU, 2006). Furthermore, the country remains heavily reliant on donor organizations, a situation contentiously referred to as 'recolonization' (De Renzio and Hanlon, 2007). Donor aid has, more recently, moved to coordinated budget support, which is widely regarded as a better funding mechanism than highly visible capital projects (Clement and Peiris, 2008).

Nevertheless, Mozambique is still reliant on loans from institutions such as the World Bank, recently receiving $143 million in loans for development projects (AIM, 2010b), and is also heavily reliant on foreign investment from countries such as Portugal, Italy, Spain, Norway, China and South Africa (AIM, 2010c).

Research methods

In order to investigate the impacts of privatization in Mozambique and the current status of public sector work, this chapter draws on in-depth research findings from fieldwork visits in 2005, 2006, 2007 and 2009. In total, 58 people were interviewed. Due to the difficulties of working in a developing country, and the main language being Portuguese, the sampling strategy involved purposive and snowball sampling. Each research visit was accompanied by a review of policy documents and news reports, facilitating the triangulation of data sources (Denzin, 1989). In 2005, fieldwork consisted of 27 in-depth interviews seeking to investigate the political and economic context and the broader impacts of privatization, and included those with senior officials in the government departments of International Affairs; Port and Railways (CFM); Transport; Industry and Commerce; and Investment Promotion, in addition to senior members of the employer federation (CTA); the trade union federation (OTM); and donor agencies such as the Department for International Development and United States Agency for International Development, shedding light on the economy, politics and employment. Fieldwork in 2006 involved a further 12 in-depth interviews which included more detailed examination of the process of privatization and employment reform. These interviews were undertaken with the director and also the senior editor of the English Newsdesk of the Mozambican news agency, academics at two universities and two research institutes, and senior government officials in the departments of Trade, Industry, National Standards, Commerce and Privatization. In 2007, fieldwork involved six meetings with key informants met previously, in order to probe further into employment relations and labour markets, and in 2009 additional interviews were conducted with two directors of OTM, in addition to cabinet members of the organization representing the informal sector, and senior members of the Mozambican news agency. Each of the field visits was conceived as part of a longer project, and revisiting the same people facilitated the building of relationships. Each interview lasted between one and two hours. The data were, in almost all cases, tape-recorded, and whole interviews were transcribed. The in-depth nature of the interviews, and use of careful accounting procedures such as multiple sources of data, full transcriptions and memos, led to confidence that the research was internally valid and rigorous. After each stage, responses were analysed using a software package that facilitates open and axial coding through hierarchical coding, first NUD*IST and, in the later stages of the analysis, NVivo (Richards and Richards, 1994). Analysis of data enabled the questioning of prior assumptions and the detection of additional insights.

The following sections outline how the findings address the research questions outlined above: what has been the impact of privatization on the levels and conditions of employment in Mozambique? And what is the current status of public sector employment relations in terms of unionization, recruitment, job security, pay and equity?

Privatization and the impact on employment in Mozambique

After the socialist era, there was rapid and systemic privatization in Mozambique, in common with changes in other former socialist countries such as those in Eastern Europe, where weaknesses in state firms and the loss of markets helped to drive reforms (Pitcher, 2002). Mozambique's privatization was preceded by the liberalization of prices, devaluation of the local currency and cuts in state expenditure (Torp and Rekve, 1996). State companies were badly neglected during the war, and the government drastically reduced subsidies to state enterprises prior to privatization (see Pitcher, 2002). The Mozambican government in 1987, under pressure from the World Bank and the IMF and facing economic difficulties, agreed to privatize over 1,400 state owned companies (Director A, OTM, 2005). As a director in the Ministry of Industry and Commerce (2005) commented,

> [The World Bank] came here in order to help the country- to reconstruct the country- but sometimes they take decisions that are very difficult to manage. But we, as a country, try to do our best to follow the recommendations, as without this, it is difficult to get credit.

This implies that privatization was not the chosen strategy of national government, forming part of a coherent policy, but imposed externally, in a hasty and careless fashion (Cramer, 2001) with a lack of adequate regulatory structures (Castel-Branco et al., 2001).

A number of criticisms may be made about the process of privatization, which resulted in outcomes far removed from the theoretical predictions of institutions such as the World Bank (George, 1990; Zack-Williams and Mohan, 2005). For example, existing elites used their position to shape the process of privatization, while those who benefited included former colonial agricultural companies and Indian import–export businesses (Pitcher, 2002). Enterprises were sold cheaply in order to encourage domestic bidders, some (well-connected) veterans were allowed to buy public assets at reduced prices to avoid political trouble, and private businessmen who had profited from the war undertook joint ventures with foreign investors (Castel-Branco et al., 2001). Coupled with this, there was inadequate evaluation of new owners, who often lacked the capital or knowledge necessary to effectively revive companies. More critically, the buyers of privatized companies relied on, yet did not repay, donor loans (Hanlon, 2004). International institutions could be blamed for encouraging rapid privatization, but the national government may also be criticized for not ensuring adequate regulatory structures or the careful assessment of new owners. While privatization afforded opportunities for politically well-connected individuals to enrich themselves throughout this process, the bulk of Mozambicans, lacking such connections and access to capital, were sidelined.

The medium and longer-term outcomes of privatization have been varied. The sugar and textile industries have shown signs of investment and recovery over time, but others have failed through insufficient rehabilitation (senior editor, Mozambican News Agency, 2007). Many of the targets of privatization simply collapsed: nine of the 13 privatized companies in the north of the country closed, resulting in hundreds of job losses in historically impoverished regions (Pitcher, 2002). While, in some instances, this was due to mismanagement, in other cases these collapses reflected the adverse effects of other neo-liberal policies, such as the dropping of tariff barriers. As a result of such failures, the government took companies back into state ownership, paying the creditors. Indeed, in one case, a company was privatized twice, and twice failed (Director, Privatization Department, 2007).

The impact of privatization on employment

In common with other aspects of privatization (see Nellis, 2008; Josiah et al., 2010), the impact of privatization on employment has been variable. In the case of the durably competitive industries, such as beer, there were improvements in wages and working conditions (beer mostly consists of water, so local producers had a natural competitive advantage). However, increases in employment generally benefited workers from the purchasing country, as in the case of South African owned companies (Pitcher, 2002: Jerome, 2004). More generally, however, privatization directly resulted in higher unemployment: 'More than 200,000 workers were unemployed as a consequence of privatization. Some of them are in the informal sector now, and many are unemployed' (Director A, OTM, 2007). Other workers who had been retrenched simply reverted to subsistence agriculture.

A different form of private sector involvement has been through concessioning, involving the transfer of either all, or parts of, management or operations to the private sector, ironically a dominant practice during the first centuries of Portuguese colonialism (see Haines and Wood, 1995). While this process can mean that accumulated assets ultimately remain in state hands, outsourcing may also be associated with the privatization of profits, a lack of reinvestment and the ongoing retention of risk by the public sector. In the transport sector, this has been the dominant form of privatization. As at September 2004, the privatization or concessioning of transport had resulted in approximately 4,000 people being made redundant, 7,000 taking early retirement, and about 6,000 becoming self-employed (CFM Corporate Profile, 2001). In the ports and railways company there was overall a 67 per cent reduction of the labour force (ITWF, 2008), and in some cases there has been a serious lack of investment in people or infrastructure, such in the example of Maputo port (Director, CFM, 2005; AIM, 2010d). However, in some cases historic overstaffing rather than concessioning has been blamed for job loss. Moreover, in some cases, workers have benefited from concessioning:

> Beira (port) is one of the best concessions that we have because they invest and employment a lot of people. In this concessions agreement, there is new money, and they have kept some CFM staff with better conditions than before.
>
> (Director, CFM, 2005)

It can also be noted that donors have proven reluctant to invest in maintenance or the necessary human resources other than in highly visible capital projects, and many failures associated with infrastructural projects have been in human resource development, with funding shortfalls for training institutions and education and training of job seekers.

Privatization has entailed profound changes in the governance of organizations. Public sector work traditionally offered secure terms and conditions of employment, a culture of professionalism, standardized pay systems, and, at least in procedure, if not in practice, promotion on merit and seniority (see Brewster and Wood, 2007). In contrast, evidence of privatized enterprises in Mozambique suggests that the agenda has – outside a few high-profile, often foreign-owned firms – shifted to the release of value to owners, either through cost-cutting and closer control, or simply through the liquidation of assets. In many other instances, terms and conditions of employment have been squeezed (see Webster and Wood, 2005; Webster et al., 2006).

After the large swathe of privatization in the 1990s, the outsourcing of services to the private or voluntary sectors has not been widespread, with the notable exception of customs (outsourced to Crown Agents). Unlike countries in the industrialized north, such as the UK, government departments in Mozambique generally tend to avoid contracting out services (director, Privatization Department, 2007). In some government departments, such as the National Directorate of Industry, senior personnel were not aware of any outsourcing in their ministries, while in the ministries of Education, Health and Labour most workers were employed internally. However, interviewees from the Bureau of Standards and News Agency referred to outsourcing of cleaning services and security by some government departments, and there had also been outsourcing of municipal services such as refuse collection. In these cases, low-paid workers were more greatly affected than higher-paid workers. The future trajectory of privatization and marketization is unclear, although there has been strong pressure from the IMF and the World Bank to continue private sector involvement in infrastructure, particularly in the postal, transport, air and telecommunications sectors, and to 'rightsize' the civil service (IMF, 2006) – a term that is often euphemistically used to imply job cuts.

Public sector employment relations in Mozambique

The next sections probe public sector employment relations in more detail, and investigate the different dimensions that are arguably fundamental to sustainable employment in Africa: unionization, recruitment, job security, pay and equity (Brewster and Wood, 2007; Debrah and Mmieh, 2009).

Unionization

Workers in the public sector benefit from representation by trade unions, which is not generally the case in small and medium enterprises

(SMEs) (the dominant organizational form) in the private sector. However, the National Civil Service Union is not recognized for the purpose of collective bargaining, and is not allowed to organize workers unless it gains prior permission from the government, emphasizing the complexity of the situation in Mozambique. Bargaining rights in the public sector may improve through proposed changes to legislation. However, these changes have been long awaited. The OTM have been lobbying for changes to legislation since 2000, and delays are reportedly due to the government's concern that public sector workers will be able to go on strike if the proposed law is passed (Director B, OTM, 2007). In addition, the right to strike is referred to in the Labour Law 2007 as 'a basic right of workers. Workers shall exercise the right to strike in order to protect and promote their legitimate social-labour related interests' (Labour Law, Section vii, Article 194). However, workers in essential services are already prevented from going on strike; a wide range of occupations are excluded from this option, including: medical, hospital and medicinal services; water, power and fuel supplies; postal and telecommunication services; funeral services; loading and unloading of animals and perishable food stuffs; air space and meteorological control; the fire service; cleansing services; and private security, while 'public enterprises and any other public corporate entity whose employment relationships are governed by this law shall be considered as services directed at meeting essential needs of the purposes of the regime in this article' (Labour Law, Section vii, Article 205).

Furthermore, those engaged in casual work are unlikely to be represented by unions, suggested by the findings of a survey of 177 large employers, that workers in this type of insecure work belonged to a union in only 20 per cent of unionized workplaces (Webster et al., 2006). Additional constraints on union organizing include the devastation of infrastructure during the war (Director B, OTM, 2009). The country is long and thin, and roads are sometimes impassable, particularly during the rainy season; colonial priorities which focused primarily on the extraction of natural resources, and, later, export trade servicing neighbouring states in the interior, has meant that east–west transport links are generally much better than north–south ones (Wood and Dibben, 2005). Although a majority of public sector workers are based in the capital city, Maputo, a large proportion are also based in the provinces and districts, especially within the city of Beira on the east coast and Nampula in the north of the country.

Moreover, there is a general culture in Mozambique of non-compliance with employment law; even in instances where workers enjoy legal organizational and bargaining rights, many employers admit to ignoring legislation (Webster and Wood, 2005; Webster et al., 2006). In particular, there is a general lack of compliance with health and safety legislation:

> You go to work for a cashew company. After five years of working there you don't have hands because they have been eaten by acid from cashew shells.
>
> (Director, Research Institute, 2007)

Part of the reason for the lack of compliance might be the limited role of the labour inspectorate, acknowledged in the Labour Law (2007). This means that organizations can flout the law without punishment.

Job security

Jobs remain more secure in the public sector than in the private sector, where large-scale job cuts have taken place over the past two decades (Webster et al., 2006). The employment security offered by public sector work is of particular importance in rural areas, where there is less waged work and employment tends to be seasonal. While privately owned sugar cane and cashew nut industries together employ around 30,000 people in rural areas, the railways alone employ around 30–40,000 people. Although it is low-paid, public sector employment contributes towards economic development due to a greater degree of job security than is available in the private sector, in the informal sector, or in migrant work. This job security is vital since it enables those living in rural areas to invest a small proportion of their income into niche agricultural products, enabling them to build a future for themselves and their extended families (Director of Research Institute, Mozambique, 2007; Hanlon, 1996).

When questioned about job security in the public sector, interviewees referred to how this was a feature of the culture in Mozambique. However, contentiously, security of tenure was irrespective of performance: instead of discipline for capability or conduct, employees have tended to be moved to another job or retrained. If problems recurred, then more training was provided. The lack of punishment could be related to a 'humanistic' rather than 'instrumental' attitude towards employees characteristic of African culture – seeing people as having a value in their own right rather than being an end in themselves (Jackson, 2002, p. 1008). However, an alternative explanation is the systemic inadequacies in the vocational system. First, indigenous workers were given inferior schooling during colonial times. Second, vocational training has been neglected in recent years due to an emphasis on primary schooling. The overall technical and vocational education training system is, moreover, still fragmented and uncoordinated (OECD, 2008).

Remuneration

Within Mozambique, there is the possibility in the public sector of a fixed salary for life: if an employee holds the same position for at least ten years then he or she can apply to the government to fix his or her salary, in contrast to private sector workers, who may be subject to arbitrary cuts. Moreover, in contrast to the private sector, the public sector is not as marked by the ignoring of statutory minimum wage levels (Webster and Wood, 2005; Webster et al., 2006). Promotion prospects can also be good: every three years an officer might normally be promoted, subject to the development of further skills (Professor, Eduardo Modlane University, 2005).

Terms and conditions often appear to be better in the public sector than the private sector; however, it is important to note the structure of industry in Mozambique, which is marked by a small number of private sector firms and a huge number of small firms (Wood et al., 2010). Small firms tend to be marked by informality, and most workers earn below the minimum wage (ILO, 2009). In contrast, some large private sector employers offer relatively high wages and benefits, including housing, healthcare and training, and good health and safety practices (BHP Billiton, 2004; Sartorius et al., 2011). Yet, jobs within such companies tend to be competitive, and very scarce. Meanwhile, additional benefits of public sector work include retirement pensions and health insurance, which, although at low levels, mean that public sector workers are often better off than their counterparts in private sector companies (Castel-Branco, Director of Research Institute, 2007).

Although pay in the public sector may be less than in some large private sector companies, employment in the public sector can, nevertheless, contribute towards poverty reduction, as shown by the following statistics: in 2002 the poverty rate for households headed by a public sector employee was only 33 per cent, compared to 56 per cent if working in private services, 65 per cent if in industry and 73 per cent if employed in agricultural or domestic work (Clement and Peiris, 2008).

Employment equity

A further advantage of public sector employment is its generally better record on equity, which is of particular significance in Mozambique due to the existence of racism during colonial rule (Director of Mozambican News Agency, 2009). During that time, black Mozambicans were not provided with unemployment and pension schemes, unions or minimum wages (O'Laughlin, 2000).

Racial divisions still exist (ILO, 2009). However, these appear to be particularly prevalent in the private sector. Portuguese owners who fled after the ending of colonial rule have since returned and taken ownership of large companies. There have, moreover, been reports of Portuguese workers being treated better than Mozambicans within the same company:

> The government has [recently] discovered that some Portuguese [in the banks] are paid twice as much as Mozambicans. They have the same skills and qualifications but are paid more... It is the same as during colonial times – they pay less if workers are black. If they protest they will be dismissed.
>
> (Director, Mozambican News Agency, 2007)

Similar issues have occurred within South African owned firms:

> South African white firms... are very discriminatory against people who work for them. Mozambican workers of the same standard are on very different salaries. Although Mozambicans earn much more (there) than they would earn elsewhere in Mozambique, they earn much less than foreign workers.
>
> (Director of Research Institute, 2006)

As noted above, more recently there has also been substantial foreign direct investment in Mozambique from a range of other countries including Italy, Spain, Norway and China (AIM, 2010c). As yet, there is a lack of evidence of labour conditions within these foreign owned firms in Mozambique, with the exception of one firm, where attempts have been made to embrace diversity management (Sartorius et al., 2011). However, recent evidence from countries such as Zambia indicates that, where some countries have invested heavily in the country, this has had negative outcomes on working practices for indigenous workers (Gadzala, 2010).

Table 3.1 summarizes some of the apparent differences in employment relations between the residual areas of the public sector and the private sector.

Table 3.1 Employment relations in the public and private sector in Mozambique

Area of employment relations	Private sector	Public sector
Unionization	Better organizational and bargaining rights under the law. Union recognition and bargaining in many larger firms, but this is generally absent in SMEs. Widespread non-compliance with collective agreements.	No union recognition. However, possibility of legal reform in this area.
Job security	Insecure employment and employment protection, particularly in small firms and the informal sector. Legislation generally not enforced.	High job security and career for life model, but some outsourcing in basic service areas. IMF pressures to 'rightsize the public sector'. Risk of ongoing privatization which might lead to further retrenchments and informal sector working.
Reward	Large-scale non-compliance with official minimum wages. Pay generally low. Employees may face arbitrary wage adjustments. Some instances of better practices among large firms, including collective bargaining around pay and working conditions.	Wages may be fixed on the basis of seniority. Possibility of investment of secure public sector wages in small-scale agriculture in rural areas.
Employment equity	Evidence of racial discrimination in pay and promotion opportunities, evident since colonial times.	Generally, good track record in terms of employment equity.

The tabular summary of findings highlights important distinctions between public and private sector employment relations, indicating the influence of wider socio-economic, political and legal structures, and the way in which a lack of state regulation can impact on employment relations (Blyton and Turnbull, 2004; Debrah and Mmieh, 2009). However, it is also necessary to draw attention to the hidden complexities that a simplified analysis can tend to hide, such as the extreme differences in working practices and levels of unionization between small and large firms. Moreover, within foreign owned firms, the HR practices exhibited are likely to vary according to the influence of national, host and organizational culture, and also the role of existing institutions within host countries. These variations can be conceptualized under the broad terms of hybridization and cross-convergence, and form useful avenues for future research (see, for example, Horwitz, 2010). Although some evidence has emerged on sectoral differences in the use of HR practices (Wood et al., 2010), there is, as yet, a lack of evidence on variations in HR practices according to firm ownership in Mozambique.

Conclusions

Privatization has had dramatic effects on industrialized and emerging economies, both generally and in terms of employment relations. In each of these contexts, the aim has been to achieve increased efficiency in the management of people and in terms of the utilization of capital. However, a range of empirical evidence reveals the complexity of this issue. In the case of Mozambique, with the notable exception of a few large enterprises, the primary focus in the private sector has been on squeezing wages, cutting employment, reducing investment in people and infrastructure, and/or liquidating assets.

In summary, the findings point towards a problematic privatization process in Mozambique, with associated failings in terms of people management. Although there have been some examples of successes, there have also been many instances of privatized companies failing. Regulatory structures have been inadequate, both in terms of employment protection and collective rights, and in managing the process of privatization. This could suggest a failure of indigenous governance, but many problems can be traced back to the over-hasty nature of neoliberal reforms and the weakening of capacity as a result of budgetary cutbacks. Such limitations range from a weak technical and vocational training infrastructure through to an inability to enforce the law.

Although it is difficult to make generalizations from country-specific studies, the Mozambican case has more general import, as it helps to reveal the dynamics of sustained post-conflict growth from an extremely low base and the implications for work and employment, with possible lessons for various other sub-Saharan African countries such as the Democratic Republic of the Congo, Liberia and Sierra Leone (Jones, 2008). The case of Mozambique merely strengthens arguments for the need for better regulation to accompany all aspects of privatization, including the concessioning and contracting out to tender of public sector enterprises and functions; in employment, as with other dimensions, it is not sufficient simply to rely on trust relationships without an adequate underpinning of detailed contracts, and mechanisms to enforce them (Parker and Hartley, 2003). Further, the findings also cast light on the essential contribution of core public sector work as an exemplar of best practice in areas such as equal opportunities, wage levels and employment security (Clement and Peiris, 2008).

The drive towards introducing new forms of private sector involvement into public sector provision seems likely to continue, in both advanced and emerging economies, irrespective of a growing body of evidence that points towards a decrease in employment levels and poorer HR practices. Contrary to prescriptions for further privatization, these findings reinforce the need to treat claims about what privatization can achieve with a healthy degree of scepticism.

In addition to the immediate consequences for employment relations highlighted above, we may conclude this chapter with a broader concern. The shrinking pool of 'good' work in Mozambique creates a persistent crisis of consumer demand, making it very difficult to promote economic activity outside the export of primary commodities and trade; most Mozambicans lack the means to consume, and hence remain locked in a subsistence and quasi-barter economy. What does this mean in terms of people management? As we know, there is a lot more to Human Resource Management (HRM) than simply squeezing costs; promoting better HRM may make for greater sustainability within the organization and also has important consequences across an economy. Mozambique may appear to be very far removed from highly developed liberal market economies such as Britain and the USA. However, policy makers and managers in the latter countries would do well to heed the lessons held out by such emerging economies: sustainable, as adverse to speculative, growth across an economy cannot be secured through freezing or cutting the wages of the bulk of employees and via successive waves of redundancies, whatever the short-term gains.

Acknowledgements

The initial stage of this research was supported by the Royal Geographical Society (with the Institute of British Geographers) with an Engineering and Physical Sciences Research Council (EPSRC) Geographical Research Grant: EPSRC 1/05. The authors would also like to thank Ken Kamoche, Paul Mosley, Stuart Ogden and Ian Roper for their comments on previous drafts.

References

AIM Report (Mozambique News Agency) (2010a) 'Government Launches Austerity Measures to Subsidise Bread Prices' No. 409. 20 September 2010. www.poptel.org.uk/mozambique-news/newsletter/aim409.html. Accessed 18 January 2013.

AIM Report (Mozambique News Agency) (2010b) 'Four World Bank Loans' No. 410. 5 October 2010. www.poptel.org.uk/mozambique-news/newsletter/aim410.html.

AIM Report (Mozambique News Agency) (2010c) 'Foreign Direct Investment Soars by 400 Percent' No. 407. 17 August 2010. www.poptel.org.uk/mozambique-news/newsletter/aim407.html.

AIM Report (Mozambique News Agency) (2010d) 'New Leader for CFM' No. 404. 22 June 2010. www.poptel.org.uk/mozambique-news/newsletter/aim404.html.

AIM Report (Mozambique News Agency) (2010e), 'Strong Economic Growth Continues' No. 405. 12 July 2010. www.poptel.org.uk/mozambique-news/newsletter/aim405.html.

AIM Report (Mozambique News Agency) (2011) 'Economy Growing at over Eight Percent' No. 427. 20 June 2011. www.poptel.org.uk/mozambique-news/newsletter/aim427.html.

ALRN. (African Labour Research Network) (2002) 'Privatization-African Experiences'. www.alrn.org.

Appiah-Kubi, K. (2001) 'State-Owned Enterprises and Privatization in Ghana', *The Journal of Modern African Studies*, 39 (2), 197–229.

Bayliss, K. and T. McKinley (2007) 'Privatising Basic Utilities in Sub-Saharan Africa: The MDG Impact' (Policy Research brief: no. 3) Brasilia, Brazil. UNDP International Poverty Centre. http://www.unpeilac.org/documentos/IPCPovertyInFocus23.pdf, accessed October 16th, 2013.

Beaumont, P., J. Pate, and M. Fischbacher (2007) 'Public Sector Employment: Issues of Size and Comparison in the UK', in P. Dibben, P. James, I. Roper, and G. Wood (eds) *Modernising Work in Public Services* (London: Palgrave Macmillan).

Birdsall, N. and J. Nellis (2003) 'Winners and Losers: Assessing the Distributional Impact of Privatization', *World Development*, 31 (10), 1617–1633.

Blyton, P. and P. Turnbull (2004) *The Dynamics of Employee Relations* (New York: Palgrave Macmillan).

Bortolotti, B., M. Fantini, and D. Siniscalco (2003) 'Privatization around the World: Evidence from Panel Data', *Journal of Public Economics*, 88, 305–332.

Brewster, C. and G. Wood (2007) 'Introduction: Comprehending Industrial Relations in Africa', in C. Brewster and G. Wood (eds) *Industrial Relations in Africa* (London: Palgrave), 1–14.

Budwhar, P. and Y. Debrah (eds) (2001) *HRM in Developing Countries* (London: Routledge).

Castel-Branco, C., C. Cramer, and D. Hailu (2001) *Privatization and Economic Strategy in Mozambique*. Discussion Paper 2001/64. United Nations.

CFM (Portos e Caminhos de Ferro de Mozambique) (2001) Corporate Profile.

Clement, J. and S. Peiris (eds) (2008) *Post-Stabilization in Sub-Saharan Africa: Lessons from Mozambique* (Washington, DC: International Monetary Fund).

Conley, H. (2002) 'A State of Insecurity: Temporary Work in the Public Services', *Work Employment and Society*, 16 (4), 725–737.

Cooney, S., P. Gahan, and R. Mitchell (2011) 'Legal Origins, Labour Law, and the Regulation of Employment Relations', in M. Barry and A. Wilkinson (eds) *Elgar Handbook of Comparative Employment Relations* (Cheltenham: Edward Elgar), 75–97.

Cramer, C. (2001) 'Privatization and Adjustment in Mozambique: A "Hospital Pass?" ' *Journal of Southern African Studies*, 27 (1), 79–105.

CTA (Confederacao das Associacoes Economicas de Mocambique) (2005) *For a Better Business Environment: More Enterprises, Better Enterprises*. 8th Conference of the Private Sector, Maputo, October 2004.

Debrah, Y. A. and F. Mmieh (2009) 'Employment Relations in Small and Medium-Sized Enterprises: Insights from Ghana', *International Journal of Human Resource Management*, 20 (7), 1554–1575.

Denzin, N. (1989) *The Research Act: A Theoretical Introduction to Sociological Methods* (New Jersey: Prentice Hall).

De Renzio, P. and J. Hanlon (2007) *Contested Sovereignty in Mozambique: The Dilemmas of Aid Dependence*. Global Economic Governance Working Paper 2007/25, University College Oxford.

Dibben, P. (2010) 'Union Change, Development and Renewal in Emerging Economies: The Case of Mozambique', *Work, Employment and Society*, 24 (3), 468–486.

Dibben, P. and P. James (2007) 'Introduction: Is Modern Better?' in P. Dibben, P. James, I. Roper, and G. Wood (eds) *Modernising Work in Public Services* (London: Palgrave), 1–2.

EIU (Economist Intelligence Unit) (2006) *Mozambique at a Glance 2006–7* Country Report Mozambique, August 2006.

Fashoyin, T. (2007) 'Industrial Relations and the Social Partners in Kenya', in G. Wood and C. Brewster (eds) *Industrial Relations in Africa* (London: Palgrave), 39–52.

Gadzala, A. W. (2010) 'From Formal to Informal Sector Employment: Examining the Chinese Presence in Zambia', *Review of African Political Economy*, 37 (123), 41–59.

George, S. (1990) *A Fate Worse than Debt* (New York: Grove Weidenfeld).

Haines, R. and G. Wood (1995) 'The 1994 Election and Mozambique's Democratic Transition', *Democratization*, 2 (3), 362–376.

Hanlon, J. (1991) *Mozambique: Who Calls the Shots?* (London: James Currey).

Hanlon, J. (1996) *Peace Without Profit: How the IMF Blocks Rebuilding in Mozambique* (Oxford: James Currey).

Hanlon, J. (2004) 'Do Donors Promote Corruption? The Case of Mozambique', *Third World Quarterly*, 25 (4), 747–763.

Horwitz, F. (2007) 'Trans-Continental Trends and Issues', in G. Wood and C. Brewster (eds) *Industrial Relations in Africa* (London: Palgrave), 207–218.

Horwitz, F. (2010) 'Evolving Human Resource Management in Emerging Markets', Keynote Address to the International Symposium on Human Resource Management and the Creation of Effective Organisations in Africa, Nottingham Trent University, 13–14 September 2010.

Horwitz, F., V. Browning, H. Jain, and A. J. Steenkamp (2002) 'Human Resource Practices and Discrimination in South Africa: Overcoming the Apartheid Legacy', *International Journal of Human Resource Management*, 13 (7), 1105–1118.

Hyden, G. (1987) *No Shortcuts of Progress* (Nairobi: Heinemann).

ILO (International Labour Organization) (2009) *National Profile of Working Conditions in Mozambique* (Geneva: International Labour Office).

IMF (International Monetary Fund) (2004) *International Financial Statistics*, August 2004.

IMF (2006) *Republic of Mozambique. Fifth Review under the PRGF*, 1 December 2006.

IMF and IDA (International Monetary Fund and International Development Association) (2006) *Republic of Mozambique Poverty Reduction Strategy Paper*, 14 November 2006.

ITWF (International Transport Workers' Federation) (2008) *Facing Up to the Free Market*, July 2008.

Jackson, T. (2002) 'Reframing Human Resource Management in Africa: A Cross-cultural Perspective', *International Journal of Human Resource Management*, 13 (7), 998–1018.

Jerome, A. (2004) Infrastructure Privatization and Liberalization in Africa, 4th Seminar on International Development, University of Balearic Islands, Spain, September 2004.

Jones, S. (2008) 'Sustaining Growth in the Long Term', in J. Clement and S. Peiris (eds) *Post-Stabilization in Sub-Saharan Africa: Lessons from Mozambique* (Washington, DC: International Monetary Fund), 82–125.

Josiah, J., B. Burton, S. Gallhofer, and J. Haslam (2010) 'Accounting for Privatisation in Africa? Reflections from a Critical Interdisciplinary Perspective', *Critical Perspectives on Accounting*, 21 (5), 374–389.

Kamoche, K. (2002) 'Introduction: Human Resource Management in Africa', *International Journal of Human Resource Management*, 13 (7), 993–997.

Klerck, G. (2007) 'Labour Regulation in Namibia', in G. Wood and C. Brewster (eds) *Industrial Relations in Africa* (London: Palgrave), 98–110.

Mangwiro, C. (2008) 'World Bank Upbeat on Mozambique's Economy', *Mail & Guardian* online. www.mg.co.za. Accessed 21 July 2008.

Marsden, D. (2007) 'Pay and Rewards in Public Services', in P. Dibben, P. James, I. Roper, and G. Wood (eds) *Modernising Work in Public Services* (London: Palgrave).

Moody, K. (1997) *Workers in a Lean World* (London: Verso).

Nellis J. (2008) 'Privatization in Africa: What Has Happened? What Is to Be Done?' in G. Roland (ed.) *Privatization: Successes and Failures* (New York: Columbia University Press), 109–135.

OECD (2008) African Economic Outlook. http://www.oecd.org/dataoecd/13/6/40578303.pdf

O'Flynn, J. and J. Alford (2008) 'The Separation/ Specification Dilemma in Contracting: The Local Government Experience in Victoria', *Public Administration*, 86 (1), 205–224.

O'Laughlin, B. (2000) 'Class and the Customary: The Ambiguous Legacy of the Indigenato in Mozambique', *African Affairs*, 99, 5–42.

Pamacheche, F. and B. Koma (2007) 'Privatization in Sub-Saharan Africa – An Essential Route to Poverty Alleviation', *African Integration Review*, 1 (2), 1–22.

Parker, D. and K. Hartley (2003) 'Transaction Costs, Relational Contracting and Public Private Partnerships: A Case Study of UK Defence', *Journal of Purchasing and Supply Management*, 9 (3), 97–108.

Pitcher, A. (2002) *Transforming Mozambique: The Politics of Privatization, 1975–2000* (Cambridge: Cambridge University Press).

Pollert, A. and I. Hradecka (1994) 'Privatization in Transition: The Czech Experience', *Industrial Relations Journal*, 25 (1), 52–62.

Przeworski, A., M. Alvarez, J. Cheibub, and F. Limongi (2000) *Democracy and Development* (Cambridge: Cambridge University Press).

Richards, L. and T. Richards (1994) 'From Filing Cabinet to Computer', in A. Bryman and R. Burgess (eds) *Analysing Qualitative Data* (London: Routledge), 146–172.

Sachdev, S. (2001) *Contracting Culture: From CCT to PPP* (London: Unison).

Sartorius, K., A. Merino, and T. Carmichael (2011) 'Human Resource Management and Cultural Diversity: A Case Study in Mozambique', *International Journal of Human Resource Management*, 22 (9), 1963–1985.

Stiglitz, J. (2002) *Globalization and its Discontents* (London: Penguin Books).

Tangri, R. and A. Mwenda (2001) 'Corruption and Cronyism in Uganda's Privatization in the 1990s', *African Affairs*, 100 (3978), 117–133.

Teicher, J., Q. Alam, and B. Van Gramberg (2006) 'Managing Trust and Relationships in PPPs: Some Australian Experiences', *International Review of Administrative Sciences*, 72 (1), 85–100.

Torp, J. and P. Rekve (1996) 'Privatisation in Developing Countries: Lessons to be Learnt from the Mozambican Case', *Transformation*, 36, 73–92.

Van Johnston, R. and P. Seidenstat (2007) 'Contracting out Government Services: Privatization at the Millennium', *International Journal of Public Administration*, 30 (3), 231–247.

Van Slyke, D. (2003) 'The Mythology of Privatization in Contracting for Social Services', *Public Administration Review*, 63 (3), 296–315.

Webster, E. and G. Wood (2005) 'Human Resource Management Practice and Institutional Constraints: The Case of Mozambique', *Employee Relations*, 27 (4), 369–385.

Webster, E., G. Wood, M. Mtyingizana, and M. Brookes (2006) 'Residual Unionism and Renewal: Organized Labour in Mozambique', *Journal of Industrial Relations*, 48 (2), 257–278.

Woldu, H. and P. Budhwar (2011) 'Cultural Value Orientations of the Former Communist Countries: A Gender Based Analysis', *International Journal of Human Resource Management*, 22 (7), 1365–1386.

Wood, G. and P. Dibben (2005) 'Ports and Shipping in Mozambique: Current Concerns and Policy Options', *Maritime Policy and Management*, 32 (2), 1–19.

Wood, G., P. Dibben, C. Stride, and E. Webster (2010) 'HRM in Mozambique: Homogenization, Path Dependence or Segmented Business System?' *Journal of World Business*, 46 (1), 31–41.

Zack-Williams, T. and G. Mohan (2005) 'Africa: From SAPs to PRSP', *Review of African Political Economy*, 106, 501–503.

Part II

Multinationals and People Management in Africa

4
Knowledge Appropriation and HRM: The MNC Experience in Tanzania

Ken N. Kamoche and Aloysius Newenham-Kahindi

Introduction

The extant literature on knowledge appropriation, corporate control and transfer within multinational companies (MNCs) tend to focus on the role of the firm, unit and subsidiary levels, often emphasizing on firms' capabilities, knowledge assets and knowledge processes with little emphasis on how these are related to the capability of individual behaviours, social contexts and team cultures across different societal contexts (Hedlund, 1994; Snape et al., 1998; Mudambi et al., 2007; Abrahamson and Eisenman, 2008). In these circumstances, appropriation is normally understood as 'the allocation of rents where property rights are not fully defined' (Grant, 1991, p. 128). In the case of managing human resources (HR), there exists an ambiguity over what constitutes a resource and the ownership of control over resources. We argue in this chapter that the management of corporate culture and HR can be understood in terms of an 'appropriation regime' that functions through mechanisms of control to strengthen the organization's capacity to secure the benefits from the utilization of resources. We also argue that the perspective of appropriation raises valuable questions about whose interests are served, and how power is implicated in the process of diffusing and appropriating knowledge (e.g. Kamoche, 2006; Frenkel, 2008; Pinnington et al., 2009).

Examining a subsidiary context of Tanzania, this chapter aims to fill a gap in the literature on knowledge appropriation through the management of human resources (HRM) and technology through the process of surveillance of HR in the workplace. The unit of analysis used in this chapter is the organization: the MNCs' control mechanisms and the way they diffuse HRM values through their corporate culture (see Pinnington et al., 2009). Previous work has discussed the role of subsidiary relations in terms of 'ethnocentricity', in indicating the pursuit of efficient social exchange relations (e.g. Allen, 1994; Merton, 1996; Gerhart, 2004), often organized by MNC headquarters before being standardized across global operations (Malnight, 1995; Bartlett and Ghoshal, 2000; Bartlett and Beamish, 2011). Similarly, in this context of MNE headquarters and subsidiary relations, Frenkel (2008) has used post-colonial theory, where power is seen as a relational construct derived from the mutual identity between 'colonized' and 'colonizer', to examine the transfer of knowledge and practices in MNCs. He claims that 'by representing knowledge from the first world as the only knowledge worth transferring, and by portraying its adoption by the foreign third world affiliate as a step towards better management, the MNC re-imposes the taken-for-granted hierarchy that justifies the first world's political and economic domination' (Frenkel, 2008, p. 930). We here acknowledge the importance of knowledge transfer, which for Frenkel (2008) is central to the post-colonial debate, and start by questioning why MNCs are concerned with transferring knowledge: hence our focus on knowledge appropriation.

We draw on both ethnocentricity and post-colonial theory, and take the debate further by applying Foucault's social theory to examine how power is used in the MNC–subsidiary relationship with particular regard to the management of people at the organizational level, and to capture the effects of the processes of control on individuals. Foucault's (1991) work allows us to shed new light on the way two MNC banks used technology both as a form of surveillance, to cast an enduring gaze on the labour force, and a management tool, to secure compliance and knowledge appropriation, and the consequences of the sustained and intrusive monitoring processes on an unaccustomed labour force. In Foucauldian terms (Foucault, 1991, p. 170), the 'appropriation regime' and capacity to secure benefits from the utilization of resources occurred through an art of 'correct training', in order to achieve discipline and to bind people together; through training on their movement, bodies and souls to a single unit. Particularly, we aim to illustrate and compare the ways in which both banks solidified their appropriation regime through the use of technological surveillance to enhance work commitment and employee retention.

Technology-based surveillance is not limited to developing countries (see Mir and Mir, 2009; Upadhya, 2009). This chapter points out the need for MNCs to pursue an approach that recognizes the complexity of the local context across subsidiaries. The context in which this study was carried out (data collected during a time of rapid industrial and techno-logical transition) makes this chapter relevant for emerging economies eager to attract foreign direct investment (FDI) and where the disci-plinary effects of technology are likely to have far-reaching effects. Hence, while the two MNCs found the Tanzanian institutional environ-ment extremely favourable for them, their operations raised important concerns about the implications for the local labour force.

Theoretically, the appropriation regime incorporates the sometimes competing interests of a variety of stakeholders, as a result of the ten-sions built in the creation and utilization of knowledge (Bowman and Swart, 2007; Pinnington et al., 2009), and to the extent that organiza-tions' ability to appropriate tacit knowledge is restricted by ambiguity over property rights (Grant, 1991). In practice, though, it is commonly assumed that knowledge is produced for the benefit of the organization, and that the organization is the one which defines the appropriation regime. Therefore, organizations create, secure and retain the outcomes (or 'rents') that result from utilizing knowledge, for their own use (i.e. Teece, 1986; Bogner and Bansal, 2007). Successively, employees are then co-opted into this enterprise, and recompensed in proportion to their contribution to the collective effort of creating productive knowledge. This can be regarded as a disciplinary process in which employees are co-opted through 'training', as urged by Foucault (1991, p. 129); it exposes employees to 'standard habits', 'timetables' with conventional activi-ties, 'good habits' and 'orders', which in turn either 'punish' or 'reward' those who evolve according to the corporate culture. Therefore, the employment relation, in this context of knowledge appropriation, is a key for analysing the ways in which power is implicated in these pro-cesses of knowledge transfer, and how individuals contrive to oppose the normalizing effects of Foucauldian subjection (Kamoche et al., 2011). An appropriation regime characterized by plurality would, therefore, offer enduring learning and motivational opportunities for employ-ees to achieve sustainable benefits, thus providing further incentives for them to contribute to organizational performance (Kamoche and Mueller, 1998; Delbridge et al., 2008). Hence, an effective mechanism for leveraging HR for organizational performance would be, as we empha-size in this chapter, an appropriation regime that embraces both the interests of the organization and the employees' aspirations (Monks and Scullion, 2001; Kamoche, 2006; Frenkel, 2008; Tian et al., 2009).

This chapter contributes important issues in the study of MNC–subsidiary relations within the context of knowledge appropriation in the study of HRM with respect to the power/knowledge paradigm. This study is still relatively under-researched within the context of Tanzania, a country that has been in transition from the socialist ideology to the uncertainties of globalization. This chapter also contributes to the debate on cross-national relations among stakeholders, cross-cultural management and the internationalization of MNCs, through the critique of the strategy, the practices and the management philosophy adopted by MNCs in a subsidiary context of Tanzania.

In the sections that follow, we analyse the challenge of knowledge appropriation, set out the building blocks of our theory (knowledge appropriation and the discipline of surveillance), and then offer a concise introduction to the Tanzanian (i.e. subsidiary) context. Finally, we examine the two case studies and conclude with some recommendations for further research.

Knowledge appropriation through HRM

Although the literature is still distant in dealing critically with the challenge of knowledge appropriation through the management of people, researchers are beginning to acknowledge the relation between knowledge management and HRM (i.e. Storey and Quintas, 2001; Currie and Kerrin, 2003; Collins and Smith, 2006; Kamoche, 2006). With increasing internationalization of businesses, HRM in the context of a firm's strategy, structure and choices is now being recognized as a critical discipline in management studies (Monks and Scullion, 2001). Others have indicated the necessity to balance the economic need for integration with the pressures for local responsiveness (Bartlett and Ghoshal, 2000), and the importance of a 'fit' between corporate strategy, HR policies and the overall corporate culture (Scullion, 2001; Collings, 2003). While global competitive strategies and resources are significant determinants of MNCs' success, the management of knowledge through people remains a challenge for firms operating in foreign countries (Bartlett and Ghoshal, 2000; Kamoche, 2006; Bartlett and Beamish, 2011).

If we present the management of the knowledge possessed by people as part of an appropriation regime that brings together the (potentially divergent) interests of a variety of stakeholders, it becomes clear that a transitional economy like Tanzania presents major challenges for MNCs. These challenges include deploying expatriates with the necessary cultural sensitivity and willingness to learn from the local knowledge, and developing truly transnational companies that attempt to achieve a balanced approach between organizational goals and those of the host country, something that both ethnocentricity and post-colonial theory have identified as a significant challenge in both management and international business theories. Some researchers have highlighted the need for more research that strengthens the theoretical underpinnings of HRM (Kamoche et al., 2004). Horwitz et al. (2002) identified, in the context of Afro-Asia business relations, the importance of 'crossvergence' and hybrid approaches that acknowledge the complex nature of international business relations across diverse cultures. These insights are particularly relevant to the cultural context of Tanzania regarding developing hybrid practices and acknowledging the potential for reverse diffusion whereby MNCs are prepared to learn, adapt and positively engage with the local context rather than merely attempting to impose their own claimed global best HRM practices (see Frenkel, 2008; Khanna and Palepu, 2010).

The discipline of electronic surveillance and Foucauldian 'normalization'

The use of information and communications technology (ICT) as an instrument of management control within MNCs has created new demands on institutional configurations within the knowledge appropriation regime. For instance, as far as banks are concerned, electronic control systems have enabled services to increase the efficiency and control of work (Abolafia, 1996; Heiskanen and Hearn, 2004). The resultant subjection is manifested in the process of 'normalization' (Foucault, 1984). How normalization enables the analysis of power relations in a transnational organization (Ahonen and Tienari, 2009) is an example of normalization process. Kamoche et al. (2011) have also considered how it manifests itself within the context of careers that become a contested territory, pitting the employee's quest for employability against the organizational quest for flexibility. The functions and delivery systems of new financial services through the sometimes bewildering use of ICT represent a functional system of banking regulations and services (Abolafia, 1996; Cetina and Preda, 2005), and also constitute a manifestation of normalization, in the way technology influences the subjectivity of individuals made to submit to power structures (Foucault, 1984).

Employees performing formalized and standardized financial tasks constitute a case example of 'internal labour market' relationship that supports management influences in organizations (Grint, 1998; Kunda,

1992). Such management influences represent the 'hegemonic organization of work' and 'bureaucratic systems' that maintain obligations, power and control over employees (Burawoy, 1984, p. 247; see also Poster, 1990; Timmons, 2003), often with unexpected outcomes. Some believe that, in certain highly ordered service organizations, such as call centres and banking, the attributes of ICT are one of the most fundamental social transformations in work behaviour (Sewell, 1998; Hansen, 2004; Abrahamson and Eisenman, 2008). They consider the effects of ICT as not being restricted exclusively to technology, but extending to the social dynamics and relations that it establishes in people and organizations. We demonstrate in this chapter how the integration and intensification of work processes in two MNCs were achieved through the use of an ICT system. We use Foucault's (1991, p. 172) view of organizations as tools of 'hierarchical surveillance' (e.g. panoptic institutions) to illustrate the effects of MNCs' control in a Tanzanian context.

The complexity of ICT, the reality of interactions connecting the digital and the material world, and the mediating cultures that organize the relations between these technologies and users exemplify the 'electronic control system' in organizations (Foucault, 1991; Sewell, 1998). Electronic monitoring can be fairly passive, when workplaces are monitored by security and electronic cameras, for example, or highly active and intrusive systems, such as when supervisors keep track of work performance electronically and send warning messages to employees. The potential contests inherent in this form of electronic surveillance are tied to the argument that knowledge is both the creator and the creation of power (Foucault, 1984): it creates an environment in which both the MNC and the employee engage themselves to reaffirm and legitimize their claims to knowledge. Foucault (1991) views technology as a 'corpus of knowledge' in which a hierarchical power relation seeks to extend its rhythms, network of relations, precision and task regularities to establish a disciplinary regime upon the subjects in the workplace.

Often, the rhythms are well calculated, organized and technically thought out. Although they may be subtle, they remain a powerful source of physical order. Foucault goes on to argue that work environments are similar to 'prison institutions' which create space between two worlds: the place for the individual transformation of his/her soul and conduct, and also where individuals are recompensed individually as a way to reinsert them morally and materially into the strict world of the economy. By embracing ICT, the use of symbols in such forms as appraisal and reward systems has become an important tool to cement disciplinary control by inculcating and reaffirming the normative rules of the bureaucratic organization. As such, morals are reformed, industry invigorated, instruction diffused, and the power of the 'panopticon' understood and internalized by its subjects (Foucault, 1991, p. 206).

Host nation's institutional context: from *Ujamaa* to a market economy

Tanzania, like other developing nations, is characterized by a diversity of complex cultures that preserve a strong element of traditionalism, patriarchal values and *weak/void institutions* that offer limited protection of employee rights in the employment relationship (see DeSoto, 2000). In 1967, the government became the main source of employment and job creation. This followed after the introduction of *Ujamaa*, a socialist command institutional system, as a strategy to bring about economic and social development (Kitching, 1989). Towards the end of the 1980s, however, this socialist ideology proved incapable of reducing social problems such as poverty and high unemployment. The ideology became economically unsustainable as a result of hard internal and external economic shocks (Kitching, 1989). The World Bank and International Monetary Fund came in to offer new alternatives in order to bring about economic rejuvenation. This led to the influx of FDI, which was previously mostly unknown, across many sectors.

The presence of MNCs in Tanzania had an impact on the design and implementation of new forms of work systems, HRM policies and the way technology was used at work (Rutinwa, 1995; Mapolu, 2000). These practices were not always well received, but, as we show below, were often in conflict with the extant cultural norms, beliefs and practices. Thus, Tanzania needed the FDI and MNCs to create employment and economic prosperity, offering low-cost labour and a variety of labour relations and tax incentives. However, it was not easy to attain a balance between the needs of the employees anxious to secure jobs and those of MNCs with virtually a free hand in the management of employee relations.

Methodology

In order to investigate the most modern (i.e. in use of ICT systems at work) global firms investing in Tanzania, an extended study was carried out between August 1998 and March 2004, with a data update follow-up in 2008. Because they were the most prominent MNC banks in terms of both public profile and size, employing hundreds of local employees across the country, the American (Citibank) and South African (Standard Bank) firms were selected. The choice of Standard Bank was intended to help us determine the extent to which an African bank's ethos and practices were compatible with the institutional environment of a fellow African country, while Citibank offered a significant juxtaposition of a western MNC. Our intention was to examine how these MNCs appropriated knowledge through HRM and the potential cultural conflicts associated with these processes.

Both banks claimed to follow global 'best practices' in managing HR and financial services, in a neo-liberal market system characterized by compliance with the stock market ethos, centralized hierarchical organizational structures, shareholder orientation, and standardization of HRM policies and work values (see Dore, 2000). Our purpose was also to identify both the similarities and the differences in the way they embedded themselves in the local context and to discover how an American and an African MNC negotiated the cultural context, and the role and implications of technology in these processes.

Semi-structured interviews (with bank and branch representatives, expatriates and local employees), archival documents and observation of workplace behaviour were the methods used to collect data. An exploratory research approach was used, which depended to some degree on the grounded theory approach, to the extent that the study did not begin with a set of hypotheses or a predetermined theoretical framework. Similarly, the data were analysed with a view to leading towards theory construction as the 'story' unfolded, and to generate insights for further theoretical articulation (Glaser and Strauss, 1967; Strauss and Corbin, 1998). This approach appeared appropriate for the relatively under-researched Tanzanian context.

During fieldwork, new questions and themes emerged and further enriched the data collected. Questions were asked on how HR activities, such as recruitment, training and career development, were conducted. The objective was to explore the lived experiences of the employees by focusing on their typical day's work, their expectations and the 'psychological contract', their opinions of the employers, forms of social interaction, and the nature of training and socialization they went through. No questions were asked about knowledge appropriation.

The data were analysed using inductive techniques, taken through numerous iterations until particular concepts, key categories, common themes and insights began to emerge. These were checked against the data such that a precise and unique picture emerged of the characteristics of each case. The analysis was guided by replication rather than

sampling logic (Yin, 2003), and sought to critique and extend existing theory. Data were triangulated through different research methods
consistent with case study research, such as official archival documents and observation of employees' behaviour (including by their
employers). Specifically, the following were observed in both banks:
how employees navigated the day-to-day organizational/cultural practices; the employee response to technologically based surveillance; the
way they interacted with customers and socialized with their employers,
for example, during lunch breaks; the way they replied to customers'
queries on the telephone; and how they handled the pace of work in
general. This approach reinforced the grounded theory while enhancing
the reliability of the data (Eisenhardt, 1989). The findings below demonstrate how the banks sought knowledge appropriation through HR and
cultural practices that were underpinned by a process of normalization.

Research findings – Case 1: Citibank

Citibank has been operating in Tanzania since 1995. During fieldwork, it
had three main branches, located in Dar es Salaam, Mwanza and Arusha.
Given the nature of sector and customer services in which the bank was
involved in the country, the use of advanced ICT had significant impacts
in the way organizational systems were structured and standardized, and
the degree of compliance to standard operating procedures required of
both management and employees (e.g. see Kunda, 1992; Hedlund, 1994;
Sewell, 1998).

Organizational setting and identity: Americanization of the workplace

As part of its 'modernizing influences', the workplace environment
was unambiguously American in terms of both culture and work
ethics (Burawoy, 1984; Poster, 1990; Tian et al., 2009). Each branch
was equipped with communal lounges where employees could read
American newspapers and watch CNN and MTV-USA during the lunch
break in a relaxed atmosphere; no local television channels were
allowed. Besides branch representatives, all employees were required to
have lunch at the branch canteens. They were not authorized to bring
in meals from outside. Tight security checks ensured they complied with
this regulation.

The bank enhanced a sense of identity (Burawoy, 1984; Kunda, 1992)
by expecting employees to comply with a formal dress code. Employees
were also required to speak with an American accent, especially when

they spoke on the phone to their bank and branch representatives, expatriates and customers. There was an organized process for socializing between employees and bank representatives. In each branch, employees were expected to join the bank's recreational scheme free of charge and attend at least once a week; the bank subsidized the expenses of employees' transportation. Bonuses were granted to those employees who attended the recreational scheme regularly. According to the bank representatives' opinion, recreational schemes provided a healthy and balanced lifestyle for their employees, and a chance to 'get together' in a relaxed atmosphere away from the pace and intensity of the work. At each branch, resource centres served as a training ground for new and ongoing programmes, and were made available to students from selected colleges and universities that were seen as a source of future recruitment.

We see the above forms of socialization and identity creation as a mechanism to realize knowledge appropriation by getting employees to align their everyday lives and sense of who they are with the bank's corporate objectives. Remarkably, their mandatory nature and the use of financial tools to reinforce culture were strengthened further by the use of expatriates. This was justified on grounds of their experience in business management training and their ability to diffuse best practices in line with the corporate culture (Teece, 1986; Kamoche and Mueller, 1998). As a bank representative in Dar es Salaam put it:

> Due to the competitive nature of the banking industry, the role of expatriates from the head office is crucial for our business success and development. They have the necessary skills and know-how to run businesses.

The expatriates were the ones to arrange the recreational activities much of the time, thus encouraging team building in the workforce. Their main responsibility, however, was to provide training to the locals, an indication of a deeper need to transmit international 'best practices' and to inculcate the corporate culture. Most expatriates held key posts in ICT, budget control, project management and the overall tasks of training local employees, exerting significant personal and cultural authority through direct supervision, and by ensuring compliance with formalized procedures. Induction training, recreational activities and other HR functions were management tools designed to 'infiltrate' into the culture of the host society (i.e. see Poster, 1990; Grint, 1998; Timmons, 2003) and were consistent with the process of normalization

(Foucault, 1984). Both banks used sophisticated software packages that were designed, updated, tested and developed in the head offices to train and turn employees into 'specialists', expecting that subsidiaries with a high expatriate presence would more closely comply with the management practices of the head offices. For Foucault (1991, pp. 171–172), hierarchical structures, such as head offices, serve as tools of discipline to convert the subjectivity of individuals in the workplace. They make use of technology to ensure that individuals are effectively observed, measured, categorized and normalized. Hence, bank representatives in both banks revealed that the number of expatriates was expected to increase in the near future.

CASE 2: Standard Bank

Standard Bank claimed to be Africa's leading financial institution in providing financial services and products to more than 17 African countries. Its business operations were in Dar es Salaam, Arusha and Mwanza, assisting customers mostly in the mining, tourism and construction sectors.

Organizational setting

Standard Bank's representatives (including those at branch levels) and expatriates mostly came from South Africa, with a minority from Namibia. As in Citibank, there was an integrated organizational system in and across workplaces (see also Monks and Scullion, 2001); both bank and branch representatives had regular reporting systems to the head office on all matters, including HRM policies, financial reports and detailed information on customers. However, in contrast to Citibank, employees could easily chat and visually interact with one another. The ambience at work was clearly more relaxed and the employees seemed to be under less pressure than at Citibank. The country head office and branches had resource centres fitted with both local and foreign magazines, videos and textbooks, all for training purposes. Some videos had been translated into the local language, Swahili. All employees and visitors were subjected to high security checks upon arrival, as in Citibank. The organizational systems largely matched those of Citibank. Strategic management and business activities in the host nation, including HR functions, were controlled directly from the head office in Johannesburg before being passed to the country head office in Dar es Salaam. The head office had complete operational control over the country operations and played an important role in the implementation of HRM policies (see e.g. Abolafia, 1996). One of the main responsibilities of the country head office in Dar es Salaam was to implement key decisions made at the head office, such as those relating to ICT, financial services and the appointment of bank and branch representatives in key positions, and the appointment of expatriates.

In Foucauldian terms, the two banks executed their 'obligation' by intermediating the relationship with the head office leadership and their potential customers abroad. Additionally, the high degree of centralization in decision-making rendered control by bank representatives difficult; hence the need for technologies of surveillance, which, consequentially, further strengthened the centralization. Communication patterns established in both banks also reflected Sewell and Wilkinson's (1992) 'electronic panopticism' (also see Thompson and van den Broek, 2010) and Poster's (1990) 'super-panopticon' (see also Spicer et al., 2009), which describe disciplinary monitoring and technological control.

Appropriation of knowledge through HR functions

In both banks, branch representatives played an important role in managing HR policies. As indicated in secondary data, HR departments received guidance from their head offices which required high levels of efficiency and centralization processes, especially in recruitment and training (see also Monks and Scullion, 2001; Collings, 2003; Pinnington et al., 2009). The pursuit aim of centralization by the head office resonates with Foucault's (1991, p. 201) use of a 'panopticon' to indicate how organizations induce a state of permanent visibility in their corporate culture.

In both Citibank and Standard Bank, new members were taken through a process that laid the foundation for eventually facilitating knowledge appropriation through HRM, a three to five-day induction course that involved briefing candidates on the banks' vision, mission statements and strategies. Expatriates were tasked with making sure that the new recruits had all the necessary information and knowledge to smooth their entry into the organization and facilitate their progression to an acceptable satisfactory performance level (see Table 4.1).

According to Kunda (1992, pp. 8–14), 'training in organizations resembles "rituals", where organizational culture is used to bring about integration and value consensus that leads to employee loyalty and work commitment'. Training encouraged teamwork, and was guided by training needs, quality, productivity and efficiency, but also contributed

Table 4.1 Citibank and Standard Bank

Similarities – Organizational systems	Appropriation (through HRM)
Centralized system from the head offices	Enabled expatriates to transfer corporate culture from the head offices
Interconnected ICT system	Enabled employees to be trained to think and perform tasks in rationalized work system, i.e. emphasis on standardized efficiency
Use of electronic database to monitor financial activities	Enabled the deployment of so-called modern 'best practices' of HRM practices within the banking industry, including regular report systems to head offices
Application of modern electronic monitoring system, e.g. surveillance systems	Enabled the 'normalizing gaze' of the banks' corporate culture, i.e. appropriation and utilization of culture through the management of HR
Differences – Citibank	*Standard Bank*
Management policies: emphasized a strict adherence to HRM policies as directed by head office	HRM policies directed from head office but also responded to local contexts, i.e. leadership, gender
Age specific: must be between 18 and 35 age category	Must be over 35 with work experience
Global responsiveness: strict individualized management approach:	Local responsiveness: mix between individualized and collective/team approach:
• promotion based on competence regardless of gender and age • use of western management practices, American accent required in communication with international customers	• promotion mainly based on age (older), and gender (mainly male) • use of *Ubuntu* and *Indaba* ideologies to 'fit' with local realities

to establishing rapport between employees and managers (Thompson and van den Broek, 2010). According to bank representatives, the final approval on content came from the head office, thus indicating an ethnocentric approach in shaping the type of knowledge that was required and how it was created through training policies.

Both banks had formal and well-documented appraisal systems, used to determine salary rises, bonuses, profit or benefit schemes and promotion for local employees, designed at the head offices. Employees were evaluated quarterly or annually depending on the decision of branch representatives, the appraisal itself varying from general frameworks to highly standardized systems that closely captured every aspect of performance. However, some significant differences were observed. Standard Bank had both group and team appraisal. Assessment criteria were based on a group work-related attitude, such as whether teams had internalized the corporate values of the bank on collective management and leadership approach. Individual assessments were unusual and were, in fact, discouraged. However, age and gender were considered essential. New recruits were supposed to have previous working experience before joining the bank, and to be over 35 years old, and there was a preference for males. A small number of women, however, were hired for administrative tasks. Team appraisals determined group bonus and group benefit schemes, while individual appraisals, when they took place, were for determining promotion and salary increase. At Citibank, managers considered individual characteristics such as numerical competence, age (a preference for 18–35-year olds), communication skills, quality of work, initiative, leadership, trust and innovation (see Table 4.1). There were no group rewards. Instead, the branch HR managers individually called successful employees to inform them about their award confidentially, a practice designed to avoid harmful competition and nourish belief in perceived fairness. In fact, it damaged trust and created a culture of suspicion, yet it achieved normalization based on the knowledge people possess that, in turn, regulated the value the bank placed upon them. Therefore, both banks chose different approaches to shape the subjectivity of their employees by means of HRM: Standard Bank normalized and attributed value to employees through their perceived commitment and internalization of a group ethos, while Citibank relied on individual performance and attributed employee value accordingly.

On the basis of the above data, the rigidity of both Citibank's and Standard Bank's formal structures in the host nation reveals how the banking sector was systematically integrated in its organizational system, which also enabled the banks to be highly structured in their delivery of services (Monks and Scullion, 2001; Kamoche, 2006). All activities appeared to be converted into one focal visibility by surveillance and coordination systems, in both banks. According to Foucault (1991, p. 202), panoptic institutions tend to create fictitious relations where subjects are isolated from those in power and are continuously subjected to visibility. Furthermore, those in power can easily survey their subjects, adjust their behaviour and impose upon them the methods they see fit. This pursuit of visibility worked as a strong control mechanism whose aim was to ensure knowledge appropriation between employees who were in no position to resist its disciplinary effects. Still, the use of expatriates to attain these ends did not necessarily reflect the nature of labour market conditions in Tanzania.

The extent and impact of knowledge appropriation initiatives

In this section, we consider the degree to which both banks achieved the goals of knowledge appropriation by examining what the process represented to the employees. Mostly, employees exposed to an assortment of new forms of organizational models within the banking sector, such as standardized and automated work systems, were frequently overawed and overwhelmed by the sheer scope of the operation and the power of the ICT. As one employee reported:

> I came to realize how this bank [Citibank] was really integrated across its business operations. I have come across clients from all over the world... Yes, it is very interconnected.

Yet, most employees continued to be unfamiliar with the specifics of the banks' organizational structures and how these structures operated a very firm and centralized monitoring system (Bartlett and Ghoshal, 2000). Regarding the work systems, the relationships between local employees and bank representatives were characterized as centralized and task-specific (Monks and Scullion, 2001; Delbridge et al., 2008). Work was designed so that organizational structures delineated social relationships between different areas of responsibility (Scullion, 2001). Employees were instructed to preserve the integrity of the work systems; to internalize the need to preserve 'secrecy' in all work activities, and to guard against disclosure to outsiders. An interviewee at Citibank reported:

> I can understand why the bank [...] is very strict towards its policy of confidentiality on financial information. It seems this is a very sensitive business where any financial information can have repercussion to the bank and the customers.

Employees accepted the reasoning for confidentiality and did not see it as a problem. However, the process could be bewildering. This was revealed to us by the interviewee at Citibank:

> Well, there are so many regulations here, though. They keep coming and going. Sometimes it is difficult to know where the boundaries lie. For example, we have to recycle all papers we use and we cannot take them outside the building. But what really comes out pretty often is the requirement to preserve and not to release financial information to outsiders.

Accepting the necessity to keep computer passwords and software databases safe was one thing. Coming to grips with the constant CCTV surveillance was quite another (see also Burawoy, 1984; Kunda, 1992). CCTV surveillance raised significant concerns about the extent of the electronic monitoring, as well as the level of intrusion into their private lives (see Sewell, 1998). A Citibank employee reported:

> At the beginning we seemed not to care much about the presence of all these electronic cameras at work. The foreign managers kept saying they needed to protect their property from forgery, terrorism and crime. We never knew where the boundaries were. It came to our attention only when the bank representatives gave our first performance appraisal feedback at the end of the year. In the appraisal, each one of us came out expressing shock... It seemed they were monitoring our work and movements every day. They knew [the bank representatives] how often we came late to work, who was not working properly, who deserved disciplinary action, and who spent more time in the canteen watching CNN television programmes!

Both banks utilized a system of over-specialization that seemed to serve as a knowledge protection and isolation mechanism. Employees at Citibank revealed that they did not understand the broader content of work in different departments other than their own units. An employee asked to distinguish between fund accounting and corporate finance reported:

> Well, I have no idea what people do in fund accounting. We sometimes process account payments together and pass the information

to foreign fund managers. I would not know in detail what they do over there. We just do the work!

Another said:

I know very little of what they do in different departments. The only thing that I am aware of is that our activities are very much interconnected. Sometimes we see this when we have brainstorming or 'Test Train Test' interactions where we gather bits and pieces of information from different departments.

When asked about the implications of work specialization in their units, one employee replied:

As a woman working in customer services for the last 16 months, I feel I need to do something different than this. I have been doing the same job for a long time. I need a challenge. My main concern is that if my contract is not renewed, I may easily get employed in another private bank, like Standard Bank, but the likelihood is that they may give me a job in the same area again.

Over-specialization was ironically one of the things that attracted job seekers to Citibank in the first place: the training they received. The respondent above continued saying:

Well, this is the only bank [Citibank] that offers intensive training in the country. Everyone knows about that. The experience I get here will be seen as more valuable in another bank than to be employed in a different job area.

There were mixed responses regarding what work specialization meant for the employees. Age and gender seemed to be critical. For instance, younger employees were willing to learn more diversified skills, particularly when they anticipated changing jobs (that signifies their approach to and motivation for appropriating knowledge), but older employees were more settled in their specialized work. Older employees at Standard Bank demonstrated satisfaction with their work and did not see constant training as critical in accomplishing multi-skilling:

I have been working here for the last three years. I enjoy my job, it is manageable. I do not see that [boredom with specialization] as

a problem. It will be very hard for me to work in different departments where I have to go through many training with computers
and working experience. This job is fine with me.

Overall, while the interview material presented here reveals much dissatisfaction with the working environment in both banks, the analysis
found little effort to meet the normalizing gaze with the potential for
resistance or subversion. Responses from local employees on issues, such
as repetitive and boring work, on intrusive surveillance, or on how
the organizational systems were systematically coordinated, reveal that
these job characteristics were all broadly accepted as part of everyday
life (see also Burawoy, 1984; Hansen, 2004).

Employees tended to justify their experiences as part of their unavoidable exposure to the exigencies of the modern workplace, thus demonstrating the banks' success in legitimizing their appropriation regimes
and normalization process through HR and cultural practices.

As previously mentioned, there were some significant differences in
the use of these mechanisms. In Standard Bank, some local employees
revealed that HR recruitment and career development had adopted local
patterns and reflected the nature of management and leadership systems
in the society. A clerical employee at a Mwanza branch said:

> We do not see many differences between other local firms and private
> in this bank, especially when it comes to seniority, promotion and
> teamwork. The bank is very accommodating and everyone seems to
> be happy. The only difference between this and local firms is that this
> bank pays very well.

However, some employees who had left Citibank and joined Standard
Bank were less optimistic about HRM policies in Standard Bank.

> In the last 17 months since I joined this bank I have not seen much
> training happening here. In Citibank, we had frequent training. It is
> really a quiet place to work here.

> This bank does not promote you in the same way as I experienced at
> the other bank [Citibank]. For most of young men and women who
> work here the prospect of promotion can be really an enduring slow
> process... Well, first of all, when you join the bank they do not take
> your leadership skills seriously. Secondly, when it comes to leadership
> and promotion the big potatoes [i.e., older men] get the nod and you
> cannot question about that. It is the norm here and outside but what
> can you do if you are in this situation?

Asked why she still worked at the bank, she said:

> The bank gives you a guaranteed permanent job! The pay here is also great and jobs are much more stable compared to where I worked before.

Similar research has demonstrated how work has become rule bound, automated and monitored, and how it operates through the irresistible appeal of seductive financial and motivational techniques that secure commitment at the cost of self-sacrifice (Kunda, 1992), which resonates with this finding. Likewise, Poster (1990) has shown how 'super-panopticon' institutions are practically inescapable working environments where employees have to 'put up with it', a notion that Sewell and Wilkinson (1992) have described as employees being reduced to 'resigned behavioural compliance' in the workplace. Compliance at Standard Bank was rationalized regarding job security and high pay, while Citibank ensured compliance through surveillance.

Dealing with cultural conflict

The paradox of inappropriate African values

Citibank's focus on American culture stands in stark contrast to that of Standard Bank, which was described as consistent with African values. Standard Bank describes itself in published records, including its website, as 'African', with values based on the vision of *Indaba* and *Ubuntu* (Stanbic, 2006), concepts currently emerging in the southern African management debate. *Indaba* is about consensual decision-making and generally involves leadership that comes with experience and age, while *Ubuntu* denotes a sense of 'togetherness as one people' (Mbigi, 1997). These values were, as our findings show, more acceptable to the older generation and specifically to men, who preferred stable career prospects, but were not always welcomed by women and younger workers. Thus, while the bank's intention was to show sensitivity to local norms by adopting HR practices informed by South African cultural values, to a segment of its labour force these values were just as distinctly foreign as the American ones imposed by Citibank. This argument demonstrates the risk of assuming cultural homogeneity across the African continent. Prior research has indicated the sheer diversity across the continent (Kamoche et al., 2004; Newenham-Kahindi, 2011) that is just as likely to create a challenge at the national level as those practices brought in from western nations. Bank representatives at Standard Bank reported:

> We are... [Standard Bank management] collective and open, and we show concern for our employees. We live and work as one family together... and this works pretty well for us.

> We are an African bank... as such, we work as a family where respect, mutual trust and team work become our central aim in managing business and our employees.

By contrast, most employees pointed to Citibank as exercising more fairness regarding promotion and training.

> The more you work hard, come to work on time and make fewer mistakes in your work the greater the likelihood of being promoted and getting a salary increase. An individual success approach is highly encouraged in the bank.

The disadvantage to this, however, was the lack of job security, as this same respondent went on to describe:

> Well, most things are good here. But there are things that do not please us at all. There is no guarantee whether or not you will be in the bank for the next six months. We are all contracted employees, and we have to sign each time to agree with the terms and conditions of employment. So, when you think about it, it is not a secure working environment.

Thus, the young men and women who worked at Citibank appeared to be satisfied with the HR practices concerning training, promotion and career development. Apart from the prospects of lack of job security, Citibank was the preferred option: its 'western values' that emphasized merit, experience and competence, as opposed to age, were more consistent with those of the young men and women for whom the traditional African patriarchal system seemed oppressive. We noticed some forms of conflict between the younger and the older employees in their responses to Standard Bank's application of HR policies. The older employees expressed concern about the younger ones' dissatisfaction with the bank's approach to *Ubuntu* and *Indaba*. They feared that their stability and job security were endangered by the younger employees' desire to change the culture and prevailing values. The older employees had absorbed the culture, and hence established themselves as subjects who were regulated by power relations through a process of subjection (Foucault, 1984).

The limits of American values

Acculturation for the purposes of appearing 'professional' was a source of apprehension:

> I am a graduate of journalism and communication studies. Right from the day I started learning English, locals or foreign teachers taught me. But here, the foreign expatriates teach us to speak with an American accent. We are constantly told that when you have to deal with customer 'X' in Europe or America you need appropriate customer relations... [meaning an American accent], otherwise customers won't understand what you are talking about. It is absolutely ridiculous to have to adjust your voice when you enter the building.

Asked if there was anything else that was very American, this interviewee said:

> Yes, they have all these textbooks and teaching materials from America. The accountancy themes and concepts we use in the workplaces...and the distance exams we do are all regulated in America.

The Americanized norms of communication with customers raised particular issues for female employees:

> I have just got married, and the manager told me that smiling at customers is the best gesture...he is a complete nutter...you wouldn't believe what they are imposing over here...how can I keep smiling at customers? People [reflecting] will think I am enticing men around me, something that goes completely against my culture.

Probed for further examples, she said:

> Well, there is another thing we are not really happy with it. Going for swimming classes, walking, jogging, and playing sports. I am no longer a kid to go swimming. Swimming is for kids not a graduate like myself. I have worked so hard to reach where I am, and to be told to do exercise after work...I do not understand it.

For some female workers, what Citibank managers considered a way to maintain a healthy lifestyle, such as engaging in keep fit recreational activities, was an unnecessary intrusion into their private lives, and inconsistent with the way they construed themselves and the image they had of successful professionals in this culture. It was at odds with how they believed an African woman should behave in public, especially when it involved 'inappropriate' clothing like swimming costumes, shorts and trainers. We found no evidence that the bank had asked for the employees' opinions as to whether these forms of socialization and recreation were acceptable to the employees or not. The foregoing exemplifies the conflict between the two cultures and how centralized MNC management can come to be construed as insensitive to local cultures and customs (Bartlett and Ghoshal, 2000; Kamoche et al., 2004; Mudambi et al., 2007). This is an important critique of MNC 'best practices' and their perception as universal (see also Snape et al., 1998).

Discussion

The foregoing exemplifies how two banks used contrasting HR approaches that were legitimized on the basis of their specific cultures. Still, each cultural rationale faced some opposition, demonstrating the difficulties of achieving acceptability either for the 'American way' or for the 'South African way' in the Tanzanian context. Our purpose was not to impute sinister motives on the part of the banks, but, following Frenkel (2008), who argues that MNC knowledge transfer practices are not neutral with regard to power, and need to be revealed rather than concealed, we sought to interpret the effects these processes and practices had, and how they constituted a form of Foucauldian subjection.

We found that the HR functions at Standard Bank emphasized team/group work as the locus of knowledge creation and the repository of knowledge. Bank representatives and expatriates succeeded in tilting the knowledge appropriation regime in favour of their organizations, by standardizing procedures in training and career development, specifying the capabilities that shape the management of work rather than relying on the discretion of individuals (see also Kamoche, 2006). The highly formalized structure for training and career development at Citibank was particularly remarkable: we argue it was designed to ensure that knowledge did not reside in a few individuals, but was distributed among the teams/groups. This helped strengthen the organization's appropriation regime and meant that employees whose contracts were not renewed did not unduly interfere in the workflow or take away with them valuable knowledge.

On the other hand, Standard Bank pursued HRM policies via team/group initiatives and cultural practices based on some traditional African values (see Mbigi, 1997). However, it failed to acknowledge that the collectivist ethos that favoured older (mostly male) workers did not appeal to the younger staff and female staff, who wished for more frequent training and a faster pace of inclusion in promotion, career development and leadership. These findings highlight the complexities when MNCs attempt to impose new organizational and managerial cultures that are at odds with the prevailing norms and values (Kamoche et al., 2004; Mudambi et al., 2007). They also reveal the inadequacy of ethnocentricity and post-colonial theory in explaining the structure of power relations of an African MNC *within* the African context, in contrast with the more familiar 'first-world–third-world' context (Frenkel, 2008).

At Citibank, the approach to knowledge appropriation was underpinned by the use of expatriates to train locals and inculcate culture, the socialization and creation of an Americanized culture and ethos. This approach was appreciated by those who valued the merit-based HR approach, but for others the lack of job security and inculcation of American values remained a source of friction. At Standard Bank, the knowledge appropriation regime was rationalized according to traditional African values that only appealed to a segment of the labour force. In either case, the selected approach ensured that the knowledge appropriation regime, though unfavourable to some of the workforce, nevertheless served the bank's purpose. The process was rationalized on the basis of the banks' internal quest for efficiency and promoted on the basis of organizational/corporate culture to reinforce the knowledge-appropriation regime to meet customers/clients' demands (i.e. as external forces), but with little consideration of the local cultures. Therefore, similar financial tools were implemented by both banks: standardized operational routines, rationalized training (i.e. with firm-specific skill development), with a view to aligning employee behaviour to the corporate culture (Monks and Scullion, 2001; Collings, 2003).

Drawing from Foucault, we showed how MNCs dealt with their subjects, with the intent to change and shape their behaviour (see also Timmons, 2003, pp. 143–152). The banks' HR coordination mechanisms combined with ICT become powerful instruments for inculcating 'obedience' through 'normalization' (Foucault, 1991). Heiskanen and Hearn (2004, pp. 148–167) proposed that standardization of work, closer observation of employees and seating arrangements in the workplace do not only work to realize order and efficiency of work, but actually aim to sustain the nature of power relations in organizations. This resembles the view that knowledge transfer replicates geopolitical power relations (Frenkel, 2008) at the macro-level. Citibank's inculcation of fitness consciousness, American accents and characteristics eroded the employees' culturally embedded construction of their own identity, and also normalized them into establishing their identity as pseudo-American. Their compliance with this normalization was, in turn, legitimized through higher wages and training. By revealing these realities and paradoxes as seen through the eyes of the local employees, our study made a significant contribution; as Frenkel (2008) has observed, the voice of workers in 'third world countries' is never heard, since most MNC studies focus on managers.

Still, in spite of the potential power of the 'normalizing gaze' (Foucault, 1991), which not only recognizes unacceptable breaches but also develops profiles of computer usage (Sewell and Wilkinson, 1992) as well as chronicling behaviour, as we observed at Citibank in particular, panoptic power is not yet all-pervasive (Grint, 1998). Similarly, Heiskanen and Hearn (2004) have documented resistance to panoptic power in call centres. In our case analysis, for the Tanzanian workers, the supervisory gaze was both bewildering and unavoidable, and virtually inescapable (Poster, 1990). Especially for employees on short-term contracts, it left little space for resistance, and little job security, while helping to reinforce the organization's capacity to appropriate knowledge. We argue that the success of this normalizing gaze was attributable to the asymmetrical power relations as much as to the extant labour market conditions and the weak institutional environment, all of which left the local bank employees in a relatively vulnerable position.

Implications and conclusions

We have reasoned that knowledge appropriation cannot be conceptualized as an unproblematic process of tightening control or even the more superficial notion of retaining 'rents' from the utilization of HR assets. It is actually much more complex than this, with significant implications for research, management practice and policy. In pursuing these ends, we acknowledge there are some limitations in this study. First, the original data may seem dated, which is why we undertook a follow-up field visit and have emphasized that the data need to be interpreted against the background of an economy that is still transitional today.

The 2008 visit actually revealed little change on critical issues like gender and age inequality in either bank. This accentuated important policy implications, particularly the need for effective labour legislation in an economy in which MNCs exert substantial power over employees with limited job security.

A second limitation is the use of only two case studies, which might not have completely captured the reality of the MNC experience in Tanzania. However, we have concentrated on drawing lessons that can generate additional theory from these two illustrative case studies, seeing that our goal was not to achieve generalizability across populations. Clearly, there are important theoretical and managerial implications in the application of ethnocentric HR and cultural practices (e.g. Allen, 1994; Gerhart, 2004), not only in the banking sector, but across the economy in general. In addition, our study advanced the critique of MNC behaviour by analysing an African MNC in which the colonial discourse is absent, thus underscoring the analytical legitimacy of the Foucauldian perspective adopted here.

There will be demand for additional research in HRM and knowledge appropriation, using a range of theoretical approaches and research methods, as the Tanzanian economy continues to open and become an integral part of the global economy. This takes into consideration the recent inflow of Chinese firms in the construction, trading and manufacturing sectors not only in Tanzania, but in much of Africa. Such research will further test the sustainability of the theories discussed here, given China's unique context as a developing country, albeit one with considerable (mostly state-owned) MNC clout. This chapter raises further policy and managerial implications regarding the need for effective employee relations so as to achieve a better balance between the MNCs' needs for organizational control and the employees' needs for training, job security and respect for their culture. Future research might consider other sectors such as mining, tourism and construction, which are dominated by MNCs in Tanzania. Hence, our study will hopefully engender further research in the design of knowledge appropriation mechanisms that achieve a meaningful balance between the needs of various stakeholders (see Table 4.1).

This chapter demonstrated the challenge to the organization's appropriation regime on the basis of contextual validity, thus leading to further research into the legitimacy of HR practices and the use of cultural tools to accomplish narrowly defined organizational ends. We drew eclectically from Foucault's social theory to describe how HR and cultural practices achieve normalization and lead employees to comply with the structure of power relations, thus strengthening the banks' knowledge appropriation powers. Further research might consider the ethical implications of this 'subjection', the long-term effects of the erosion of local cultures and marginalization of identity, as well as the existence of non-visible forms of resistance among employees in similar developing country contexts. Scholars might also analyse how the extensive use of ICT for surveillance, while economically efficient and operationally legitimate due to security concerns, can tackle the tensions and conflicts that jeopardize the very commitment management is seeking to achieve due to the erosion of trust and erosion/marginalization of identities. A significant implication and avenue for further research is the viability of hybrid practices that merge suitable MNC 'best practices' and local practices at the subsidiary level, therefore allowing the MNC to overcome ethnocentricity. This will require a reassessment of the current structure of power relations that were realized and reaffirmed through surveillance and HR practices. This argument reinforces the need to pursue policies that stand for harmonization, diversity and inclusivity in the workplace. This chapter will hopefully lead to further research that draws from other areas of contemporary social theory, given Tanzania's (and indeed Africa's) history and its current engagement with a global economy.

References

Abolafia, M. T. (1996) *Making Markets: Opportunism and Restraint on Wall Street* (Cambridge, MA: Cambridge University Press).

Abrahamson, E. and M. Eisenman (2008) 'Employee Management Techniques: Transient Fads or Trending Fashions?' *Administrative Science Quarterly*, 53(4), 719–744.

Ahonen, P. and J. Tienari (2009) 'United in Diversity? Disciplinary Normalization in an EU Project', *Organization*, 16(5), 655–679.

Allen, S. (1994) 'Race, Ethnicity and Nationality: Some Questions of Identity', in H. Ashfer and M. Maynard (eds) *The Dynamics of Race and Gender: Some Feminist Interventions* (London: Taylor & Francis), 85–105.

Bartlett, C. and P. Beamish (2011) *Transnational Management: Texts, Cases, and Readings in Cross-Border Management* (6th ed.) (London: McGraw-Hill).

Bartlett, C. and S. Ghoshal (2000) *Transnational Management* (3rd ed.) (Boston, MA: Irwin McGraw-Hill).

Bogner, W. C. and P. Bansal (2007) 'Knowledge Management as the Basis of Sustained High Performance', *Journal of Management Studies*, 44, 165–188.

Bowen, D. E., C. Galang, and R. Pillai (2002) 'The Role of Human Resources Management: An Exploratory Study of Cross-Country Variance', *Human Resource Management*, 41(1), 103–122.

Bowman, C. and J. Swart (2007) 'Whose Human Capital? The Challenge of Value Capture when Capital is Embedded', *Journal of Management Studies*, 44, 488–505.

Brocklehurst, M., C. Grey, and A. Sturdy (2010) 'Management: The Work that Dares Not Speak its Name', *Management Learning*, 41, 7.

Bryman, A. (2004) *Social Research Methods* (London: Oxford University Press).

Burawoy, M. (1984) 'Karl Marx and the Satanic Mills: Factory Politics under Early Capitalism in England, the United States, and Russia', *American Journal of Sociology*, 90, 247–282.

Callaghan, G. and P. Thompson (2001) 'Edwards Revisited: Technical Control and Call-Centres', *Economic and Industrial Democracy*, 22(1), 13–37.

Cetina, K. K. and A. Preda (2005) *The Sociology of Financial Markets* (London: Oxford University Press).

Citibank (1997) *Personal Investment Brochure* (New York: Mezzanine).

Collings, D. (2003) 'Human Resource Development and Labour Market Practices in a US Multinational Subsidiary: The Impact of Global and Local Influence', *Journal of European Industrial Training*, 27(2), 188–200.

Collins, C. J. and K. G. Smith (2006) 'Knowledge Exchange and Combination: The Role of Human Resource Practices in the Performance of High-Technology Firms', *Academy of Management Journal*, 49, 544–560.

Currie, G. and M. Kerrin (2003) 'Human Resource Management and Knowledge Management: Enhancing Knowledge Sharing in a Pharmaceutical Company', *International Journal of Human Resource Management*, 14, 1027–1045.

Delbridge, R., M. Hauptmeier, and S. Sengupta (2008) 'Human Relations Special Issue Call for Papers: Beyond the Enterprise – Broadening the Horizons of International HRM', *Human Relations*, 61, 1809.

Dore, R. (2000) *Stock-Market Capitalism: Welfare Capitalism, Japan and Germany versus Anglo-Saxons* (Oxford: Oxford University Press).

Eisenhardt, K. M. (1989) 'Building Theories from Case Study Research', *Academy of Management Review*, 14, 532–550.

Foucault, M. (1984) 'What Is Enlightenment?' In P. Rabinow (ed.) *The Foucault Reader* (London: Penguin), 32–50.

Foucault, M. (1991) *Discipline and Punishment: The Birth of the Prison* (Harmondsworth: Penguin).

Frenkel, M. (2008) 'The Multinational Corporation as a Third Space: Rethinking International Management Discourse on Knowledge Transfer through Homi Bhabha', *Academy of Management Review*, 33(4), 924–942.

Gerhart, B. (2004) 'Culture in Management Research: Nation and Industry Differences Matter (But, What about Organization Differences?)', *Working paper*, School of Business, University of Wisconsin-Madison.

Glaser, B. and A. Strauss (1967) *The Grounded Theory* (Chicago: Aldine).

Grant, R. M. (1991) 'The Resource-Based Theory of Competitive Advantage: Implications for Strategy Formulation', *California Management Review*, 33, 114–135.

Hansen, S. (2004) 'From Common Observation to Behavioural Risk Management: Workplace Surveillance and Employee Assistance 1914–2003', *International Sociology*, 19(2), 151–171.

Hedlund, G. (1994) 'A Model of Knowledge Management and the N-form Corporation', *Strategic Management Journal*, 15, 73–90.

Heiskanen, T. and J. Hearn (2004) *Information Society and the Workplace: Spaces, Boundaries and Agency* (London: Routledge).

Horwitz, F., K. Kamoche, and I. K. H. Chew (2002) 'Looking East: Diffusing High Performance Work Practices in the Southern Afro-Asian Context', *International Journal of Human Resource Management*, 13(7), 1019–1041.

Kamoche, K. (2006) 'Managing People in Turbulent Economic Times: A Knowledge-Creation and Appropriation Perspective', *Asia Pacific Journal of Human Resources*, 44(1), 25–45.

Kamoche, K., Y. Debrah, F. Horwitz, and G. N. Muuka (2004) *Managing Human Resources in Africa* (London: Routledge).

Kamoche, K. and F. Mueller (1998) 'HRM: An Appropriation-Learning Perspective', *Human Relations*, 51(8), 1033–1060.

Kharun, T. and K. G. Paletu (2010) *Winning in Emerging Markets: A Road Map for Strategy and Execution* (Boston, MA: Harvard Business Press).

Kitching, G. (1989) *Development and Underdevelopment in Historical Perspective: Populism, Nationalism and Industrialism* (London: Routledge).

Malnight, T. W. (1995) 'Globalization of an Ethnocentric Firm: An Evolutionary Perspective', *Strategic Management Journal*, 16, 119–141.

Mapolu, R. (2000) Poverty and Economy in Tanzania. *IDM Paper Series –Institute of Development Studies* (Dar Es Salaam: University of Dar Es Salaam).

Mbigi, L. (1997) *Ubuntu: The African Dream in Management* (Randburg, South Africa: Knowledge Resources).

Merton, R. K. (1996) 'On Social Structure and Science', in P. Sztompka (ed.) *Ethnicentrism* (Chicago: University of Chicago Press), 339–359.

Mir, R. and A. Mir (2009) 'From the Colony to the Corporation: Studying Knowledge Transfer across International Boundaries', *Group and Organization Management*, 34(1), 90–113.

Monks, K. and H. Scullion (2001) 'An Empirical Study of International Human Resource Management in Irish International Firms', *Personnel Review*, 3(5), 536–553.

Mudambi, R., S. Mudambi, and P. Navarra (2007) 'Global Innovation in MNCs: The Effects of Subsidiary Self-determination and Teamwork', *Journal of Product Innovation Management*, 24, 442–455.

Newenham-Kahindi, A. (2011) 'Human Resource Strategies for Managing Back-Office Employees in Subsidiary Operations: The Case of Two Investment Multinational Banks in Tanzania', *Journal of World Business*, 46, 13–21.

Nonaka, I. (1994) 'A Dynamic Theory of Organizational Knowledge Creation', *Organizational Science*, 5, 14–37.

Pinnington, A. H., K. Kamoche, and Y. Suseno (2009) 'Property in Knowledge Work: An Appropriation-Learning Perspective', *Employee Relations*, 31(1), 57–80.

Poster, M. (1990) *The Mode of Information* (Cambridge: Polity Press).

Rutinwa, B. (1995) *Legal Regulations of Industrial Relations in Tanzania* (Labour Relations Unit: University of Cape Town) (Southern Africa Labour Monographs no. 1/95).

Scullion, H. (2001) 'International Human Resource Management', in J. Storey (ed.) *Human Resource Management* (London: International Thompson), 352–382.

Sewell, G. (1998) 'The Discipline of Teams: The Control of Team-Based Industrial Work through Electronic and Peer Surveillance', *Administrative Science Quarterly*, 43, 397–428.

Sewell, G. and B. Wilkinson (1992) 'Someone to Watch over Me: Surveillance, Discipline and the Just-in-Time Labour Process', *Sociology*, 26(2), 279–282.

Snape, E., A. Wilkinson, and T. Redman (1998) 'Performance Appraisal and Culture: Practice and Attitude in Hong Kong and Great Britain', *International Journal of Human Resource Management*, 9(5), 841–861.

Spicer, A., M. Alvesson, and D. Kärreman (2009) 'Critical Performativity: The Unfinished Business of Critical Management Studies', *Human Relations*, 62(4), 537–560.

Standard Bank in Tanzania (1999) http://corporateandinvestment.standard bank.co.za/cib/country-offices/africa/Tanzania, accessed October 16th, 2013.

Storey, J. and P. Quintas (2000) 'Knowledge Management and HRM', in J. Storey (ed.) *Human Resource Management: A Critical Text* (London: Thomson Learning), 339–363.

Strauss, A. and J. M. Corbin (1998) *Basics of Qualitative Research: Techniques and Procedures for Developing Grounded Theory* (Thousand Oaks, CA: Sage).

Teece, D. J. (1986) 'Firm Boundaries, Technological Innovation and Strategic Management', in L. G. Thomas III (ed.) *The Economics of Strategic Planning* (Lexington, MA: D.C. Heath), 187–199.

Tian, J., Y. Nakamori, and A. P. Wierzbicki (2009) 'Knowledge Management and Knowledge Creation in Academia: A Study Based on Surveys in a Japanese Research University', *Journal of Knowledge Management*, 18(2), 76–92.

Thompson, P. and D. van den Broek (2010) 'Managerial Control and Workplace Regimes: An Introduction', *Work, Employment and Society*, 24, 1.

Timmons, S. (2003) 'A Failed Panopticon: Surveillance of Nursing Practice via New Technology', *New Technology, Work and Employment*, 18(2), 143–153.

Upadhya, C. (2009) 'Controlling Offshore Knowledge Workers: Power and Agency in India's Software Outsourcing Industry', *New Technology, Work and Employment*, 24(1), 1–18.

Yin, R. K. (2003) *Case Study Research Design and Methods* (London: Sage).

5
Human Resource Management in Southern African Multinational Firms: Considering an Afro-Asian Nexus

Frank M. Horwitz

Emerging market MNCs in the Afro-Asian context

Van Agtmael (2007, pp. 10–11) predicts that 'in about 25 years the combined gross national product (GNP) of emergent markets will overtake that of currently mature economies causing a major shift in the centre of gravity of the global economy away from the developed to emerging economies'. He argues (op. cit., p. 12) that, by the middle of this century, emerging markets in aggregate will be nearly twice as large as the current developed economies. Emerging markets account for more than 50 per cent of global economic output, and emerging market multinational companies (MNCs) like Tata, Infosys and Wipro of India, Exarro Resources, Naspers, SABMiller, Sasol and Sappi from South Africa, Haier in China, Petrobas in Brazil, and Hyundai and Samsung in Korea, are now global players (Horwitz and Mellahi, 2009).

South Africa has joined the BRICS group of leading emerging market countries (Brazil, Russia, India China and South Africa). The 'next 10'emerging markets in terms of population and economic growth include the economies of the CIVET, the acronym coined by Michael Geoghegan, former chief executive of HSBC, to cluster another group of middle-income emerging markets: Columbia, Indonesia, Vietnam, Egypt, Turkey (McRae, 2010). The BRICS and CIVET markets are arguably likely to attract more growth in foreign direct investment (FDI) than established markets, given the rising purchasing power of these populations and potentially high returns on investment over time.

These are, however, complex transitional societies, often with diverse demographic and ethnicity mixes and difficult challenges of human development. From this complexity and diversity emanate firms that are steeped in working with these issues in order to survive and, indeed, prosper. This arguably provides a measure of resilience which, this chapter argues, positions them strongly and adroitly in international markets. But, for economic development and growth to be sustainable in the long term, there are still massive human resource and infrastructural development challenges to be overcome in most African countries (Kamoche et al., 2004, p. xvi).

There is a paucity of published work on HRM in MNCs in transitional economies, particularly comparative analysis of those from Africa and East Asia (Zupan and Kase, 2005; Horwitz, 2012), with some notable exceptions such as Budhwar and Debrah (2001), van Agtmael (2007) and Judge et al. (2009). This chapter identifies what HR challenges need to be addressed, particularly by Africa's own rapidly growing MNCs. This is a key purpose of this chapter. With rapidly growing trade and investment between Africa and Asian countries such as India and China, a further purpose of this chapter is to propose an Afro-Asian framework or typology of HRM, analytically using illustrative case examples from southern African emerging markets.

Socio-economic development and growth in Africa

Regarding Africa itself, 'six of the ten fastest growing countries in the world in 2000–2010 were in Africa. Angola grew faster than anywhere else on the planet. Some of this new prosperity is the result of better economic policies, but more is the consequence of a boom in commodity prices' (*The Economist*, 12 February 2011, p. 12). Today the stereotype of Africa as a 'hopeless continent' is misplaced. *The Economist*, which described it as such in 2001, recently stated that 'Africa is now near the top of the agenda for the world's leading business. Africa as a whole has continued to advance and is expected to grow by at least 4.3%' (*The Economist*, 2 October 2010, p. 74). This is a higher growth rate than Brazil. *The Times* (23 March 2011, p. 2) refers to an 'Africa rising', though noting that infrastructural problems remain in many countries. 'If Africa were a country it would already be as big as Russia and India' (Robertson and Pitel, op. cit., pp. 38–39). China has overtaken western countries as the single largest investor in Africa. South Africa was invited in 2011 to join the emerging market BRICS group. This could have a significant impact on its trade and investment with these countries and raises the interesting question about the diffusion of HRM practice between these emerging market giants. Table 5.4 shows the top 50 ranked African companies by country, sector, turnover and profits. Of these, 38 are from South Africa.

China, with an interest in Africa's raw materials, such as coal and oil, has become the largest foreign investor in Africa in the past five years. A deal to build a US$8.3 billion railway line in oil-rich Nigeria has been announced, together with joint China–African exploration of energy development. China has cancelled US$10 billion in bilateral debt forgiveness from African countries. Trade tariff reduction and training and development programs, as well as further infrastructural development, are part of regular policy-level talks between China and African governments, including South Africa, Angola and Nigeria. Africa in 2006 also attained the largest increase in tourism growth, at 10.6 per cent, making it the highest growth region in the world for tourism. Sub-Saharan Africa, in spite of its poverty, may begin to see some relief in this regard, with a 12.6 per cent rise in tourism in 2006 (*Cape Argus*). African MNCs have become significant direct investors in other emerging markets: examples include SAB Miller, which has become the second largest brewing MNC globally, with operations in Eastern Europe, China USA and elsewhere, and other South African MNCs such as Khumba Resources (mining and iron ore) and Naspers (media communications) have significant operations in China. Murray and Roberts, a construction and property development MNC, has significant interests in the Middle East. This may, however, be a somewhat normative belief. While there are, indeed, some similarities between African and east Asian cultures, there are also fundamental differences between them.

Most poignant is whether African countries, including the more developed South Africa, have the skills capacity and appropriate HRM strategies to meet the challenge of higher economic growth and global competitiveness (Horwitz, 2009, op. cit., p. 463). African countries, including Africa's largest economy, South Africa, still lag other leading emergent markets such as Brazil and China regarding FDI. Nonetheless, all 94 US-based emergent market mutual funds have stakes in South African companies, making it a destination of choice given its relative stability and steady economic growth (Lynch, 2006). Key to sustaining and improving this is the extent to which political democratization, the rule of law, institution-building and HRM development are speeded up. There are positive signs, with fewer conflicts over the past five years, and HIV/AIDS infection has dropped, but corruption, especially in sub-Saharan African countries, still retards economic growth, human resource development and organizational capacity building.

Towards an Afro-Asian HRM framework

Comparative work has been done on emerging market HRM and knowledge worker attraction and retention issues between East Asia and Africa (Horwitz et al., 2006), developing the notion of an 'Afro-Asian nexus' in diffusion of HRM policy and practice in emerging market MNCs. This analysis seeks to delve deeper than the much-used convergence/divergence frameworks, positing that the latter's polar extremes do not reflect the integrative alternative of cross-vergence (Ward et al., 1999, op. cit., pp. 466–473) and institutional analysis. This results in a need for closer attention to process dynamics in the design and implementation of HRM and the allied concept of reverse diffusion.

The cultural/institutional complexity of emerging markets precludes over-simplified analysis. Developing a six-factor typology of an 'Afro-Asian nexus in HRM', focusing on emerging market MNCs in the southern African context with particular reference to Asian influences, this chapter thematically explores emergent themes in HRM. It evaluates:

(1) the extent to which good HRM practice is converging on the continent with the influence of East Asian firms,
(2) indigenous thought systems and contextual factors,
(3) the diffusion of HRM practice,
(4) process implementation factors,
(5) talent management and diversity, and
(6) contingency factors.

Human resource issues that have been identified in the emerging economy literature include the inappropriate use of foreign HRM policies and practices, burgeoning literature on use of expatriate skills, reliance on particularistic practices driven by local institutional and legislative regimes, nepotistic considerations, lack of transparency in often highly politicized decision-making, and a concern with procedural and transactional HRM rather than strategic issues (Kamoche et al., 2004, pp. 1–2). Other than in South African firms and some multinational energy firms, managing people strategically in Africa is rare, but an insistent need.

The analysis provides a qualitative approach in seeking to fill a gap in the literature in respect of integrating both the importance of contextual variables and Afro-Asian comparative International Human Resource

Management (IHRM) (Horwitz et al., 2006). Consideration has to be given as to whether these practices are adopted 'as is', or with some modification, or comprehensively redesigned, with due consideration, therefore, of cross-vergence issues.

The need for integrative frameworks for effective cross-cultural diffusion and adoption requires critical evaluation of variables key to implementation (Warner, 2000). The growth of emerging market MNCs raises the question of contingency approaches and mediating variables affecting organizational-level application of HRM practices in different markets.

Considering indigenous thought systems and HR practice

An enduring theme in emergent market HRM is the appropriateness of western management principles and practices. There are challenges to MNCs and local firms which adopt practices with little consideration of their suitability or relevance (Kamoche et al., 2004; Horwitz, 2009, op. cit., p. 464). African indigenous thought systems variously reflect high collectivism and group solidarity tendencies. Indigenous models of leadership and organization emphasizing the notion of *ubuntu* or humaneness, group decision-making and interdependence struggle to assert themselves in the face of a converging global business orthodoxy (Mbigi, 2000). These notions have similar precepts to the Confucian emphasis on family *guanxi* networks/social capital and cohesion found in Chinese firms.

The importance of collective solidarity is seen in the network of inter-relationships, extended family and mutual obligations not dissimilar to the paternalism found in Chinese, African and Taiwanese MNCs. In the case of certain African MNCs, this results in a sense of communalism and traditionalism, which is not unlike the Confucian influence on east Asian MNCs' culture. Hence some researchers, like April and Shockley (2007) and Jackson (2004), propose an epistemological shift away from the predominant western management theories to alternative ones based on Asian and African perspectives in MNCs from these economies. These include cultural heterogeneity as a source of mutually beneficial win–win cooperation, a polyocular vision with regard to what constitutes 'objective' truth, the mental connectedness the worker shares with group members, and the idea that the individual assumes a relational existence and identity whose raison d'etre is located within the community to which he/she belongs. Just as the African notion of *ubuntu* is not widespread in parts of modern Africa, so, too, are the tenets of Confucianism not hegemonic in East Asia. Caution is, however, necessary in potentially confusing a desired future vision with current empirical reality. At the same time, like east Asian countries, there is a high need to develop people (Kamoche et al., 2004).

A conceptual perspective within which an Afro-Asian context can be suitably framed is that posited by Jackson (2004, pp. 20–22) – a typology of western instrumentalism, African humanism and east Asian attributes as a useful contextual framework for a proposed Afro-Asian HRM typology (Table 5.1 below). Values such as adherence to social obligations, collective trust, deference to rank and seniority, sanctity of reciprocity and good social and personal relations are

Table 5.1 The six-factor Afro-Asian typology, following Jackson (2002)

	African renaissance	East Asian
Organizational orientation and culture	People and results management – internal stakeholder focus Balancing stakeholder interests	Social cohesion, harmony seeking People management – in and out group relations Managing results defined by stakeholder interests
Management motivators	Diverse but seeking sense of belonging Personal and group/team development	Corporate oriented development Harmony, stability and security
Organizational commitment	To the group – collective solidarity	Corporate objectives and purpose, results orientation, work and family
Management principles	Internal and external locus of control Status and achievement orientation Either Theory X or Y – cross-national and cross-cultural diversity Core purpose business model – core business competency focus, divesting non-core assets, e.g. AngloGold Ashanti, MTN telecommunications	Strong external locus of control. Theory Y (in or own group) Theory X (out or external groups) Trust of internal group and members Relational aspects of decision-making Status through seniority and 'face'

Table 5.1   (Continued)

	African renaissance	East Asian
		Diversified business model – multi-sector and multi-industries, e.g. Tata
Human resource practices	Consultation and participation Negotiation with groups such as trade unions, e.g. in South Africa and Botswana Relatively open communications	Consultation (*ringi* in Japan) Communicating information aimed at consensus seeking Processes aimed at seeking harmony

relevant. African *ubuntu* or humanism may arguably reflect a conceptual proximity to Confucian humanism and Chinese *quanxi*. But an unrealistic, idealized or, indeed, romanticized conception may not have significant empirical or managerial support. There is also a latent assumption of both homogeneity and unique distinctiveness, which obfuscates the reality of interregional, intercountry and interethnic diversity. Wells (2003) notes differences between African and Asian MNCs in that their competencies are developed in countries that have distinct disadvantages due to erosion of natural resources and insufficient domestic investment in infrastructure, including physical and human capital.

In countries like South Africa, where the regulatory and institutional framework for employment relations remains relatively strong, this, together with local cultural factors, may militate against unchanged adoption and development of HRM practices in emerging market MNCs. The need for a contingency approach also arises from preoccupation with cross-cultural analysis and the convergence thesis.

Cultural context and HR practice

Cultural factors may also limit or assist the adoption of HRM practices such as performance-related pay and merit promotion, in that deference to seniority, service and age remains important in countries where family control of large enterprises remains strong, for example, Malawian and South African retail firms in Africa. Yet, within a country and national cultural context, variation between MNCs' and local firms' propensity to adopt HRM occurs. However, MNC influence may extend beyond HRM. MNC influence on global integration and work practice standardization may reveal cross-cultural convergence of HRM practices within MNCs through adoption of 'best global practice', compared with a higher degree of divergence in local firms. South African Breweries' jointly owned breweries in Poland have successfully implemented best operating practices and management know-how on systems, process and technology based on Japanese practices and its experience in emergent economies, and South African restaurant groups in Singapore and the UK, such as Nando's, draw on home-country practices. Identical HRM practices cannot be transferred intact. As previously argued, a degree of cross-vergence appears inevitable and, indeed, necessary.

This supports Jackson's (2004) framework and is based on historical racial and ethnic disparities. However, an emergent black middle class has begun to occupy decision-making roles. Class mobility is likely to have an impact on managerial culture and inform strategic choices about appropriate organizational culture, business and HRM practices in the African context. Organization and national culture in many African countries tend to reflect considerable diversity and pluralism, with procedural regulation of conflicts in South Africa particularly. The latter lends support to the post-instrumental model in Jackson's framework. The advent of democracy, especially in South Africa, and the 'glasnost' effect of global competition beg the ongoing question as to the inevitability of HRM convergence and global hegemony of 'best practice' over local exigencies. In practice, hybrid models appear more likely in MNCs from these countries.

There has been a resultant reassessment of management practices in local, especially southern African, firms, but this investment has also seen the diffusion of low-cost HRM practices in Chinese firms in the region. As stated earlier, Chinese firms' investment in Africa now constitutes the biggest share of FDI on the continent. Positively, this has been accompanied in many instances by investment by Chinese firms in development of local infrastructure and facilities, such as hospitals, in countries such as Angola and Tanzania. Hybrid forms of HRM may occur in nomenclature, design, content and implementation processes. In South African MNCs, indigenous African terms are now being given to adapted east Asian practices, often in preference to using Japanese terminology, for example, the Zulu term *Indaba* groups for Total Quality Management teams or *sebenza* problem-solving teams.

Indaba refers to 'debate in groups'. The former term means work or workplace. Human resource strategies need, therefore, to be firm-specific. Though the African notion of *ubuntu* is not widespread in parts of modern Africa, some view it as a basis for fostering an Afrocentric managerial culture with aligned HRM practices (Jackson, 2004). The notion of *ubuntu*, literally translated, means 'I am who I am through others'; this is in contrast to the western tenet of 'cogito ergo sum' – 'I think therefore I am'. It is this contrasting of a form of communal humanism with individualism and instrumentalism which has a normative appeal for advocates of an African economic and cultural renaissance.

An important allied theme is diversity management. It is erroneous to assume homogeneity within specific countries, too, since many African countries have diverse ethno-cultural communities (Kamoche et al., 2004, p. xvi). In countries like Zambia and Ghana with extensive privatization of state-owned enterprises (SOEs), the HRM landscape has been reshaped in significant and enduring ways. Many Zambian SOEs, for instance, have been bought by South African companies, whose managers apply employment practices based on those of the parent company. The southern African region (in particular Botswana and South Africa) has emerged as a catchment area for talent from other parts of Africa, in particular east and central Africa. African countries variously have their own policies of localization, Africanization, and, in some countries like Zambia, Zambianization. South Africa has employment equity legislation and a recent strong focus on broad-based Black Economic Empowerment BEE) to enhance share ownership and other forms of employee empowerment. Industry charters are developed setting targets for BEE in sectors such as insurance, mining, oil and energy. The basis of these policies is to redress employment skills and access to managerial, professional and economic opportunities by groups previously denied these opportunities.

Managerial styles, HRM practices and preferences for particular types of conflict resolution may be mediated by ethnicity factors, including the degree of cultural ethnocentrism, and tolerance or intolerance of diversity. Firm-level employment practices in some countries like Kenya and South Africa have in some sectors reflected preferences for particular ethnic groups or family members of an ethnic group. Post-independence governments have promoted policies variously referred to as Africanization, localization and employment equity, requiring designated employers to employ over a specified number of historically disadvantaged employees (in some cases minority groups and in others majority groups, for example, in Namibia and South Africa) and to set targets and timetables for improving diversity, removing unfair discrimination practices and representation of the workforce at all levels. These tend to focus on numerical change to enhance representation at all levels of an organization. Qualitative changes in workplace attitudes, institutional culture and leadership styles are, however, equally important.

Human resource practice research and diffusion in African multinational firms

Wocke et al.'s (2007, p. 829) study of four South African MNCs, namely Nando's International (fast foods), Sasol (synthetic fuels and chemicals), SABMiller (beer) and MTN International (ICT), concludes that focus on implementation of corporate HR strategies from the parent's perspective shows that MNCs differ in:

(1) scope and level of abstraction of their corporate HR strategies. This is primarily due to differing business models (emphasizing global integration or local market responsiveness);
(2) the need to accommodate national culture (extending from limited to very high levels of adaptation);
(3) type and role of organizational culture, often transferred by deployment of expatriates in the MNC, which variously impacts on the level of convergence of HR practices; and
(4) degree of convergence of international HRM practices.

In all four cases a large degree of variance in these factors was found. Wocke et al.'s (2007) study found a range in the extent of convergence of international HRM practices from high convergence (Sasol) to low convergence with evidence of 'cross-vergence' in Nando's (op. cit., pp. 840–841). Their research also shows some measure of support for the construct of 'cultural distance', whereby implementation of HRM practices from parent to host country may vary, inter alia, because of deep cultural differences. In all four cases a large degree of variance in these factors was found. Sasol, South Africa's MNC in the synthetic fuels industry converting coal into petroleum, has become the world's leader in this process, diversifying into chemicals, with operations in China, Europe, Nigeria and the USA. South African Breweries, which bought Miller beer (now SABMiller) from the food arm of Phillip Morris, has a large presence in other countries, from Africa to Eastern Europe, Russia and China, in most cases through joint ventures or acquisitions, and has become the second largest global brewer.

Following Wocke et al. (2007) above, cultural context factors may also limit or assist the adoption of HRM practices, such as performance-related pay and merit promotion, in that deference to seniority, service and age remains important in Japan and countries where family control of large enterprises remains strong, for example, chaebols in South Korea and Malawian firms in Africa. In the southern African context it appears that 'as is' adoption is rarely effective and that either some or extensive modification occurs, thus reflecting the need for sensitivity to local circumstances. However, managerial practices are somewhat traditional, based on low labour cost/cost reduction methods, and cannot be considered 'high-performance'.

Comparative research on performance management in South African and Uganda organizations identifies the need for a much higher level of 'performance literacy' at both organizational and public policy levels (Magoola and Horwitz, 2010). A qualitative study of South African Breweries, the Rand Water Board and Uganda Revenue Authority identified the following key success factors for raising 'performance literacy' and hence improvement in African organizations:

- organizational member alignment: diffusion of performance management knowledge and skill
- mechanisms or processes for organizational and individual learning
- participative and effective maintenance of performance management systems
- enabling institutional/regulatory mechanisms in both intra and pan-African diffusion of performance management processes. This is frequently absent or poorly developed in African countries, reflecting a significant barrier to effective performance management.

Another study (Grzeschke and Moehring, 2004) also investigated HRM practices in South African multinational companies. In both external MNC and emerging local multinational firms, human resource practitioners considered the most important workplace challenges to be performance improvement, employment equity, training and development, and managing trade union expectations. Training and development are seen by both managers and frontline employees in the services industry as vital in addressing the skills gap and developing the capacity to meet competitive demands (Horwitz et al., 2006).

Job evaluation, performance management systems and work process redesign are increasingly important facets of HR work in emerging market MNCs. Although western managerial practices have prevailed for decades in African countries, there is an increase in southern and east African firms adopting Japanese and east Asian practices (Horwitz, 2009, op. cit., p. 465). These include lean manufacturing, just-in-time methods and other operations management measures to reduce product defects, stock holdings, inventory and waste. Quality and productivity improvement measures have sought to benchmark international standards in South African hospitality MNCs, the Sun International and Protea Groups. Increasingly, the ideas of lean thinking have gained currency in African firms such as Bell Equipment, Nampak Management Services and South African Breweries (SABMiller). Use of flexible work practices, including functional forms of flexibility such as multi-skilling and performance-based pay, is more common in MNCs in Africa. African organizations tend to emphasize collective and procedural relations, whereas Asian MNCs have more distinctive, often diffused, HRM practices based variously on group cohesion, individual relations and, in the case of Chinese and Taiwanese clothing and textile firms, low-cost work practices and employment practices; this especially with the recent growing influence of Chinese state-run enterprises and Taiwanese MNCs in African markets such as Angola, Sudan and South Africa.

Effective diffusion requires sensitivity to the cultural context (Horwitz et al., 2004). It is posited that MNC influence on global integration and work practice standardization, reveals a cross-cultural convergence of HRM practices within MNCs through adoption of 'best global practice'; this in contrast to a higher degree of divergence in local firms.

Some 18 South African MNCs are among the top 200 emergent market companies (Morgan Stanley Capital International Inc., 2003). Not only has China become the single biggest foreign investor in Africa (trade between South Africa and China is upwards of \$12 billion per annum), but research on African MNCs has also seen South African firms increasingly investing and doing business in China. Several of these, such as SAB Miller, have joint venture operations, investments and growing market share in China. Horwitz et al. (2005) examined perspectives of 13 MNCs from South Africa in respect of variables considered important in labour and markets in China. The following six focus areas were found to be important for business effectiveness in this market: understanding its market complexity, importance of joint venture partners, *guanxi* relationship networks, human capital, language and culture, and regulatory

Table 5.2 South African MNC perceptions of key success factors in Chinese labour markets

---

- Understanding its market complexity, importance of joint venture partners
- *Ubuntu* (African), *guanxi* (Chinese) relationship networks
- Human capital, including developing local skills capacity
- Culture and language
- Regulatory and institutional environment

Source: Horwitz et al. (2005).

environment. South African firms perceive themselves as having particular strengths for operating in China, ascribed to cultural sensitivity from experience in a multicultural society, business experience in a developing context, reasonable salary expectations and flexible work practices. However, these are generalizations, and there are likely to be exceptions (Table 5.2).

Southern African MNCs expecting to perform well in other emerging markets will, therefore, increasingly need to recruit and develop quality local staff and managers. The most effective way of achieving this is by offering a highly competitive salary and good career prospects. Economic reforms and the influx of other emerging market MNCs are bringing a more strategic approach to human resource management in China, with a greater emphasis on merit-based recruitment and career development. An important lesson is to ensure that employees recruited by a joint venture partner are often willing to receive incentive pay. Emerging market MNCs may, therefore, have particular strengths in operating in other emerging markets (Horwitz et al., 2005) or what Judge et al. (2009) describe as an 'organisational capacity for change' in transitional economies. These findings are also consistent with Wocke et al. (2007).

It appears that the adoption of east Asian HRM in southern African firms derives from both increased investment and the consequent influence these firms have in Africa, and an emergent managerial belief in southern African firms that there is much to be learned from Indian, Chinese and Japanese managerial practices, particularly as these might have a higher likelihood of adoption in the African cultural context, while it may be argued that Chinese HRM, other than in outside MNCs, may tend to not be based on the International Labor Organization notion of 'decent work'. Large Indian emergent market MNCs like the Tata Corporation, ICICI Banking and Mittal Steel, and Korean

MNCs such as Hyundai, are significant direct investors in African markets, while South African MNCs such as SAB Miller (which has become the second largest brewing MNC globally with operations in Eastern Europe, China, the USA and elsewhere), Khumba Resources (mining and iron ore) and Naspers (media communications) have significant operations in China. Murray and Roberts is a South African construction and property development MNC which has grown significant interests in the Middle East. This may, however, be a somewhat normative belief. While there are indeed some similarities between African and east Asian cultures, there are also fundamental differences between them. In this section we attempt to formulate a rationale for a more critical analysis of the diffusion of practices between these two regions.

HRM process implementation factors

A qualitative approach can be adopted in seeking to fill a gap in the literature in respect of integrating both the importance of contextual variables and Afro-Asian comparative IHRM (Horwitz, 2012). It is important to identify process implementation factors, such as the extent to which HRM is introduced (1) 'as is' – transplanted intact cross-culturally, or (2) with some adaptation based on local culture and factors, such as labour relations institutions, or (3) whether these practices are significantly transformed because of local exigencies, and (4) the nature and degree of convergence which may occur. Strategies may vary greatly with differing demands in the global environment. Conflicting demands may occur as emerging market MNCs attempt to enhance their capacity to be locally responsive while also maintaining influence over global corporate structures, for example, by fostering a global corporate culture with associated human resource practices (Horwitz and Melahi, 2009).

A conceptual perspective within which an Afro-Asian context can be suitably framed is that posited by Jackson (2004, pp. 20–22) – a typology of western instrumentalism, African humanism and east Asian attributes – as a useful analytical framework. The latter concept reflects values such as sharing, adherence to social obligations, collective trust, deference to rank and seniority, sanctity of commitment, and good social and personal relations. As discussed above, these arguably reflect a conceptual proximity to Confucian humanism and Chinese *Quanxi*, with social cohesion and cooperative rather than adversarial and competitive relations. However, there is a danger in presenting both

African and east Asian systems in this way. An unrealistic, idealized or, indeed, romanticized conception may not have significant empirical or managerial support. Second, there is a latent assumption of both homogeneity and unique distinctiveness, which obfuscates the reality of interregional, intercountry and interethnic diversity. Hence, a cross-divergence perspective is important.

It appears that the adoption of east Asian HRM in southern African firms derives from both increased investment and the consequent influence these firms have in Africa, and an emergent managerial belief in southern African firms that there is much to be learned from Indian, Chinese and Japanese managerial practices, particularly as these might have a higher likelihood of adoption in the African cultural context.

Talent management, diversity and patterns of diffusion

Van Agtmael (2007, op. cit., pp. 227–247) refers to a revolution in 'cheap brainpower' in discussing emergent market MNCs. Yet the demand for qualified staff continues to outstrip supply in most emerging markets. Turnover is higher, poaching is rampant and pay packages often overheated. A World Bank survey revealed that a shortage of skills was the factor most identified by management in the over 800 firms questioned as strongly retarding their further development (*The Economist*, 2007).

This is similar to a 'systematic shrinkage of skills', which may require importing certain high-priority skills in the short term (Abedian, 2007). Poor knowledge and education about the opportunities for technical training, together with perceptions that artisan and technical work is somehow of a lower status than graduate qualifications, continue.

While improving the supply side production of graduates, technicians, artisans and health care professionals from emerging market tertiary education institutions is critical, for corporate leaders the challenge lies in attracting, motivating and retaining intellectual capital. Talent management research in environments of uncertainty, complexity and 'unknowability of transitional economies' like South Africa shows that professional workers at high skill levels in knowledge-intensive industries rate the factors shown in Table 5.3 as critical to work motivation, effective utilization and retention (Sutherland and Jordaan, 2004; Horwitz et al., 2006; Judge et al., 2009, p. 1746).

Table 5.3 Talent management factors in transitional economy contexts

---

- Organizational capacity or 'readiness' for change and resilience – a 'meta-capability'
- Emergent strategies – adaptiveness rather than robust organizations (Judge et al., 2009, p. 1741)
- Opportunity to plan and control work which is challenging and demanding
- An 'engaging' culture with direct communications, collegial peer and boss relations and 'decent work'
- Human resource development, and, in certain BRICS and CIVET firms, flexible remuneration

---

Source: Adapted from Horwitz and Mellahi (2009).

Skills requirements in organizations should also be closely aligned with an organization's strategy. As positive indications of economic growth are now occurring, concomitant social development and service delivery are clearly dependent on an ability to motivate and retain scarce skills in the context of a shortage of specialized and professional skills. Getting to this point, though, begins with understanding and addressing the unique needs of scarce skills knowledge and professional workers today, which include:

> market-related pay and benefits and employment practices; intrinsic work factors such as job satisfaction and peer group relations, recognition and reward; personal and professional development and doing work which might be at the leading edge in an industry or sector.
>
> (Horwitz and Mellahi, 2009, p. 273)

However, a purely market-driven approach to skills development is not likely to be effective in emergent market MNCs. The notion of a developmental state occurring in emerging markets such as China, Korea and South Africa as well as in more developed Asian states such as Singapore, committed to developing the country's human resources in joined-up partnerships with the private sector and organized labour, can remove the many constraints to international competitiveness, such as skills development and better education (Soko, 2007). This appears consistent with a stakeholder approach posited in the African Renaissance element in Table 5.1, adapted here in the proposed Afro-Asian HRM nexus typology.

Table 5.4 Rankings 2010 (1–50)

Rank	Rank	Difference	Company name	Country	Sector	Turnover 2009–2010	Net Change (%)	Profits
1	1	–	SONATRACH	Algeria	Petroleum	47,479,918	–33.49	3,820,683
2	2	–	SONANGOL	Angola	Petroleum	22,442,400	–15.63	4,325,600
3	3	–	SASOL	South Africa	Chemicals	18,583,050	35.10	1,840,023
4	4	–	THE BIDVEST GROUP	South Africa	Retail	15,157,520	29.58	392,094
5	5	–	MTN GROUP	South Africa	Telecoms	15,092,695	39.34	2,313,646
6	11	+5	EKSOM	South Africa	Electricity	9,600,397	68.82	488,048
7	62	+55	SANLAM	South Africa	Insurance	8,179,664	293.01	685,020
8	17	+9	SHOPRITE HOLDINGS	South Africa	Retail	7,997,328	58.85	269,404
9	10	+1	VODACOM GROUP	South Africa	Telecoms	7,891,689	35.35	566,244
10	14	+4	PICK'N PAY STORES HOLDINGS	South Africa	Retail	7,379,305	39.2	160,288
11	8	–3	IMPERIAL HOLDINGS	South Africa	Diversified	7,318,434	23.86	204,657
12	18	+6	VODACOM SOUTH AFRICA	South Africa	Telecoms	6,799,107	35.53	ND
13	20	+7	STEINHOFF INT. HOLDINGS	South Africa	Diversified	6,476,753	36.09	505,979
14	22	+8	MASSMART HOLDINGS	South Africa	Retail	5,814,611	37.78	163,254

15	+4	BARLOWORLD	South Africa	Diversified	5,693,718	15.08	99,632
16	−7	SAPPI	South Africa	Paper	5,369,000	−8.43	−177,000
17	+10	TELKOM	South Africa	Telecoms	5,164,010	34.16	508.433
18	−3	ORASCOM TELECOM	Egypt	Telecoms	5,064,790	−3.42	379,472
19	−6	ANGLO PLATINUM CORP.	South Africa	Mining	4,981,195	−7.12	421,717
20	+11	TRANSNET	South Africa	Transport	4,800,940	35.28	412,954
21	–	GROUP ONA	Morocco	Diversified	4,684,968	1.48	381,540
22	+15	AVENG	South Africa	Diversified	4,553,101	45.49	281,895
23	+16	MURRAY & ROBERTS HOLDINGS	South Africa	Construction	4,551,847	54.44	315,115
24	+11	MTN NIGERIA	Nigeria	Telecoms	4,493,011	34.76	ND
25	+8	MTN SOUTH AFRICA	South Africa	Telecoms	4,469,148	30.33	ND
26	+14	SPAR GROUP	South Africa	Retail	4,348,781	53.92	100,468
27	−15	SUEZ CANAL AUTHORITY	Egypt	Sea transport	4,289,500	−20.30	ND
28	+4	SAB MILLER SOUTH AFRICA	South Africa	Beverages	4,214,000	21.69	ND
29	+7	ANGLOGOLD ASHANTI	South Africa	Mining	4,145,041	31.77	−372,373
30	+16	GOLD FIELDS	South Africa	Mining	3,921,496	61.32	207,030
31	−3	ORASCOM CONSTRUCTION IND.	Egypt	Construction	3,861,027	3.45	461,994

Table 5.4 (Continued)

Rank	Rank	Difference	Company name	Country	Sector	Turnover 2009–2010	Net Change (%)	Profits
32	7	−25	DE BEERS CONSOLIDATED MINES	South Africa	Mining	3,840,000	−44.25	−743,000
33	29	−4	MAROC TÉLÉCOM	Morocco	Telecoms	3,807,241	3.52	1,227,167
34	58	+24	NASPERS	South Africa	Media	3,774,690	74.13	532,809
35	24	−11	DATATEC	South Africa	ICT	3,738,026	−10.82	29,974
36	30	−6	GRINDROD	South Africa	Sea transport	3,733,441	4.75	126,972
37	25	−12	IMPALA PLATINUM HOLDINGS	South Africa	Mining	3,521,633	−11.39	811,616
38	23	−15	ARCELOR MITTAL SOUTH AFRICA	South Africa	Metal, Steel	3,451,122	−18.16	−64,444
39	34	−5	NAFTAL	Algeria	Petroleum Services	3,437,127	0.41	130,025
40	41	+1	SOUTH AFRICAN AIRWAYS	South Africa	Air Transport	3,420,977	22.65	51,551
41	16	−25	SAMIR	Morocco	Refinery	3,382,081	−34.64	69,647
42	43	+1	EDGARS CONSOLIDATED STORES	South Africa	Retail	3,353,782	25.99	−142,100
43	54	+11	KUMBA RESOURCES	South Africa	Mining	3,155,867	39.85	940,370
44	52	+8	NETWORK HEALTHCARE HOLDINGS	South Africa	Health	3,132,138	36.40	236,070

45	+6	OLD MUTUAL LIFE ASSURANCE CO.	South Africa	Insurance	3,113,129	35.48	725,332
46	−40	OFFICE CHÉRIFIEN DES PHOSPHATES	Morocco	Mining	3,011,760	−59.80	ND
47	−10	ALLIED ELECTRONICS CORP.	South Africa	Electrical Equipment	3,011,340	15.08	73,207
48	+2	LIBERTY GROUP	South Africa	Insurance	2,965,770	26.11	31,818
49	+10	WOOLWORTHS HOLDINGS (WHL)	South Africa	Retail	2,955,564	39.42	169,846
50	+5	THE ARAB CONTRACTORS	Egypt	Construction	2,764,000	22.90	223,000

Source: The Africa Report No. 27, February 2011.

Cross-cultural variation in the labour market and skills supply for addressing market needs is an important consideration by emerging market MNCs in the decision regarding their own FDI. An MNC seeking a low-wage, low-skill host country for a low-cost labour-intensive work process may seek to invest in CIVET economies with these features. Most African countries have regional economies with an oversupply of manual, relatively unskilled workers, and dualistically a shortage of artisan, technical, financial and managerial skills. In South Africa this was exacerbated by the apartheid legacy, which until recently deliberately reserved access to skilled work on a racial basis. Migrancy and the flight of knowledge workers from Africa or between African countries is becoming critical as more African countries seek to attract, develop and retain key skills to grow their economies and compete both domestically and globally. In Africa, the main labour-receiving countries are Botswana, Mauritius and South Africa. An allied issue is the widespread move towards labour market flexibility and an increase in sub-contracting and outsourcing as work is externalized. The casualization of the labour market is increasing even in countries with more regulated legal regimes, such as South Africa. Numerical and temporal flexibility and even pay flexibility have a profound effect on employment security, the psychological contract and workplace arrangements.

Talent management research in South Africa shows that professionals in knowledge-intensive firms rate opportunity to plan and control their own work, challenging and stimulating work, sound workplace relations, work–life balance, personal development and growth more highly than remuneration (Horwitz, 2012). Good working conditions, career opportunities and competitive pay are vital. For example, well-trained nurses have been lost to hospitals in Britain and Dubai, resulting in serious shortages in South African hospitals. Engineering and occupational therapy skills are being lost as better opportunities occur abroad. Budget constraints, together with poor HRM practices and, in some instances, poor application and unintended consequences of employment equity measures, have made retention problematic.

Yet these problems are reversible with progressive policies, implementation of good HR practices and leadership commitment. Retention of needed talent requires organizations to create a challenging and stimulating work environment, employee engagement, opportunities for personal growth and development, flexible and competitive remuneration, offering stretching and interesting assignments/projects, and collegial, supportive peer relations (Horwitz et al., 2006).

Contingency approaches

The growth of emerging market MNCs raises the question of contingency approaches to organizational-level application of HRM practices in different markets. This supports Jackson's (2004) framework and is based on historical racial and ethnic disparities. However, an emergent black middle class has begun to occupy decision-making roles. Class mobility is likely to have an impact on managerial culture and inform strategic choices about appropriate organizational culture, business and HRM practices in the southern African context. However, organization and national culture in many African countries tend to reflect considerable diversity and pluralism, with procedural regulation of conflicts in South Africa particularly suggesting elements of the stakeholder approach in respect of the posited framework of an Afro-Asian nexus. The advent of democracy, especially in South Africa, and the 'glasnost' effect of global competition begs the ongoing question as to the inevitability of HRM convergence and global hegemony of 'best practice' over local exigencies.

In practice, hybrid models are most likely in MNCs in these countries. African workplace practices are more collectivist than individualist, often with strong masculine and patriarchal cultures. This supports the cross-cultural and contingency features of the proposed Afro-Asian nexus typology. HRM practices such as team working based on group and collective behaviour and norms operate effectively, especially if reward systems are designed for group or team performance and performance management objectives. These issues reflect important concerns about the way people are managed and the impediments managers have to overcome before HRM can come of age. Multinational corporations through their local managers are increasingly adopting contemporary management ideas and HRM practices. Given collective decision-making and extended family orientations in many African cultures, adaptation of HRM practices is expected to contribute to achieving organization objectives. Managers have to satisfy stakeholders with conflicting interests. These realities suggest that the application of standard management tools cannot always be expected to work, underlining the value of a contingency approach.

Up to a third of formal sector employees work in parastatal or government-linked organizations in many African countries. Here there is often insufficient procedural discipline and underdeveloped HRM. However, managers generally recognize the need to apply practices that are effective, developmental and appropriate. It is important to understand social and institutional circumstances within which managers operate, the challenges they face, and how they respond to these. As mentioned earlier, this underlines the need to understand the African context and indigenous thought systems. Jackson (2004, p. 18) argues that paradoxical value systems – western instrumental and individualist versus humanistic systems – are often found in tribal and rural communities. But collective orientations can enable team-based practices and group incentive systems, suggesting support for the contingency variable in the Afro-Asian nexus typology.

Conclusions

This chapter underlines the need to strengthen analysis beyond descriptive cross-cultural adoption to within cultural variables, such as the degree of homogeneity or diversity within the culture adopting HRM practices. This is important to enable both comparative description and rigorous qualitative analysis. Both impact on the process and design of HRM policies and practices. Given the diverse practices and organizational cultures of MNCs in southern Africa, countries with a large underclass population may face a double transitional challenge – to redress workplace inequalities and to simultaneously and speedily develop their skills capacity to compete in a harsh global economy.

Skills formation and entrepreneurial development are vital, especially in African countries with huge transitional challenges (Horwitz and Mellahi, 2009; Horwitz, 2012). National skills policies in South Africa have introduced mechanisms such as a 1 per cent of payroll levy to finance human resource development in order to meet national, sector and organizational development objectives. The priority of practical policy initiatives by government, private sector firms, and labour market institutions such as sector training authorities and bargaining councils must be large-scale initiatives to train and retrain for enhancing employability in the changing labour market.

Human resource development and education in skills and competencies, including 'performance literacy', will be critical to their global competitiveness. Several sectors need both high and low-level skills. The former are in the information economy and high-value adding occupations, while the latter are in services sectors such as hospitality. Hybrid forms of HR based on MNC and local firm practices may occur in nomenclature, design, content and implementation processes. Even firms in countries within the same market economic type will experience some degree of localization in HRM practices and policies and therefore need to adjust the role of HRM accordingly (Horwitz and Mellahi, 2009).

Southern Africa, like east Asia, reflects a diverse tapestry of political economies and social, cultural and institutional systems. The same HR practices, for example, performance appraisal, or those pertaining to cross-border mergers and acquisitions, that could build trust in one country context may fail to do so in another – each HR practice that an MNC considers implementing should be filtered through a 'localization mesh' that identifies clashes with local values, resource capabilities (such as technical and managerial competencies), culture and institutional/regulatory environment. This analysis, according to the above authors, should allow modifications that will render the practice 'culturally fit', given that 'understanding the HR-performance relationship essentially requires exploring the heterogeneities of implementation' (Khilji and Wang, 2006, p. 1173). The proposed Afro-Asian typology or framework would, therefore, appear to have relevance in analysing case examples of southern African MNCs, given the pertinence of HR development, cultural diversity, need for adaptive contingency approaches to HRM, and the influence of Asian firms in Africa and, indeed, African firms such as SABMiller, MTN and Naspers in other emerging markets, including China.

It is debatable how long the paradigm of emerging markets and the developed/developing construct will be able to explain the fundamental shift of power under way. The economic primacy of the once-called West – now called the industrialized North – is no longer a given, and these nations are no longer able to take unilateral decisions affecting emerging economies. Managing people strategically has become more important given the increased globalization of markets, including labour markets, positive economic growth on the continent, increased FDI, especially from China, and the mostly adverse impact of World Bank and International Monetary Fund economic structural adjustment programmes (SAPs) on formal employment security in many African countries (with exceptions such as South Africa) (Horwitz, 2009, pp. 472–473).

While there is some evidence of a rise in employment relations institutions such as collective bargaining and dispute resolution, strong independent trade unions not linked to the state or employers are exceptions. Positively, though, tripartite corporatist engagement is not uncommon, for example in South Africa. This supports the stakeholder component in an Afro-Asian nexus typology, though there are union concerns about exploitative Chinese labour practices in several African countries. Yet, 'for aeons the prospect of China and Africa coming closer together had seemed otherwordly' (*The Economist*, 23 April 2011, p. 76). It is now a reality.

References

Abedian, I. (2007). Quoted in Mangxamba, S. 'Look East, government urged', *Cape Argus*, 27 August 2007: 18.

'Africa Rising'. (2011). *The Times*, 23 March 2011: 2.

April, K., and Shockley, M. (Eds) (2007). *Diversity: New Realities in a Changing World*. London: Palgrave MacMillan, 1–13.

Budhwar, S. P., and Debrah, Y. A. (2001). *Human Resource Management in Developing Countries*. London: Routledge.

Economist Briefing (2011). 'The Chinese in Africa – trying to pull together'. *The Economist*, 23 April 2011: 76.

Economist Intelligence Unit (EIU) (2007). *Global Corporate Network Survey* (16 August).

Grzeschke, C., and Moehring, D. (2004). 'Human resource practices in multinational companies in South Africa', Graduate School of Business, University of Cape Town, MBA thesis (November): 1–60.

Horwitz, F. M. (2012). 'Evolving human resource management in Southern African multinational firms: towards an Afro-Asian nexus'. *The International Journal of Human Resource Management*, 23 (14): 2938–2958.

Horwitz, F. M. (2009). 'Managing Human Resources in Africa – emergent market challenges', in J. Storey, P. M. Wright, and D. Ulrich (Eds), *The Routledge Companion to Strategic Human Resource Management*. London: Routledge, 462–477.

Horwitz, F. M., Chan, T. H., Quazi, H. A., Nonkwelo, C., Roditi, D., and van Eck, P. (2006). 'Human resource strategies for managing knowledge workers: an Afro-Asian comparative analysis'. *International Journal of Human Resource Management*, 17 (5): 775–811.

Horwitz, F. M., Ferguson, M., Rivett, I., and Lee, A. (2005). 'An afro-Asian nexus: South African multinational firm experiences in Chinese labour markets'. *South African Journal of Business Management*, 36 (3): 29–40.

Horwitz, F. M., and Mellahi, K. (2009). 'Human Resource management in emerging markets', in D. G. Collings and G. Wood (Eds), *Human Resource Management: A Critical Approach*. London: Routledge, 263–295.

Horwitz, F., Nkomo, S., and Rajah, M. (2004). 'HRM in South Africa', in K. Kamoche, Y. Debrah, F. Horwitz., and G. Muuka (Eds), *Managing Human Resources in Africa*. London: Routledge, 6–7.

Jackson, T. (2004). *Management and Change in Africa*. London: Routledge, 1–48.

Jackson, T. (2002). 'Reframing human resource management in Africa: a cross-cultural perspective'. *International Journal of Human Resource Management*, 13 (7): 998–1018.

Judge, W. Q., Naoumova, I., and Douglas, T. (2009). 'Organizational capacity for change and firm performance in a transitional economy'. *The International Journal of Human Resource Management*, 20 (8): 1737–1752.

Kamoche, K., Debrah, Y., Horwitz, F., and Muuka, G. N. (2004). *Managing Human Resources in Africa*. London: Routledge.

Khilji, S. E., and Wang, X. (2006). 'Intended and implemented HRM: the missing linchpin in strategic human resource management research.' *International Journal of Human Resource Management*, 17 (7): 1171–1189.

Lynch, D. (2006). 'South African government tries to unlock the economy'. *USA Today*, 27 October 2006: 25.

Magoola, I. W., and Horwitz, F. M. (2010). 'Performance poverty or poverty of performance leadership? The centrality of performance leadership and procedural justice in Africa's quest for development'. *Journal of Management Policy and Practice*, 11 (5): 155–168.

Mbigi, L. (2000) 'Making the African renaissance globally competitive'. *People Dynamics*, 18 (11): 16–21.

McRae, H. (2010). 'The subtle hand we must play on trade'. *The Independent*, 27 July 2010: 5.

Morgan Stanley Capital International Inc. (2003). 'Reported by Shevel, A.' *Sunday Business Times*, 17 July 2003: 3.

Robertson, D., and Pitel, L. (2011), 'If Africa were a country, it would be as big as Russia and India'. *The Times, Business Africa*, 23 March 2011: 38–39.

Soko, M. (2007). 'The developmental state can work'. *New Agenda – South African Journal of Social and Economic Policy*, 26 (2nd quarter: 5): 60–62.

Sparreboom, T. (2004). 'Skills development information systems in demand driven markets: the case of South Africa'. *South African Journal of Labour Relations*, 28 (1): 130–131.

'Spread of wealth'. (2011). *The Economist*, 12 February 2011: 12.

Sutherland, M., and Jordaan, W. (2004). 'Factors affecting the retention of knowledge workers'. *South African Journal of Human Resource Management*, 2 (2): 55–64.

'The beast goes on safari'. (2010). *The Economist*, 2 October 2010: 74–75.

van Agtmael, A. (2007). *The Emerging Markets Century*. London: Simon & Schuster, 10–13, 97–98, 140–152, 228–250, 282, 288–289, 339, 342.

Ward, S., Pearson, C., Entrekin, L., and Winzar, H. (1999). 'The fit between cultural values and countries: is there evidence of globalization, nationalism, or crossvergence?' *International Journal of Management*, 16 (4): 466–473.

Warner, M. (2000). 'Introduction: the Asia-Pacific HRM model revisited', *International Journal of Human Resource Management*, 11 (2): 171–181.

Wells, L.T. (2003). 'Multinationals and developing countries', in T. L. Brewer, S. Young, and S. E. Guisinger (Eds), *The New Economic Analysis of Multinationals*. Cheltenham: Edward Elgar, 106–121.

Wocke, A., Bendixen, M., and Rijamampianina, R. (2007). 'Building flexibility in to multi-national human resource strategy: a study of four South African multinational enterprises'. *International Journal of Human Resource Management*, 18 (5): 829–844.

Zupan, N., and Kase, R. (2005). 'Strategic human resource management in European transitional economies', *International Journal of Human Resource Management*, 16 (6): 882–890.

6
Managing Sustainable Development through Cross-Cultural Management: Implications for Multinational Enterprises in Developing Countries

Aloysius Newenham-Kahindi

Introduction

This chapter discusses how multinational enterprises (MNEs) use their existing employees in the workplace as intermediaries, to influence local community stakeholder attitudes and behaviours during the implementation of sustainable development initiatives in communities, with the aim of shedding some light on the complexities of managing sustainable development challenges in developing countries. We illustrate how employees who are part of the community can influence local communities in corporate social responsibility issues (CSR). The majority of employees in our case studies come from the local communities where MNEs operate. We present a case of MNEs from an emerging market, South Africa, and an MNE from a developed nation that engages in extractive mining activities in East Africa, and illustrate how mining MNEs use sustainable development initiatives (e.g. CSR) to influence the attention, attitudes and behaviours of employees, both at work and within their communities where MNEs operate. Our unit of analysis in this study is the organization (e.g. the MNEs) and how it prioritizes relations with various stakeholders during CSR implementation (Husted and Allen, 2006). We use the resource dependency and institutional theories to explain the relevance application of stakeholder orientation utilized by MNEs towards local communities. Using some literature on sense-making (e.g. Weick, 1995), we argue that it is imperative for MNEs operating in developing nations, such as Tanzania, which have numerous social problems, to consider the relevance of their CSR activities with community stakeholders. The term 'local communities' used in this chapter refers to those community stakeholders who are directly or indirectly affected by MNEs' business activities, and encompasses communities of place (e.g. based on geographic locations surrounding corporate facilities or operations). These are the new battlegrounds on which MNEs' activities are contested (Calvano, 2008). This trend has enormous financial and reputational consequences for MNEs.

The increasing reach of MNEs and their business activities across countries has intensified the debate about the function of the MNE in local communities. In developing nations with high levels of institutional voids and unregulated economic activities, MNEs face numerous challenges. Extractive mining MNEs, for example, whose activities are limited within specific geographical areas, are of particular interest in addressing stakeholder relations; opposition to them has likewise become increasingly globalized and remains contentious (Kapelus, 2002). Local communities, for example, have often challenged mining MNEs on a wide range of issues such as profit flows, tax revenues, royalties, MNEs' rights to extract minerals, rights to compensation measures, rights to be engaged in community involvement, dialogue and the long-term impact on their land, as well as social issues such as jobs, the environment and farming livelihood (Calvano, 2008).

This challenge has now created pressure for MNEs to design new organizational strategies that 'make sense' within local contexts, and that create an *inclusive* engagement platform to deal with the inherent local challenges of social problems. We define the term 'making sense' as referring to the socially established organizational structures of meaning generated by MNEs in conjunction with local employees to influence positive behaviour and attention in local communities towards addressing sustainable development issues (e.g. Yue and Mills, 2008).

Following the UN Global Compact implementation in 1999, many MNEs have progressed past the simple ideology of 'giving back' philanthropy and are actively involved in combating societal ills such as poverty, disease and environmental degradation, either because they desire to do so or as a response to intense pressure to change from their stakeholders and other social actors (UNDP, 2005). The UN Global Compact provides guidelines for businesses and the role of stakeholders (as well as various social actors on social issues), and calls for change and greater positive impact on people, the planet and societies (Waddock, 2008). Many corporations no longer undertake such initiatives on their own, but, rather, join forces with other players, including employees, communities and groups such as non-governmental organizations (NGOs) (Prahalad and Hart, 2002). More specifically, the new 'rules of the game' are focused on building enduring strategic partnerships that are focused on benefiting all involved parties (Waddock, 2008). Such *responsive* behaviour towards sustainability practices aims to positively influence stakeholders and other social actors to promote public good.

The emphasis of such responsive behaviour on stakeholders is based on 'building bridges' through collaboration between strategic stakeholders. However, the hybrid form of governance within MNEs that involves a strategic use of existing employees as a means and end for influencing sustainability behaviour remains a challenging phenomenon within the management literature and MNEs operating in developing nations, especially when it comes to understanding various institutional and stakeholder behaviours.

A growing number of inclusive partnerships between MNEs and local stakeholders have been increasing rapidly over the past decade, given the promise of mutual benefit (Austin, 2000). Through these stakeholder partnerships, corporations can acquire knowledge about social issues, especially at localized levels, as well as expertise in stakeholder management (Rondinelli and London, 2003). As far as this chapter is concerned, we argue that by engaging MNEs in CSR strategies, first and foremost with employees internally, either through training or by making it part of their career growth, employees can inform firms about the importance of localizing CSR initiatives at work and in communities where they live. This approach can also lead MNEs to increase business innovation and market opportunities as they are forced to adapt to hostile conditions across various cultures (Waddell, 1999; Prahalad and Hart, 2002). The potential benefits to MNEs are likewise numerous, including gaining access to large amounts of capital and market (Oster, 1995), improved efficiencies and accountability (Calvano, 2008), and exploiting economies of scale and large distribution networks (O'Regan and Oster, 2000). Moreover, the governments of poor countries can pursue national institutional systems to improve and promote home-based sustainable development policies (Kapelus, 2002). In sum, partnership approach to CSR through locally relevant initiatives can positively impact the triple bottom line.

Despite the benefits of partnerships, however, challenges remain as to how MNEs might actively engage local communities through employees working for global firms in local communities. If the whole idea of developing sustainable CSR partnership is to *make sense* to local stakeholders, there is a need to radically rethink and redesign the role of MNEs in their societal relationships with their local employees. In particular, there is a need to internally redesign MNEs' internal CSR practices in engaging employees to influence local community stakeholders, by taking into consideration the nature of stakeholders' cultural and institutional context (Horwitz, 2000; Kamoche et al., 2004).

Theoretical discussion

Institutional theory often explains interactions with stakeholders on the basis of legal, normative and taken-for-granted standards of conduct: for example, how national systems influence stakeholder behaviour, and beliefs about the role of economic actors. In this chapter, we use institutional theory to examine community stakeholders' orientation towards sustainable development initiatives. We examine the internal organizational systems influences of MNEs, through the use of employees and interaction with external stakeholders (local communities, local government apparatus and NGOs) as an attempt to understand the role they have in a society (William and Aguilera, 2008). We also use the resource dependency theory, which is concerned with external control of organizations, to illustrate how MNEs use, control and acquire resources to attend to the demands of stakeholders. In particular, we use this theory to show how local resource pressures on extractive mining shape MNE–stakeholder partnerships. As MNEs operate across environments with diverse resources and institutional pressures, both theories provide a foundation for considering an adaption to the local context in order to acquire legitimacy and social licence to operate in specific geographical mining locations in developing nations.

As far as the resource dependency theory is concerned, MNEs are subject to multiple pressures, ranging from their head offices to subsidiary environmental pressures. While operating in subsidiaries, MNEs depend on their head offices for crucial resources such as capital, knowledge and reputation. Balancing between head offices and multiple stakeholders' demands in subsidiaries may leave MNEs in a challenging situation, such as the need to balance between internal and external challenges.

MNEs from emerging markets and sustainable development

Recent research on MNEs from emerging markets has indicated the need for drastic thinking when dealing with social issues, rather than simply following the global convergence model of CSR (Kapelus, 2002). At the same level, these MNEs have responded to the 1999 UN Global Compact standard regulations by developing diverse CSR initiative strategies that emphasize sustainability through engagement practices. Such strategies emphasize the relevance of a localized approach, where culture and other human relations values are embedded in the overall MNEs' corporate governance systems for addressing the public good (UNDP, 2005). The arrival of these MNEs from emerging markets such as India, China and South Africa, and other MNEs from South America, has been responsible for the growing interest in international comparative management studies (Child and Tse, 2001; Khanna et al., 2005), which present an alternative sectoral form of interaction within global and local contexts in dealing with CSR challenges (Waddock, 2008).

There are several factors and motivations that have contributed to the growth of institutional transformation in the MNEs of emerging markets (Khanna et al., 2005). According to Horwitz (2000) and Kamoche et al. (2004), two highly significant situational and contextual factors have contributed to the success of such MNEs in the midst of globalization: the national institutional systems and the management of the social organizational contexts. Socio-economic reforms and a series of subsequent restructurings in corporate governance and ownership structures have contributed to the growth of national systems that advocate for the creation of responsible institutional practices. The growth of these MNEs has resulted in social and economic forms of partnership to motivate home-grown businesses and innovation development in organizations (Khanna et al., 2005). All of these have had a direct impact on promoting public good.

With respect to institutional contexts, MNEs from emerging markets have traditionally been organized along social organizational systems (Mbigi, 1997; Jackson, 2004). The nature of social organizations emphasizes a culture of stakeholder orientation, humanistic values, harmonious teamwork and acceptance of responsibilities in managing business relations. This can be seen in the nature of managing stakeholder relations, in which the cultural organizational domain of a MNE is a predominant source of influence (Horwitz, 2000). For instance, in many South African organizations, the use of distinctive national, institutional and organizational cultural practices that are based on human relation traditions, such as *Ubuntu* and *Indaba* (Mbigi, 1997), seems common. Many Chinese firms tend to adopt *Quanxi* and Bamboo Network (based on relationship-building and consensus with local stakeholders; Child and Tse, 2001; Smart and Smart, 2005), and the *Jugaard* (with its human relations values that emphasize grassroots consensus seeking, consultation and involvement of key groups and individuals to influence stakeholders) is a model used in many Indian firms (Khanna et al., 2005). Each of these examples illustrates stakeholder relevance in dealing with the institutional complexities and the challenge of addressing social issues.

The term *Ubuntu* refers to an ethnic group who live in several regions of Africa. The term continues to acquire positive meaning based on revaluing African traditions and developing them into responsible management and leadership practices (Horwitz, 2000). The word *Ubuntu* is found, with slight variations in pronunciation, over a wide geographical and social region in east, central and southern Africa. For example, the largest tribe in Tanzania, the Sukuma, uses the word 'Bantu'; the term used in the Zulu tribe in South Africa is 'Abantu'; by Sesuto people in southern Africa it is 'Batho'; by the Herero people in Namibia 'Avandu'; in central Africa it is 'Ngumtu,' 'Kubuntu' and 'Edubuntu', and the Swahili people in East Africa use it as 'Watu'. In each case, the term implies 'togetherness' or 'a united group of people' for a common cause and purpose.

When used in connection with stakeholders' engagement in CSR practices in an institutional context, the concept of *Ubuntu* (or humanness) means that a person is seen not as an individual but as part of a collective society (Jackson, 2004; Kamoche et al., 2004). This concept is different from that of the western institutional domain, where a person is typically seen as an individual (Horwitz, 2000). *Ubuntu* emphasizes group solidarity and relationship-building, and provides the foundation for the way most central, eastern and southern African people think and behave (Mbigi, 1997). From a cognitive cultural perspective (Scott, 1995), for example, it is a concept that focuses on the spirit of caring and community, harmony and hospitality, respect and responsiveness that individuals and groups display for each other.

In any organization, leadership practices are essential elements in the development of institutional competencies, innovation and sustainability (Horwitz, 2000). The term *Indaba* refers to a traditional, socially constructed structure of handling and resolving any debate or conflict that may arise within a group, and it implies that leadership is defined according to experience and competence, much like the Zulu terms 'Ubaba' and 'Ukuhlonipha' (respecting of experienced elders). Such a concept and its meaning are also found in East Africa, where the largest Sukuma tribe in Tanzania call it 'Ndaba' or 'Banamhala' ('chiefs' in English or 'Wazee' in Swahili), implying that the leadership of experienced and responsible/caring elders is used to encourage and enable groups into collectively resolving problems that involve environmental, organizational structure/design, business or community issues. In *Indaba*, decision-making tends to be circular and inclusive (Horwitz, 2000; Jackson, 2004). Although the term itself is grounded on dignity and respect, any form of debate must be honoured and respected by all.

Ubuntu and *Indaba* both assume that, once stakeholders, such as employees and local communities, are well treated and their core needs are met, there will be a reciprocal response. They will feel they are part of a firm's family, will be dedicated in their work, will have a high level of accountability and trust, and will become more innovative and productive for the firm and for their own interests and families (including extended ones), and the communities in which they live (Mbigi, 1997; Jackson, 2004).

However, as suggested by resource dependency and institutional theories, the success of any stakeholder relationship will depend on the stakeholders' behaviour (e.g. employees and local communities), MNEs' capabilities to utilize their available resources, and the effectiveness of national institutional regulatory systems as mediating and facilitating tools that cooperate with MNEs to address social problems in communities.

Methodology

Research setting

South Africa's institutional context

South Africa is an example of an emerging market within the African continent. This year, it has joined the group of the fastest leading emerging economies of Brazil, Russia, India and China (BRICS). Following the advent of democratic transformation and inclusive national institutional systems in 1994, the country has been reformed to enhance business competitiveness at home and abroad, by enhancing stakeholder relationships, and opening South African firms up to African and world markets (Horwitz, 2000). The country is currently one of the major economies in Africa and other emerging markets such as in Asia. Several of its local firms' in sectors such as mining, banking, retail, communications and technology, have become major business investment players in Africa and beyond (UNCTAD, 2005).

In order to meet the challenges of globalization and local institutional contexts, several South African institutions and firms operating in heterogeneous environments in developing nations such as Africa have adapted new systems of business management (*Ubuntu*) and leadership (*Indaba*) practices, as well as certain business practices from other western developed countries (Horwitz, 2000; Kapelus, 2002). *Ubuntu* and *Indaba* business models can be seen as examples of organizational sense-making used to promote sustainable engagement initiatives, with stakeholders that are culturally understood and locally accepted.

In sum, there is a move towards the creation of enduring organizational partnerships throughout the management practices of some South African businesses and institutions, reflected in the various participative schemes in stakeholder relationships designed to engage stakeholders in authentic forms of dialogue, and to empower individuals.

Tanzania's institutional context

As a developing country in East Africa, Tanzania has one of the highest levels of unemployment and poverty in sub-Saharan Africa (UNCTAD, 2005). The nation is dominated by 'void' institutional systems and complex heterogeneous cultures (Mapolu, 2000). Like most developing countries, Tanzania exhibits elements of weak national and institutional systems for regulating MNEs' business activities, for example (DeSoto, 2000).

Most of the Tanzanian culture and institutions are based on human relations, whereby stakeholder relevance in dealing with institutional complexities is highly important (Mapolu, 2000). Like *Ubuntu* in South African institutions, Tanzania uses the local Swahili word of 'Watu' (meaning people or togetherness) to mobilize its local stakeholder relations towards enhancement of responsible behaviour among its people and addressing communal social challenges.

Since the collapse of socialist command policies in 1995 (called *Ujamaa* in the Swahili language), closely followed by the effects of globalization and technology, the country has undergone an institutional transformation to a market economy by opening up to and attracting foreign direct investment to create prosperity for its people. In order to protect the interests of MNEs and its own people, Tanzania has continued to harmonize its investment policies and institutions. The introduction of the Investment Act of 1997 was intended to encourage free market and trade liberalization in the country (Mapolu, 2000). Despite the changes taking place in the country, however, it has yet to be seen whether the government regulatory systems will play a significant role in mobilizing and protecting the interests of Tanzania's citizens (i.e. the stakeholders) and MNEs.

Case study methodology and participating firms

This chapter adopts a case study approach (Eisenhardt, 1989; Yin, 2004) to analyse how CSR initiatives were implemented by global mining MNEs in local communities in Lake Victoria Zone in Tanzania. For confidentiality purposes, the names of MNEs and interviews are disguised. Our study was conducted between March and July 2008, with follow-up data collection in May and June 2010. The interviews were mostly face-to-face and lasted from 45 minutes to two hours. Most interviews were recorded and transcribed verbatim. Archival data were also collected from all the companies, and from the host country government officials. The archival data provided complementary information and allowed our data to be triangulated. The aim of adopting a contrast between MNEs from an emerging and a developed nation in a case study approach for data collection was to provide rich description on the processes used in CSR initiatives through employees, as intermediaries, to address sustainable challenges in local communities (Yin, 2004); the reason for selecting three extractive mining MNEs, located in a specific geographic region, was to use specific CSR approaches as their preconditions for institutional and resource dependency legitimacy, and, thus, to help us capture new themes and theoretical development in CSR initiative concepts during the analysis process (Eisenhardt, 1989). All the three MNEs are located in the Lake Victoria Zone, an important economic region for mining firms. We chose to investigate global firms' investments in a single country to avoid complications that might arise from cross-country policy variations. Tanzania was chosen because it is among the most important investment destinations for South African and other global mining MNEs in Africa after Angola, Zambia, Ghana and the Democratic Republic of Congo. The three MNEs were chosen because they claimed to have deployed competitive strategies that apply diversities of stakeholder relationships when addressing social issues in the local context of a developing nation, Tanzania.

In view of the broad and exploratory nature of the research issues in this case study, we adopted a qualitative approach, in the form of semi-structured interviews, observation and the use of relevant documents, as the most appropriate ways to approach this research (Bryman, 2004). By using a case study analysis method from these MNEs, we were able to capture the dynamics of CSR through employees' engagement and how employees' reactions to CSR practices were influenced significantly by the communities in which they live. The capturing of this dynamic also helped to identify key themes and concepts that shed some light on our research objective. Furthermore, this methodology allowed us to gain in-depth knowledge of a 'process' that leads to understanding the nature of CSR implementation by MNEs, as opposed to capturing a 'snapshot' at a single point in time (Eisenhardt, 1989; Bryman, 2004).

Interview participants

Respondents were selected from individuals and groups that were expected to have useful insights about their communities and how they were affected by MNEs' CSR initiatives. They provided themes and concepts that were equally relevant in understanding the nature of stakeholder relationships that influenced attention and positive behaviour of employees towards CSR issues (e.g. Eisenhardt, 1989). For example, frequent emerging themes such as shared interests, trust, social acts, empowerment, proactive leadership, two-way collaboration, dialogue and identity were categorized as part of an *integrative* initiative within the CSR implementation process (Yin, 2004). Further, new themes were uncovered that were deemed substantial in the context of local cognitive culture of the people (e.g. Scott, 1995) in Tanzania. These included the role of cultures and community-based micro-culture functions in management and leadership styles, which fit with the *Ubuntu* and *Indaba* practices identified in the two South African MNEs.

The respondents from the South African MNEs were representatives and local employees based at subsidiary operations in different mining sites in Lake Victoria Zone. As for the other mining company, representatives were based at the country head office in Dar Es Salaam, and other interviews came from the firm's mining site in the Lake Victoria Zone in Mwanza and Geita, all in Tanzania. Specifically, the persons interviewed per organization were: MNEs' representatives and expatriates, government/ministerial representatives, local employees, NGOs and local community leaders residing close to each MNE's operations.

Procedure and interview methodology

Respondents were asked about the overall effects of corporate social responsibility policies on local social issues of poverty and unemployment as well as environmental concerns; how CSR initiatives occur and under what circumstances; the nature of each MNE's partnership initiative strategies in the local area (i.e. types of collaboration techniques used with stakeholders); the role of Tanzania's national regulatory systems in facilitating the activities of MNEs on CSR; role of various stakeholders in formulating and implementing CSR practices (i.e. social strategies); and the objective and extent of collaboration between MNEs and local communities. Respondents were never asked about the role of

Table 6.1 Sample characteristics

N	Job title/Position description
Company MNE – I	
3	Representatives from South Africa, based at the head office in Dar Es Salaam
2	Branch representatives from South Africa in Arusha and Moshi
4	Local employees (two men and two women) in Mwanza and Dar Es Salaam
2	NGOs' representatives in Mwanza and Moshi
11	Total
Company MNE – II	
2	Mining representatives from South Africa, based in Dar Es Salaam
4	Expatriates from South Africa (three in Geita and one in Mwanza)
5	Local employees (all male) all in Geita
1	Government official based in Dar Es Salaam
12	Total
Company MNE – III	
2	Mining representatives from a developed nation, based in Dar Es Salaam
4	Expatriates from developed nations (three in Geita and one in Mwanza)
5	Local employees (all male) all in Geita
1	Government official based in Dar Es Salaam
12	Total

employees as 'intermediaries' of MNEs to local communities. In addition, respondents were never asked questions about the concepts of *Ubuntu* or *Indaba*, social licence or legitimacy. In total, 36 (including one government official) interviews were conducted for the study (see Table 6.1).

Although the respondents from the three large MNEs, local communities and employees were the main focus of this study, stakeholders from a number of other organizations, such as NGOs, were also interviewed in a bid to triangulate the information received from the primary sources. Triangulation was deemed important to provide broader insights as well as better validate our results (Eisenhardt, 1989). Archival data were collected from MNEs on annual CSR investment reports, and engagement initiatives with communities (e.g. through training workshops, seminars, etc.). Secondary data from an interview with a government official at the National Investment Centre in Dar Es Salaam provided more insight into the way the local and national institutions facilitated such hybrid partnerships with MNEs and stakeholders.

Data analyses

We followed the data analysis procedures for theory building based on case studies. We first conducted within-case analyses. We synthesized the interview data with archival data for each case and recorded the implications of each case for our research questions. This process allows the unique patterns of each case to emerge. We then performed between-case analyses and searched for cross-case patterns. We paired cases to compare their similarities and differences in terms of their implications for our research questions. These within-case and between-case analyses led us to a preliminary theoretical framework to analyse the relationships among four key actors: the firms' head offices, the host country government, firms and local communities. Two researchers then coded the interview data independently to examine the validity of the preliminary theoretical framework, and reconciled the coding differences afterwards. These processes led to the final version of the theoretical framework, discussed in the following section.

In the following sections, we present data descriptions of each case and of the way CSR initiatives with employees and other stakeholders were implemented. The overall research method attempted to explore issues in context, as reported by the interviewees. In seeking to describe how a particular phenomenon occurred (Denzin, 1989), each case provided information that unveiled the nature of each company's practices in dealing with social issues. Moreover, the cases expose the ways in which CSR initiatives were transferred, adopted or learned, and implemented, and how each firm responded to its challenges differently.

Findings and conceptualization

South African MNE I

The South African MNE is based in Johannesburg, South Africa. It came to invest in Tanzania in 2002. Currently, it employs over 10,000 local employees in various mining activities. As part of its globalization processes, the company operates in many countries in Africa, Asia and Australia, serving larger companies and investors. Its international business expansion, however, has mainly been in Africa, where it has a strong local competitive advantage and a large pool of potential customers in construction and tourism sectors from its country of origin.

In response to the host nation's and local communities' social needs, the company's mission is stated through its institutionalized fundamental values of *Ubuntu* and *Indaba*, and grassroots mobilization of its overall business and corporate governance strategy in Tanzania. The grassroots approach is presented by the firm's representative in Dar Es Salaam, where the MNE country head office is based, as an effort 'to promote local-for-local innovation initiative, a process requiring the bank to not only rely on identifying local needs but also to use its own available local resources to respond to those needs'.

The firm's role in Tanzania is to use its resources and capabilities to effect change and accountability upon local communities where the company's business activities are based. Interviews found that the company's management goal on the CSR issue is to encourage and support committed stakeholders and bring them together to discuss the social issues that affect them, either directly or indirectly. As two interviewees with the MNE, a mining regional office in Lake Victoria Zone, reported:

> When we started our business, we only focused on employees and how to integrate and influence CSR practices at work. We gave our employees books and pamphlets about CSR to take with them home and to their villages where they live. We thought that over time our employees would inspire people where they live to act and respond responsibly in their communities. The whole process did not work at all. In some ways, we felt disappointed by our employees whom we have given them several CSR training as part of their career development. After a few years, we realized that it was not only to do with CSR and employees at work and their communities; other influential stakeholders were out there in communities that we needed to talk to. We started to discuss with employees and the way we could engage them to achieve sustainable development in their communities. All suggested that we need to go out there and talk to the village leaders and people. They need to know how you engage them seriously. We had several workshops organized by community elders and our employees based on the language of dialogue. Dialogue is highly valued by our company and locals.

> Through a two-way dialogue, we have come to identify common values between us. The value of listening to the influential leaders in communities before they can accept the influence of our employees

on CSR issues is very much essential for the local communities to enter any form of partnerships.

In order to achieve credibility and legitimacy in addressing social issues in partnership with stakeholders, the company reports using the language of dialogue, not as just as symbols, but as part of its core values (see Table 6.2). With this hybrid form of engagement practices, the company facilitates joint learning and knowledge sharing in partnership with its local stakeholders. As the above interview excerpt shows, this new form of institutional system, based on intercultural values, seems to move beyond symbolic engagement activities to emphasize authentic dialogue and shared language so that stakeholder interaction will appeal to the members of all stakeholder groups, and subsequently enhance accountable attitudes among them.

Since its inception in Tanzania, interviews revealed how the company has succeeded in initiating a wide range of CSR projects through its

Table 6.2 Key features of institutionalization systems of selected South African MNEs' behaviour

Feature	Description
MNEs' orientation	Building flexibility through management (*Ubuntu*) and leadership (*Indaba*) practices to address stakeholders' demands and gain social licence and legitimacy in local communities (Mbigi, 1997; Horwitz, 2000; Kamoche et al., 2004).
Motivation for globalization	Seeking new markets, customers, and resource advantages in developing/emerging countries (Kapelus, 2002; Khanna et al., 2005).
Business practices	Hybrid approach to balance between global and local strategies (Khanna et al., 2005; Bartlett and Beamish, 2008; Calvano, 2008).
Organizational culture	Cross-cultural interface as reflected by the firm's core culture, the national institutional context and stakeholders' need (Horwitz, 2000; Khanna et al., 2005).
Intercultural CSR through HRM	Bottom-up local partnership approach: emphasis on stakeholders' orientation, stakeholder input, participation, consensus seeking and relationship-building through institutionalized *Ubuntu* and *Indaba* systems (Horwitz, 2000; Jackson, 2004; Khavul et al., 2009).

social corporate responsibility division with public institutions aimed at stakeholders' empowerment, responsible leadership, authentic collaboration and a two-way dialogue to promote long-term social good in local communities. Along with employees, it has initiated many social development projects that are based on social investment (including financial, logistical or human resources-related) in partnership with local communities and the public sector. These social investment projects provide relevant information, including community-based volunteer activities and donations to community activities. Through dialogue with local stakeholders, the MNE uses local skills to initially fund these projects, with the goal of empowering the locals to manage such projects on their own.

Company representatives reported how they have learned the importance of integrating several of their CSR policies into overall corporate strategy in their business activities in communities. They included the not-for profit sector, such as the drop-in centres in Lake Victoria Zone, which were initially funded by the company through partnerships with locals NGOs. These organizations continue to provide temporary shelters for street children and orphans, offering counselling and various innovative training programs that enable these children to return to school. A number of primary and secondary schools within the company's area of operations have created scholarship funding to motivate local public institutions to improve educational standards and provide other logistical support. Some of the student beneficiaries go on to work for the company and in other mining institutions. Such projects are examples of how funding adds local sustainable benefit into the company's strategic mix, and results in gaining the social licence and legitimacy that are needed to operate in poor communities. During interviews with two company representatives in one of the mining sites, we gained the following insights regarding the use of social relationships rooted in local culture:

> We use indigenous institutional models of *Ubuntu* with our employees, which value local community culture, the environment, and the universe holistically. We use *Indaba* practices to establish a sense of community, belonging, shared heritage, and common welfare through responsible leadership. These are heterogeneous communities with complex culture. At the same time we acknowledge that, if we were to influence our CSR policies in these communities, the individual employees and the social environment need to be contextualized and reflect the cultural communities and organizations.

Employees are part of the local social network. Thus we make sure we do not manipulate these relationships because of our resources, nor marginalize individuals and groups.

Total poverty reduction is not simple... Using *Indaba* values, we use experienced elders who command significant influence in their communities, the employees we have at work, and who will communicate with us and help us to build trust with the locals. But we also use committed groups and specific individuals to further their aspirations and demands.

The above excerpts illustrate how the company has taken the concept of CSR as a 'strategic' focus to its business operations in Tanzania, by building bridges with local stakeholders within local communities (i.e. individuals or groups; Scott, 1995). The nature of the partnership with communities/NGOs, for example, shows how the company has enveloped the wider public domain in a responsive engagement manner. They do this by identifying the local elders and microcultures as being strong sources of influence in their communities, and, therefore, valuable facilitators who could mobilize CSR activities in an accountable manner (Waddock, 2008).

The company understood the significance of engaging stakeholders in authentic partnerships, and the community appreciated the company's efforts. A representative of Habitat for Humanity, an NGO, for example, stated:

The management is quite pleased to fund organizations like ours because we deal directly with the affected people, and we are not corrupt. Our relationship has provided us with valuable leadership skills to handle social needs in our communities.

Sectoral interaction involved in CSR revealed certain reciprocal benefits and implications for the company presence in local communities. Both partners (MNE and stakeholders) gained valuable knowledge from each other through the language of communication and by understanding and respecting one another's cultural values, and by turning various business opportunities into a way for the company to deliver social good.

South African MNE II

Our subject mining company is based in Johannesburg, South Africa, and has a significant degree of internationalization within the mining industry in Africa. As a commercial extractive multinational mining corporation, the company originally came to invest in Tanzania in 1995 as an exploratory mining firm, beginning its mining production in 2000. It currently employs tens of thousands of local workers at its mining sites in the Lake Victoria Zone, one of the poorest and most densely populated local communities in Tanzania and sub-Saharan Africa. With its increasing expansion in Africa, the company's strategic vision is to 'continue to remain a value-driven firm in promoting stakeholder relations with its employees, communities, business partners, governments, and civil society organizations'.

Stakeholder interaction in the mining company is focused specifically on efforts to confront the traditionally poor ethical reputation of the mining industry, with a view to making the strongest possible contribution towards the global transition of sustainable development in poor communities in the Lake Victoria Zone. The role of CSR within the company is reported during interviews by most company representatives as a 'social act' aimed at 'addressing social problems in partnership with local communities, government ministries, and committed NGOs through learning in a local context'. Our interview reports illustrate the extent of the company's organizational values in response to stakeholder partnerships to 'tackle core local social problems through job creation, and through its joint support of community/social entrepreneurs, community health services to fight against Malaria, HIV/AIDS, and environmental degradation in the communities where its mining activities are based in the Lake Victoria Zone'. The success of CSR within the company is attributed to high levels of commitment, trust and responsibility among the local stakeholders. As reported in interviews at the Geita mining site and at the Mwanza firm office:

> The company spent over half a million dollars last year [2007] to support various community social investments. The investment was directed at projects with the right and committed sectoral partners in adding value to long-term sustainable development in education and health care in our neighbourhoods.

> During our recent *Indaba* meeting, leaders from different communities and sectors asked us to support them through a microenterprise banking system to create training centres for unemployed young men and women in brick manufacturing, gardening, fishing, carpentry and plumbing. We are now finding significant accountability and commitment from local communities and groups on these

initiatives. Our environmental expatriates from South Africa have also been instrumental in collaborating with communities to harness their social needs in various capacities, involving environmental preservation, waste management, and reforestation programs.

Building an integrative corporate partnership with committed stakeholders seemed to be a priority for the company with respect to the delivery of social benefits. Interviews further identified additional sustainable development issues for the company in collaboration with the local communities and local governments in Geita:

> The company is aware that it needs to be sustainable in relation with local communities' issues. It often uses its employees, as an upper-hand source of knowledge with outside stakeholders. It uses management practices to share skills with various sectors in agro-forestry projects to produce tree seedlings, and bio-diversity projects with the main national university of Dar Es Salaam. Such projects have now created hundreds of jobs. Not only about job creation, jobs need to be sustainable, mobile and affordable. We realize that majority of local communities want skills that they can easily imitate, and that they can enable them to be self-sufficient in a long term. As a company, we strive to use our available resources to make sure we respond to these local demands. We are certainly seeing benefits for both our firm and communities in terms of better relations, job creation and mutual partnerships.

One interview drew attention to the company's Human Resource Management (HRM) policies and practices that were in place for dealing with local social issues:

> Our institutional culture strives to support and encourage our valuable employees, through training and exposure to sustainable development, to understand how to deal with and handle issues affecting the organization and the employees themselves, and the surrounding communities in a sustainable manner.

The use of employees, as intermediaries with local communities, was seen as a form of organizational capabilities to use its available resources (e.g. capital, skills) to deliver public good in a local context.

An MNE from a developed country – III

A mining firm came to operate in Tanzania in 1995. It has an integrated business operation which is governed from its head office in Toronto. Its regional head office in Africa is in South Africa. It has a country head office in Dar Es Salaam, the commercial city of Tanzania. The company operates in Lake Victoria Zone. The company appeared to be highly formalized, integrated and globalized in the mining sector. Its corporate policies on subsidiary investment decisions such as financial budgets and allocations, research and development (R&D) activities and the recruitment of expatriates in Tanzania were established at its head office, passed to its Africa regional office in Johannesburg, South Africa, then to Dar Es Salaam and, finally, to its mining site in Lake Victoria Zone.

As a global mining corporation, it possessed strategic competencies, technological capabilities and economies of scale to determine and align its organizational interests with those of subsidiary business operations in Tanzania. It had continued to embrace the welfare of Lake Victoria Zone communities, going beyond just providing jobs to providing benefits which offset the environment and social externalities of the company. Since 2008, according to interviews with managers of the company, it had begun to provide health expatriates and environmental scientists from the home country and other developed countries to visit communities and make recommendations as to what actions the company could take to improve local health and environmental conditions. The expatriates and scientists had used advanced technologies to conduct the so-called 'impact assessment' to make recommendations to the company. The purpose of such assessment strategies was to help the company to make forecasts and implement strategies that could minimize its environmental footprint and safeguard the environment and social issues at the mining sites.

Interviews further reported that the MNE was committed to making a positive difference in the communities where it operated. The company focused on responsible behaviour as its duty, creating opportunities to generate greater value for its shareholders, while at the same time fostering sustainable development in communities and countries where it operated. As a global firm, it strove to earn the trust of its employees, of the communities where its subsidiary operations were based, of the host nations' governments, or of any other persons or parties with whom the company was engaged in the sustainable development of mineral resources.

During interviews, company representatives revealed several measures already undertaken that were aimed at engagement in various cross-sector partnerships with other relevant local stakeholders. These measures were put in place to address social and ecological issues in communities where the company operated. The four executives interviewed were vehement about the need for corporate responsibility and cooperative partnerships:

> Responding to social and environmental issues in the communities where our business is based is no longer an option... we need a social framework that operates within the local communities. We follow the government investment policies. We have official legal documents as well that bind us with the government for the right and legitimacy to operate here. However, we have some challenges with some strategic mechanisms. For example, with whom should we engage seriously and in a committed manner in the communities, how and for how long? There are so many opportunistic behaviours here among local individuals, groups or even employees who claim to be committed partners but our experience so far show that they are not!

> Our ability to work within the sustainability framework will be key to getting support from local communities, and local governments in the areas. It will also allow us to initiate good projects with other local stakeholders. This is the only way we can establish good relations with the community.

> Our recent problems with local communities clearly show the need to address our presence here responsibly. There is a lot of misunderstanding and at times local communities are getting confrontational. This situation is not good for our business and our global image... indeed. However, our firm will continue to collaborate with our head office, shareholders, and the government of Tanzania to address social problems.

> Dealing with the social problems of poverty, environmental degradation and social injustices that face this area exceeds the scope of our company. We need a responsible partnership with the government. In many local communities, there are young people who need sustainable jobs, education and a livelihood. Communities need health service support and other community development projects to give them a sense of economic activities and ownerships. There is so much despair among people in these communities. Some have lost land.

Yet, among local employees working for the company, community leaders and NGOs, there was clear discontent among the members of the local communities.

> The company has a very top-down CSR policy. It spends tens of thousands of US dollars in CSR, as shown on annual company report. Also, it has initiated several development projects in our communities in education, health and infrastructure. The question is...who can afford to send their kids to these private schools and hospitals? They are completely out of our reach, and the company knows about this.
>
> We do not have jobs to access these better equipped services (education and health) nor essential means to support us to build community enterprises where we could apply our local skills in many activities. Though the company is doing very good projects here, we are still unclear with the company CSR practices. Our problems are long-term; they need serious engagement with communities.
>
> The company spends too much time talking about best internal CSR practices it has. It uses sophisticated tools and systems to address CSR issues, and brings all its expatriates from North America and Europe. Majority of us here in communities has no clue what these systems they are about! The other day, there were expatriates from developed countries. They spend time explaining to us employees how to enhance our CSR values at work...but they were beyond our capabilities! We need CSR systems that make sense to us and the local communities out there.
>
> We need a mutual partnership with foreign companies investing in our communities. There are so many potential benefits we can get from the company with respect to jobs and skill developments; also the company can learn a lot from us when it comes to negotiation strategies with our communities. If the company responds positively to our concerns, we will strive to protect its business interests here and it will operate in harmony in our communities. But the government needs to sit with local communities and tell them why the government has allowed the company to come to practise mining in their land and tell us what potential benefit it will bring in our communities. For the time being, the company is left to itself to address these issues with the local communities.

The company had used its social development department in each of the mining sites to develop practical guidelines in order to facilitate the implementation of its organizational values and missions, including building long-term relationships of mutual benefit between the operations and their host communities, and to avoid costly disputes and hostilities with local stakeholders. Yet the firm still faced serious problems and increased pressure to manage conflicts and reconcile stakeholders' demands in the Lake Victoria Zone.

Despite the company being responsive to the social and ecological problems in Lake Victoria Zone, it has continued to encounter civil unrest and violence from its employees and from the communities around its mining areas, something unheard of from the other two South African MNEs in the same Lake Victoria Zone.

Local stakeholders, government officials, NGOs, and communities: Interviews with local employees in the two companies, NGOs, local government ministries and community leaders stressed the need to secure jobs in the midst of high unemployment and increased social problems in Tanzania. Also stressed was the nature of engagement with MNEs in promoting public good. In the areas where the three MNEs operated, the local governments were actively involved in educating their citizens to embrace dialogue with the MNEs. Education was based on informing local communities of the mutual benefits and opportunities they were likely to encounter when they engaged foreign investors in their communities. Our interview with the government official in Dar Es Salaam also pointed out policies aimed at regulating funding and MNEs' engagement with local communities through its established Foundation of Civil Society (FCS) body. This body was geared to minimizing mismanagement and corruption, and educating local communities on the responsible use of resources. Tanzania, as a host nation, was a responsive partner in assisting foreign companies and local communities to enter into an inter-sector relationship on an ongoing basis.

In handling any form of institutional grievance or negotiations, the two companies from South Africa used a very different approach to the western firm, based on consensus and inclusive industrial tactics to ensure that all stakeholders involved in CSR remained satisfied with and committed to development initiatives, as guided by the *Ubuntu* and *Indaba* institutional models. The South African firms had a comparative competitive advantage over the firm from the developed country when it came to engaging stakeholders in CSR issues. This practice was echoed in our interviews by most of the local stakeholders with regard to the two South African MNEs. For instance:

> During community workshops with the companies, the collective harmony truly reflects our daily way of life, values, culture, and how we want to progress in the midst of their [the companies'] activities

in our communities. We now do not see significant conflict of interest between the foreign companies. The presence of these companies is quite beneficial for us in many ways.

The firms' engagement system makes much sense, in that we feel included, and that we [as stakeholders] can have a voice that is heard and respected. The firms use diverse approaches of engagement that includes their workers and other affected stakeholders. When a business firm is operating in your area and behaves like this way, we acknowledge its presence and contributions to the community at large.

Both companies (MNEs I & II) demonstrate how they moderate their organizational culture and those of local communities by translating their organizational commitment into the specific context of the local environment in Tanzania. Local NGOs and communities expressed the CSR success and effort in their communities by the MNE from a developed country. However, they felt that the company did not effectively use its existing local employees as intermediaries to influence local communities and NGOs on CSR issues. Furthermore, they felt that most of the firm's CSR practices are far removed from the communities' social reality. In the first instance, the company had dissatisfied employees with their working relationships with the firms, thus making it very hard to use employees to influence attitudes in communities. They felt that the company had not successfully adapted to dialogue and engagement with stakeholders that would make sense to the local communities.

Discussion

The empirical data from this research demonstrate the nature of sustainability initiatives and socially responsible business practices implemented by three multinational enterprises in cooperation with their local stakeholders (employees and communities), as well as the influence of the host nation. Given the complexities of implementing CSR in developing countries such as Tanzania, the use of the socially established structures of meaning in cross-cultural management (i.e. *Ubuntu* and *Indaba*), as reflected in the South African firms, seems to offer a different form of *organizational values* within the local context. The South African firms, with their exposure to African institutions and culture, seem to have the resources and capabilities to embed themselves in the Tanzanian situation. While these firms follow international standards and norms for dealing with social and ecological issues, as addressed by the UN Global Compact, they seem to use a diverse organizational approach in an attempt to balance between global and local challenges when they enter new markets, such as in developing countries (also see Table 6.2). The other firm, from a developed nation, persisted in utilizing its resources based on global CSR standard practices, which were perceived to be convergent with western best practices when addressing sustainable development initiatives. It implemented a sophisticated management system to interact with and operate in Tanzania which posed a different challenge and response from local stakeholders (both employees and communities).

Importantly, the case analysis of these multinational firms has provided evidence that these companies seem to have infiltrated their embedded management and leadership resources, either drawn from traditional local and corporate cultures, as in the case of the two South African firms, or using global CSR standards, as in the case of the firm from a developed nation, to produce their own innovative, hybrid model for business sustainability. Such diverging business models reflect the unique nature of each MNE, illustrating that they are not necessarily homogeneous in their handling of the global institutional governance complexities in delivering sustainable social development initiatives.

As far as the South African firms are concerned, the use of contextually relevant sustainability initiatives, and particularly the successful implementation of such practices, can be largely attributed to the stakeholder consultation model employed by these MNEs. They provide a different form of CSR practices from that of firms from developed nations. Theoretically, they are capable of utilizing their resources, competency and knowledge of the environment in order to generate legitimacy and make sense to local stakeholders. Furthermore, they have advantages based on resources developed by their firms to cope and operate in a developing countries' environment, such as in Africa (including Tanzania). Both MNEs, from an emerging market of South Africa and from a developed nation, can develop similar contextually relevant sustainability initiative advantages, but the same cannot be said of their institutional capabilities and advantages, because these are rooted in their home country environment, and the home countries of the MNEs (emerging and developed nations) differ markedly. For example, our primary data have illustrated how the two firms from South Africa are capable of responding with their CSR practices in an environment with poorly developed institutional systems in a Tanzanian context. This gives them an advantage over the MNE from developed and sophisticated institutions when both firms engage in CSR initiatives in other poor nations.

The influence of a head office in Toronto, and the persistent utilization of the convergence of global CSR best practices, could be argued as a disadvantage, preventing the firm from a developed nation from initiating new firm's resources, such as allocating assets and resources to adapt to the host nation's business practices, relationship-building with local communities, and the language to operate in developing nations. As such, while the firm claims to spend tens of thousands of US Dollars on CSR, it is unable to fully and appropriately utilize the resources necessary to legitimize its operation in poor communities. In order to reduce the challenges it faces, the firm from a developed nation requires capabilities to understand what is missing in the environment, and how to operate in an environment where legitimacy and sense-making of CSR initiatives are important when implementing sustainable development initiatives. Thus, developing socially responsible and sustainable practices through employees, as intermediaries before reaching external stakeholders, can be highly influential in gaining broader stakeholder sense-making, as well as contributing to a positive organizational reputation with both investors and employees.

Conclusion and future recommendations

Our chapter has analysed the different types of CSR initiative capabilities of MNEs in a developing nation in Tanzania. The use of both resource dependency and institutional theories helped us to explain how MNEs utilized the socio-culturally constructed stakeholder relationships differently during the CSR implementation process with local communities. While balancing their internal firms' challenges, our chapter has found that the two MNEs from South Africa had certain advantages, knowledge, resources and competencies to operate in a country with underdeveloped institutions, and where the demand for stakeholder CSR legitimacy and sense-making was important. We also found that the direct influence of the head office of a firm from a developed country had disadvantages when it came to initiating CSR practices in a local context.

In order to achieve the successful sectoral interactions witnessed in these cases, there was substantial influence of the host nation, Tanzania, and inclusion of stakeholders' world view on the practices of the MNEs. The core values of the MNEs from South Africa and their social embeddedness in a Tanzanian context seemed to appeal and make sense to most segments of the Tanzanian society (i.e. local communities, private sector organizations and the firms' employees), and thus generated local legitimacy and social licence to operate in these local communities. We argue that, for global MNEs to be successful in developing nations, they need to adapt and develop values which can be aligned with the social structures of communities where they operate – not merely symbolically, but to the extent that sustainability initiatives could be successfully implemented and maintained in the long term.

Our study took place in only one country, and focuses on three large global mining MNEs. However, we argue that the findings extend beyond these three firms. The MNEs in this study employ tens of thousands of local employees, and demonstrate generalizable strategies for the use of intercultural dimensions within the management of community stakeholders in implementing international CSR. This study has introduced the theoretical concept of 'local legitimacy' and a 'social licence model' for MNEs operating in developing nations, and how a bottom-up local partnership approach based on *cross-culture management*, starting with employees (as firms' intermediaries) and spreading to other external stakeholders, should be reinforced in the practice and study of global MNEs' role in sustainability and social responsibility issues.

The overall proposition suggested above is that, while there are global CSR standards that direct firms how to engage with stakeholders sustainably, there are varieties of initiatives that can contribute in several diverse and successful ways to the process of sustainability and social responsibility in dealing with ecosystem and societal challenges in developing countries. By adapting to different institutional contexts, MNEs should utilize and develop resources and capacities that go along cross-cultural management approaches to enhance their local legitimacy and subsequently acquire social licence to do business. Such an approach would also have a longer-term financial, reputation and competitive advantage benefit for MNEs operating in such environments.

References

Austin, J. (2000). Strategic collaboration between nonprofits and businesses. *Nonprofit and Voluntary Sector Quarterly*, 29 (Supplement), 69–97.

Bartlett, C., and Beamish, P. (2008). The future of the transnational: An evolving global role. In C. Bartlett, S. Ghoshal, and P. Beamish (Eds), *Transnational Management: Text, Readings and Cases in Cross Border Management*, 5th Ed., pp. i–iv. Burr Ridge, IL: Irwin McGraw-Hill.

Beamish, P., and Newenham-Kahindi, A. (2007). Human resource management in multinational banks in Tanzania. *Harvard Business Review* (October 29), DOI: 10.1225/907C40.

Bryman, A. (2004). *Social Research Methods*. London: Oxford.

Calvano, L. (2008). Multinational corporations and local communities: A critical analysis of conflict. *Journal of Business Ethics*, 82, 793–805.

Child, J., and Tse, D. (2001). China's transition and its implications for international business. *Journal of International Business Studies*, 32, 5–21.

Denzin, N. K. (1989). *The Research Act: A Theoretical Introduction to Sociological Methods*. Prentice Hall, NJ: Englewood Cliffs.

DeSoto, H. (2000). *The Mystery of Capital: Why Capitalism Triumphs in the West and Fails Everywhere Else*. New York: Basic Books.

Eisenhardt, K. M. (1989). Building theories from case study research. *Academy of Management Review*, 14, 532–550.

Horwitz, F. M. (2000). Management in South Africa. In M. Warner (Ed.), *Management in Emergent Countries*, pp. 214–227. London: Thomson Learning.

Husted, B., and Allen, D. B. 2006. Corporate social responsibility in the multinational enterprise: Strategic and institutional approaches. *Journal of International Business Studies*, 37, 838–849.

Jackson, T. (2004). *Management and Change in Africa: A Cross-cultural Perspective*. London: Routledge.

Kamoche, K., Debrah, Y., Horwitz, F., and Muuka, G. N. (2004). *Managing Human Resources in Africa*. London: Routledge.

Kapelus, P. (2002). Mining, corporate social responsibility and the community: The case of Rio Tinto, Richards Bay Minerals, and the Mbonambi. *Journal of Business Ethics*, 39, 275–296.

Khanna, T., Paletu, K., and Sinha, J. (2005). Strategies that fit emerging markets. *Harvard Business Review*, 85, 63–76.

Khavul, S., Bruton, G. D., and Wood, E. (2009). Informal family business in Africa. *Entrepreneurship: Theory & Practice*, 33, 1219–1238.

Mapolu, R. (2000). *Poverty and economy in Tanzania*. IDM Paper Series, Institute of Development Studies, Dar Es Salaam. University of Dar Es Salaam, Tanzania.

Mbigi, L. (1997). *Ubuntu: The African Dream in Management*. Randburg, South Africa: Knowledge Resources.

O'Regan, K. M., and Oster, S. M. (2000). Non-profit and for-profit partnership: Rationales and challenges of cross-sector contracting. *Nonprofit and Voluntary Sector Quarterly*, 20, 120–140.

Oster, S. M. (1995). *Strategic Management for Nonprofit Organizations: Theory and Cases*. New York: Oxford University Press.

Prahalad, C., and Hart, S. (2002). The fortune at the bottom of the pyramid. *Strategy and Business*, 26, 2–14.

Rondinelli, D., and London, T. (2003). How corporations and environmental groups cooperate: Assessing cross-sector alliances and collaborations. *Academy of Management Executive*, 17, 61–76.

Scott, W. R. (1995). *Institutions and Organizations*. Thousand Oaks, CA: Sage.

Smart, A., and Smart, J. (2005). *Petty Capitalists: Flexibility, Place and the Global Economy*. New York: Sunny Place.

UNCTAD (2005). *World Investment Report 2005: Transnational Corporations and the Internationalization of R&D*. Geneva: UNCTAD.

United Nations' Development Programme (2005). *United Nations Human Develop-ment Report*. Oxford: Oxford University Press for the United Nations Development Programme (UNDP).

Waddell, S. (1999). *Business-government-nonprofit collaborations as agents for social innovation and learning*. Paper presented at the Academy of Management Annual Meeting, Chicago, IL.

Waddock, S. (2008). Building a new institutional infrastructure for corporate responsibility. *Academy of Management Perspectives*, 22, 87–108.

Weick, K. E. (1995). *Sensemaking in Organizations*. Thousand Oaks, CA: Sage.

Yin, R. K. (2004). *Case Study Research: Design and Methods*. Thousand Oaks, CA: Sage.

Yue, A. R., and Mills, A. J. (2008). Making sense out of BAD FAITH: Sartre, Weick and existential sensemaking in organizational analysis. *Tamara*, 7 (1), 66–80.

7
When Two African Cultures Collide: A Study of Interactions between Managers in a Strategic Alliance between Two African Organizations

Emanuel Gomes, Marcel Cohen and Kamel Mellahi

An extensive body of research on international strategic alliances has established that the performance of strategic alliances hinges on the level and quality of interaction between managers from the different partners (Bies, 1986; Mikula et al., 1990; Kim and Mauborgne, 1993; Korsgaard et al., 1995; Konovsky, 2000; Ariño et al., 2001; Johnson et al., 2002; Luo, 2005).

Specifically, research on cross-cultural interactions in international strategic alliances has argued and demonstrated that procedural justice, that is, the perception that the procedures and governance structures used to manage the alliance are fair (Luo, 2005), and interactional justice, that is, the feeling of being treated with respect and dignity during interactions with managers from the other partner in the alliance (Bies, 1986; Bies and Tripp, 1995; Luo, 2005; Mikula et al., 1990), has powerful effects on individuals' commitment to the alliance and is a significant determinant of international strategic alliances' performance. This is because a governance structure based on procedural justice and fairness allows people from previously separate firms to have a voice in the running of the alliance and enable them to guard their self-interest (Thibaut and Walker, 1975; Luo, 2009). Ellis et al. (2009, pp. 139–140) have argued that 'fairness of processes matters because people want to be treated with respect and dignity and valued members of enduring groups ... procedural justice confirms members' standing in groups and organizations and helps build solidarity'. Further, perception of interactional justice helps create the much-needed strong relational ties between individuals to deal effectively with the challenges of integrating the two entities (Ellis et al., 2009).

This body of research has made a significant contribution to our understanding of the antecedents and determinants of procedural and interactional justice perceptions in international strategic alliances, and the consequences of managing these interactions on performance. Further, it has provided managers with guidance on how to develop remedies and solutions to alleviate the problems associated with interactions between individuals in international strategic alliances (Luo, 2009). One important shortcoming of past research on interaction between members of different cultures in strategic alliances is its exclusive focus on alliances between multinational enterprises (MNEs) from developed countries or alliances between MNEs from developed countries and partners from emerging economies. To date, scholars have overlooked strategic alliances between firms from emerging and developing countries. This is surprising, given the recent surge in emerging markets MNEs operating in emerging and developing countries. This study aims to address this gap in the literature through an empirical investigation of the underlying determinants and consequences of procedural and interactional (un)justice perceptions in a strategic alliance between a South African MNE and a firm based in the Democratic Republic of Congo (DRC). We chose a South African MNE for this study because a large number of South African MNEs have expanded into other African markets and limited research has been carried out to analyse the reasons for and, most importantly, the impact of such activity (Daniel et al., 2003a, 2003b; Goldstein and Pritchard, 2006; Wöcke et al., 2007; Miller, 2008). Daniel et al. (2003a, 2003b) wrote of the ' "South Africanisation" of the African economy', which, they argue, is 'exemplified by corporate South Africa's post-apartheid record taking over, and joining up with, existing African corporations'.

This research is important for at least two reasons. First, to the best of our knowledge, no research has examined strategic alliances between firms from within African countries. Although cross-cultural strife and misunderstandings between individuals from different cultures are often present in international strategic alliances (Luo, 2005), we believe the interaction between South African managers and other African managers adds an extra factor to the mix: in addition to cross-cultural misunderstanding there is the legacy of the apartheid era, which may accentuate interpersonal conflicts between the two groupings. A large number of scholars have reported that South African corporations have not always been welcomed in Africa, partly due to their arrogance, as well as feeling reminiscent of South Africa's past, which is inextricably linked to apartheid (Daniel et al., 2003a, 2003b; Miller, 2004, 2005; Mulaudzi, 2006; Vogel et al., 2008).

Second, and of more general significance, this study helps expand the knowledge base on management in Africa. Much of the literature on management, and more specifically human resource management (HRM), in Africa focuses on characteristics of HRM in specific African countries (Eritrea – Ghebregiorgis and Karsten, 2006; Kenya – Kamoche, 1992; Mozambique – Webster and Wood, 2005; South Africa – Wood and Mellahi, 2001) and dimensions of African leadership and management styles (Blunt and Jones, 1992). International HRM research in Africa focuses on interaction between African HRM models and western (Anakwe, 2002) and Asian (Horwitz et al., 2002a, 2002b) models (see Kamoche, 2002 for a discussion). However, research has not examined the interactions between management values and practices from different African countries.

The reminder of the chapter is structured as follows. The next section provides a brief review of relevant literature and discussion of the context of the study. This is followed by a discussion of the data collection method. The last section of the chapter provides an analysis of case study data and discussion of the findings.

Literature review and focus of the study

Cross-cultural interactions in international strategic alliances

International strategic alliances bring together individuals with different cultural blueprints, beliefs, values and patterns of behaviour to work towards a common goal (Parkhe, 1991; Danis and Parkhe, 2002), and this often results in cross-cultural clashes (Buono et al., 1985; Lyles and Salk, 1996; Meschi, 1997). Meschi (1997) argues that nearly all the problems encountered in international strategic alliances are rooted in cross-cultural factors. Scholars posit that the nature and outcomes of cross-cultural interactions in international strategic alliances are determined by three types of perceived or actual (in)justices: perceptions of distributive (in)justice, procedural (in)justice, and interactional (in)justice (Johnson et al., 2002; Luo, 2005, 2007). Distributive justice is the perception that the outcomes of the alliance are distributed fairly and equitably (Adams, 1965). Luo (2005) argues that, when the distribution of the outcome of the alliance is deemed unfair, the affected individuals tend to lower their commitment to the alliance and create an environment that damages the working relationship between the different parties. Given that distributive justice deals with strategic and financial issues, it will not be considered in this study.

Procedural justice refers to the governance structure and decision-making processes within an organization (Thibaut and Walker, 1975; Leventhal et al., 1980; Folger and Konovsky, 1989; Greenberg, 1990; Sheppard et al., 1992). Luo (2005) notes that employees experience 'feelings of anger, outrage and resentment' when they perceive that decision-making processes and governance structure in the strategic alliance are unfair and favour one party over another. When the decision-making processes and governance structures are deemed fair, however, individuals are likely to be loyal to the alliance, have high levels of team spirit and respond constructively to management requests (Luo, 2005).

Interactional justice refers to the manner and quality of the interpersonal interaction between employees from the different groupings that form the alliance (Bies, 1986; Bies and Tripp, 1995; Schuler et al., 2003). In contrast to distributive justice and procedural justice, which are based on formal structures and agreements, interactional justice is an outcome of the cultural norms, values and belief systems held by employees from the different cultures. Luo (2005) notes that employees become more attached to the alliance and have a high degree of solidarity when the various parties display social and cultural sensitivity and treat each other with fairness, respect and dignity.

The literature on management of international strategic alliances posits that managers often fail to address issues related to the forms of (in)justices during the pre- and post-agreement phases. Past research provides evidence to suggest that at the pre-agreement phase MNEs often fail to appreciate the challenges managers face in the management of a cross-culturally diverse workforce (Pritchett et al., 1997; Heifetz and Laurie, 2001; Graebner and Eisenhardt, 2004). The main reasons for failure associated with the post-agreement phase are often related to organizational, human resources and process issues such as poor communication between the different parties in the alliance, lack of decisive action from top management in defining the new direction, different leadership styles, and cross-cultural issues (Kitching, 1967; Lodorfos and Boateng, 2006; Riad, 2007).

Procedural and interactional justice perceptions and South African MNEs

A far as procedural justice and interactional justice are concerned, existing literature on management practices and culture in post-apartheid

South Africa posits two diametrically opposite propositions. On the one hand, the experience of working in ethnically diverse post-apartheid South Africa provides South African managers with the capability to work effectively in foreign cultures (Thomas and Bendixen, 2000; Wöcke et al., 2007). Wöcke et al. (2007, p. 830) note that South African MNCs had to 'contend with the management and advancement of diversity as driven by regulation', which provides them with 'capabilities that would provide an advantage when operating in different national cultures' (p. 830). Similarly, Horwitz et al. (2002a, 2002b, p. 1108) note that post-apartheid labour legislations, and in particular Act No. 108 of 1996, seek to remove and eliminate unfair discrimination in employment practices (see Horwitz et al., 2002a, 2002b for an extensive discussion of the legal framework for HR in South Africa). This viewpoint suggests that South African firms are gradually changing their traditionally discriminatory management practices and becoming more ethnically diverse (Wöcke and Sutherland, 2008), and as a result they are well placed to manage effectively across cultures. On the other hand, a number of scholars argue that there is a 'gap between legal intent and HR practice' in South Africa (Horwitz et al., 2002a, 2002b, p. 1115). For instance, white South Africans still dominate the upper echelons of most South African corporations. It is plausible, therefore, that the cultural homogeneity of top management teams in South Africa is a barrier to effective cross-cultural management in international strategic alliances. Further, South African MNEs are unlikely to provide cross-cultural training to their managers before sending them abroad. Thus, they are not equipped with cross-cultural skills to work together with partners from different cultures. Furthermore, given that most South African MNEs are newcomers to the international markets, they have yet to acquire the necessary skills to operate effectively across cultures. Finally, there is evidence, albeit anecdotal, to suggest that white South Africans hold negative stereotypes against other African cultures which may cause conflict when operating in other African countries. This viewpoint posits that the South African context is a hindrance to effective management across cultures.

In the context of a strategic alliance between two African firms, we expect high levels of perception of procedural and interactional injustices. As noted by Chang et al. (2009), there is often a high level of conflict and misunderstanding when managers from two firms both originating in developing countries interact. This is because, when MNEs from emerging economies enter western developed countries, they typically do so to learn from them, and therefore their managers are predisposed to change their practices and adopt some of the host country practices. This may not be the case when they enter another developing country, where perhaps they feel that host country practices are inferior to theirs (Chang et al., 2009). This is because, as argued by Hambrick and Cannella (1993), foreign managers typically use the relative standing of the host country economy as a proxy of the effectiveness of host country management practices. Consequently, they tend to hold management values and practices from leading economies in high regard and try to assimilate them. In contrast, they perceive those from weak economies as being dysfunctional and to be avoided. Therefore, a MNE from South Africa entering another less developed African country may try to impose its systems and procedures, resulting in procedural injustice.

Managers from the local MNE are less likely to adapt their way of doing things to the host country environment, which may result in interpersonal injustice. As noted earlier, it is plausible that managers and employees from the RDC may hold feelings of animosity against white South African managers, particularly Afrikaners, because of the legacy of the apartheid era, which may accentuate interpersonal conflicts and misunderstandings between managers from the two firms. Animosity refers here to 'remnants of antipathy related to previous or ongoing military, political or economic events' between two nations (Klein et al., 1998, p. 90). Mulaudzi (2006, p. 19) argued that Africans still retain 'some of the wariness and hostility which they displayed towards the apartheid government'. This is partly due to the legacy of the apartheid era and partly due to the fact that South African investments are seen by some Africans 'as tantamount to a recolonisation of the continent' (p. 19). Vale and Maseko (1998) have noted that 'the assumption that what is good for South Africa is good for Africa has often conjured up some uncomfortable historical encounters between Africa and South Africa's powerful establishment, encounters which, despite the miracle attached to South Africa's transformation, has scared Africa's psyche' (cited in Mulaudzi, 2006, p. 19). Similarly, Daniel et al. (2003a, 2003b) have reported that South African corporations have 'not always acted like angels. The opposite has been sometimes the case.' In support of their claim they cite reported 'dubious and questionable practices' of South African companies operating in DRC accused in a 2002 UN report of looting mineral resources during recent civil war in the country. Based on the above, we tentatively expect a high level of perception of injustice in the interaction between the two groupings in the alliance.

Methodology

Context of the study

Strategic alliances have become the preferred mode of expanding internationally (Schweiger et al., 1993; Vermeulen and Barkema, 2001). This is because strategic alliances offer a quicker way for MNEs to grow than the establishment of 'greenfield' developments and have the additional advantage of broadening the firm's knowledge and resource base (Vermeulen and Barkema, 2001). This chapter analyses the strategic alliance between the Congolese Wireless Networks (CWN) and Vodacom Group (Pty) Ltd, focusing on interactions between South African DRC managers (for an extensive discussion of the expansion of South African telecommunication firms in Africa see Games, 2004, pp. 34–43). Vodacom Group (Pty) Ltd (hereafter Vodacom) is the main service provider of communications in South Africa, followed by Mobile Telephone Networks (MTN). The acquisition of 51 per cent of the shares of the Congolese company CWN by Vodacom Group took place in December 2001, resulting in the establishment of Vodacom Congo SPRL. This majority shareholding enabled the South African buyer to take control of the Congolese firm. However, this took place within a friendly collaborative climate, as both organizations, Vodacom and CWN, signed a gentlemen's agreement aiming to maintain equilibrium between the two groups in terms of top management positions. As a result, a new company was formed under the Congolese Company Act – 'Vodacom Congo SPRL'. The strategic alliance was hailed by both sides as one of the important strategic alliances between African firms and was well received by business analysts in both countries.

The main rationale behind this alliance was international market development. Despite being the largest service provider in South Africa, Vodacom's international geographical scope was limited to only three African countries, Lesotho, Mozambique and Tanzania. In contrast, its biggest competitor, MTN, is involved in 15 African countries and some parts of the Middle East (see Figure 7.1). This relatively low degree of international expansion was partly due to an agreement with its shareholders, namely Telkom (Pty) Ltd and Vodafone plc, in which Vodacom had been restrained from acquiring telecommunications licences in the northern sub-Sahara region. This restriction was justified by the fact that the shareholders (Vodafone plc and Telkom RSA) were already operating in that region and would, therefore, want to avoid internal competition from one of their subsidiaries. As a result, Vodacom's geographical scope of action was restricted to the central and southern regions of Africa.

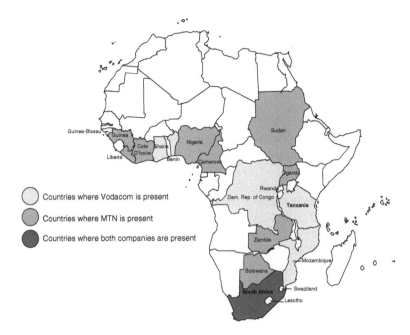

Figure 7.1 International market development of South African telecom companies in Africa
Source: Author analysis.

Moving into the DRC presented an extra challenge to Vodacom. Political turmoil, economic uncertainty, a different culture and an existing strong competitive rivalry between a few dominant incumbent firms, such as CWN, Celtel and Congo Chine, justified the choice of entering the country through an alliance with a strong local partner. The alliance provided Vodacom with access into a country with a population of approximately 58 million but where Global System for Mobile Communications (GSM) penetration is less than 7 per cent (Vodacom Interim Results, 2006). This low penetration represented a huge potential for growth.

Despite the very attractive market growth rate in the communications sector, especially mobile phones, experiencing an annual growth rate of 67 per cent, reaching a total number of 5 million subscribers (OECD African Economic Outlook, 2008), the DRC would present very serious challenges to any new entrants like Vodacom. One of the first challenges faced by Vodacom was getting necessary equipment into the host country because of poor transport infrastructure. Games (2004) reported that

Vodacom used 52 Antonov aircrafts to transport and install generators to boost power.

Other macro-environmental factors presented the company with added challenges. Due to limited investment devoted to the education system, there is a shortage of qualified and skilled labour. In 2007, the DRC was ranked 168th out of 177 countries in the category of human development and, despite recent economic growth, it remains one of Africa's poorest countries. This is coupled with a national unemployment rate of 8.9 per cent and underemployment rate of 81.7 per cent, which has fuelled social and tribal tensions in the country (OECD African Economic Outlook, 2008). In addition to this skills shortage and high political instability, the DRC is consistently ranked as one of the world's most difficult places to do business. In 2007, the DRC is ranked 168th out of 180 countries by Transparency International (OECD African Economic Outlook, 2008). This is mostly explained by the high levels of corruption, questionable business practices and weak corporate governance.

The reality at a macro-level is directly reflected at the company level, where cases of mismanagement and questionable corporate practices were reported by several Vodacom Congo employees. To this extent, one interviewee noted that 'Congolese Vodacom employees avoided complaining about any issues that related to nepotism, mismanagement, racism or tribalism', with the fear of retaliation and even job loss. In addition to lack of job opportunities outside the company, employees in Vodacom Group and their subsidiaries such as Vodacom Congo are, generally well paid, with salaries well above the industry and national average. This may discourage employees from voicing their concerns to or about their superiors: as put by one interviewee, 'It is vital of staying (sic) anonymous when complaining about a manager in this company. The whistle-blowing hotline that is supposed to be anonymous is not and local managers run the company in an atmosphere of fear and lack of trust between the two groups; the Afrikaners on one side and the Congolese on the other.'

Data collection method

The case study methodology is appropriate for this research because it builds up from rich qualitative evidence (Eisenhardt and Graebner, 2007). Evidence was captured through interviews with managers involved in the management of the alliance. According to Yin (1993, p. 59), the case study method can be defined as 'an empirical inquiry that investigates a contemporary phenomenon within its real-life context, addresses a situation in which the boundaries between phenomenon and context are not clearly evident, and uses multiple sources of evidence'. This approach enabled us to examine the intricacies of the partnership process and interaction between individuals from the parts of the alliance.

A combination of both secondary and primary data has been used in this research. We conducted 18 interviews with senior and middle managers of Vodacom Congo. All our interviewees were male. Interviews were conducted in French and English. Further data were collected in a collaboration with a manager from Vodacom Congo who had first-hand insights into the management of the alliance. All interviews were semi-structured and face-to-face. Understandably, in most cases, interviewees asked to remain anonymous and were reluctant to provide detailed information because of fear of identification and consequent retaliation. Interviews focused on the same issues to ensure internal consistency. Interview data were complemented with secondary data including the organization's communication notes, letters, newspaper articles and publicly available documents. This provided a check on the potential bias in interview data.

Background and development of the alliance

The alliance was initiated by Vodacom Group, which was looking for further expansion in Africa. The CEO at that time, Mr Alan Knott-Craig, with a delegation from CWN toured the country and visited numerous local authorities in the RDC. The pre-deal stage did not take long because both partners realized the potential of the alliance. Therefore, soon after the visit, the Vodacom Group decided to establish the joint venture and join forces with CWN. One of the main pull factors for the alliance was CWN's valid licence to operate in RDC (which cost no more than $2 million when it was obtained in 1997, when demand for the service was low (Games, 2004)), a distribution coverage through well-established dealers and sub-dealers involved in the sales of the products throughout the whole country, and an existing company with a large customer base. From CNN's perspective, the Vodacom Group had much-needed technology and know-how. Combining CNN access and knowledge of the local market with Vodacom's technology and know-how enabled the alliance to expand its network coverage significantly and increase its customer base.

Prior to entry, Vodacom Group conducted a thorough analysis of its partner's financial health (balance sheet, cash flow statement and P&L statement) and a legal due diligence process took place before Vodacom decided to buy 51 per cent of CWN shares. CWN did not contribute financially to the venture. Its contribution was limited to its customer base and the 18 years' remaining licence to operate in DRC. Although not publicly stated, our data provide evidence to suggest that CWN's non-financial resources, such as political resources, played a significant part in the negotiations.

The new firm, Vodacom Congo, benefited from synergy effects derived from the parent companies. The South African company, Vodacom, brought its high-end technology and financial resources, while the Congolese company, CWN, contributed with its well-trained local workforce and good knowledge of the market, and a well-established distribution network. Prior to the alliance, CWN was an operating telecommunications company with 20,000 customers. It was managed by Congolese staff who only knew the local languages (French, Swahili, Lingala and other dialects, which are among more than 400 dialects in the DRC). Most of the top management team had been educated in foreign colleges and universities but had limited experience working outside RDC. Once the alliance was formed, local managers were replaced by Vodacom managers, who were predominantly Afrikaners. Congolese technicians and engineers were sent to South Africa to attend training and courses provided by Vodacom Group to learn about Vodacom processes and use of new technology. Overall, the alliance was perceived as a successful venture; as one interviewee puts it, 'the acquisition seemed to have the right strategic fit ... we had the feeling that the rationale of this alliance was well thought through and both firms contributed to the enforcement of the new company strength. The existing local human resources were complemented by competent foreign experts in Information Technology, and this certainly created a competitive advantage.' Games (2004) reported that less than one month after starting operations the new company had over 50,000 customers, and five months thereafter its subscriber base had risen to 135,000 customers, growing at a rate of 1,200 new subscribers a day. Financial results were also very positive two years after the alliance was launched. The Return on Investment (ROI) was much higher than had been projected during the pre-alliance evaluation process. As stated by an interviewee, 'despite political turmoil the business success of this alliance has exceeded our expectations'. The network quality was vastly improved, and new products such as 3G, Data and other value added services have complemented the existing range of products offered by CWN before the alliance. As a result, the customer base increased from 22,000 in 2002 to 1.6 million in 2006 and to 2.6 million at the end of the 2007 financial year, making it the market leader in the RDC. Its market share rose significantly, representing a move from being number four GSM operator to number one with a market share of 51 per cent in 2008.

Interactions between South African and DRC managers

Perception of procedural (in)justice

The first shareholders' agreement in which Vodacom managers were solely responsible for the financial and operational management of the new entity planted the seeds for high perception of procedural injustice by Congolese managers. The decision-making structure provided Vodacom managers a near monopoly in all operational processes, taking responsibility for the whole management of this new venture, Vodacom Congo SPRL. Most key management positions, such as Managing Director (MD), Chief Financial Officer, Chief Information Technology Officer, Procurement Manager, and Information Systems Manager, had been exclusively assigned to Vodacom staff, who neither spoke French nor had any previous working experience in the DRC. Although the risk of procedural injustice perception was highlighted by Congolese staff during the pre-agreement evaluation and negotiation process, the issue was, as put by one interviewee, 'brushed aside' and all attention was focused purely on strategic and financial aspects. The allocation of decision-making powers made Congolese managers feel that their skills were not valued by their new organization, and they felt less valued by their team members. Congolese managers spoke of feelings of powerlessness and worthlessness and found it difficult to relate to their South African colleagues. Further, the decision-making structure meant that home country managers realized that their prospects of moving up the hierarchy were bleak. Congolese interviewees reported that most local managers were highly educated and had to take orders from what they believed to be 'less educated' South African superiors. Congolese managers reported that their South African counterparts, as put by one interviewee, did not only 'take undue credit for their work, but were given an undeserved position of power'.

Interestingly, despite the feeling of unfairness evidenced, Congolese managers did not resort to negative behaviours such as exiting the new organization or engaging in damaging behaviours such as disloyalty, reduction of efforts or acts of sabotage. On the contrary, our data suggest that Congolese managers used two mechanisms to redress the unfair distribution of power: use of voice by speaking up about their concerns in meetings and through formal channels of communication, and active action by refusing to obey 'wrong' instructions from South African superiors. The latter led, occasionally, to disciplinary hearings and dismissal on the basis of insubordination.

In 2007, a new agreement was signed by both firms. The new agreement provided a more equitable division of responsibility at top management level. South African managers and Congolese managers had a more balanced share of management responsibilities (see Figure 7.2). Now the new agreement started a process by which South African managers would be replaced by Congolese managers who were competent to perform the tasks originally held by South African managers. Data indicate that this agreement was driven by two factors. First, the new governance structure provided equitable access to opportunities and decision-making power and therefore, it was hoped, would lead to motivational effects among Congolese managers, which would subsequently enhance the commitment and morale of local managers. Second, providing Congolese managers with access to key managerial positions would help the strategic alliance to build up a unique pool of local talent that has better knowledge of the local market environment. As shown in Figure 7.2, under the new structure the South African shareholders, Vodacom Group (Pty) Ltd, kept the right to appoint the MD and CEO positions, while the Congolese shareholders, CWN, held the deputy MD and CFO positions. Interviewees reported that the new, more balanced distribution of power came just in time because the new company,

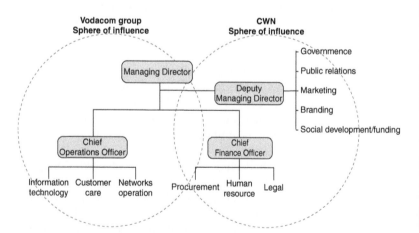

Figure 7.2 The new distribution of power
Source: Author analysis based on the new agreement.

Vodacom Congo, was, as one interviewee described it, 'on the verge of disaster'.

Understandably, and perhaps expectedly, our data suggest that Congolese staff in particular had positive attitudes towards the new arrangement 'since they saw more local staff involved in the decision-making of strategic and operational day-to-day activities'.

Further, the new structure resulted in a gradual replacement of most South African heads of department by Congolese staff. However, interviewees provided evidence to suggest that South African staff were less enthusiastic about the new structure. For instance, while according to the new structure CWN and Vodacom Group would share the responsibility and control of finance and the general administration of the organization, Vodacom managers refused to release the finance division and the deputy CEO posts to the Congolese managers. Interviewees reported that, in practice, the structure remained deeply unequal, in terms of the distribution of income and access to opportunities, particularly for Congolese line and lower-level managers, in part because their South African counterparts did not want to let go of their power. Interviewees spoke of the unwillingness of South African line managers to delegate decision-making power to their Congolese counterparts.

Perceptions of interactional (in)justice

Interviewees reported that top managers from both sides were able to work together effectively but cross-cultural clashes were evident at middle and lower management levels. As described by one interviewee, 'top management had joined their strength in a very friendly manner but the employees of both sides were more reluctant to work together because their (national) culture was not compatible'. Overall, there seemed to be a general consensus among Congolese staff that 'there was a serious degree of cultural incompatibility'. On several occasions, South African staff were criticized by local staff for their arrogance and disrespect. Congolese staff perceived South African managers to lack good manners in that they did not respect the formal dress code, nor did they address the local staff politely. One interviewee stated: 'They (South African managers) would work in their offices and meetings in T-shirts or short sleeved shirts'. Further, Congolese interviewees reported that South Africans made no effort to learn the official language of the country (French), nor did they sit with their Congolese colleagues at social functions. This was seen as a sign of disrespect towards their Congolese colleagues, as put by one interviewee: 'disrespect is evident in their talking, greeting, and constant swearing'. Congolese managers associated 'showing respect' with the way colleagues conduct themselves in terms of the language they use and the way they dress themselves. In contrast, South African managers put more emphasis on the 'task' rather than manners and personal conduct. From the South African perspective, using the Afrikaans language is more than a way of communicating – they use the language to reinforce their identity and identification of their group in a foreign culture. Interestingly, despite the animosity towards South Africa, Congolese managers did not show any reluctance to cooperate and work with their South African counterparts. To Congolese managers, the dark past of South Africa is a non-issue. However, our data suggest that both groupings perceived their espoused managerial values and norms as superior and resisted forsaking them for the sake of a harmonious working relationship.

The cross-cultural clashes illustrated above had a strong impact on the goodwill and understanding between the local and foreign managers. Most interviewees talked about a lack of mutual respect. In particular, Congolese managers felt that their South African counterparts were there to teach, but not open to learning from local managers. Interviewees also spoke about what they felt to be strong ethnocentric arrogance from some South African managers. From the Afrikaners' perspective, the cross-cultural clashes were no more than communication problems. Congolese managers, however, reported that communicating well with Afrikaners means accepting their terms and conditions.

Discussion and conclusion

We drew on extant research on interactions in international strategic alliances to examine procedural and interactive (in)justices in a strategic alliance between a South African MNE and a firm based in the DRC. The case study shows how the strong desire of Vodacom to expand into the RDC made the two partners rush to form the strategic alliance, but at the expense of taking time to know each other better and learn about the capabilities and culture of each partner. In line with past research, the present study shows that the difficulties of managing people in international strategic alliances are often underestimated compared with financial and technological issues (Schweiger and Weber, 1989; Weber, 1996; Pritchett et al., 1997; Light, 2001). This is because strategic and financial aspects are more visible and clearer to gauge, but those related to cultural differences between the companies involved are much more subtle and difficult to assess (Kitching, 1967; Leighton and Tod, 1969; Barret, 1973; Schweiger et al., 1993; Pritchett et al., 1997; Angwin, 2001).

These findings suggest that companies need to use the due diligence period to evaluate, not only the financial and strategic aspects of the alliance, but also the organizational and cultural alignment, management style and expectations between both organizations (Schweiger and Weber, 1989; Weber and Shenkar, 1996; Angwin, 2001; Light, 2001; Vermeulen and Barkema, 2001).

During the implementation stage of the alliance, the findings provided evidence of reluctance and unwillingness from the South African managers to change, or at least adapt, their deeply held beliefs, values and assumptions and ways of doing things. Past research advocates that a common pitfall that western multinationals seem to fall into in Africa is reluctance to adapt host country management practices to African culture and traditions.

This study of the strategic alliance between the CWN and South African Vodacom Group (Pty) Ltd shows that African firms make the same mistakes. This is because there is often a high level of conflict and misunderstanding when managers from two firms, both originating in developing countries, interact (Chang et al., 2009). . This perhaps explains why the South African MNE tried to impose its decision-making processes and procedures on its DRC partner, resulting in strong procedural injustice. The perceived procedural injustices exacerbated the difficulties in the working relationship between the two groupings. As a result, a significant number of local Congolese employees experienced feelings of antagonism, indignation and dislike for South African managers.

In addition to interactional injustice, the case analysis shows that interactional injustice, evidenced by poor quality of the interpersonal interaction between employees from the two organizations, created enormous post-agreement implementation difficulties. This finding challenges the argument that the ethnic diversity of South African management teams makes them well placed to manage effectively across cultures. On the contrary, the case study analysis shows that South African managers showed evidence of clannishness and a tendency to unequivocal decision-making power. Interestingly, animosities from the apartheid era did not affect working relationships between the two groupings. This finding challenges the viewpoint that past and recent conflicts and wars in Africa create considerable challenges for cooperation between African firms.

Eventually, Vodacom and CWN recognized the potential harm of perceived procedural injustice, and new management policies and structures were subsequently put in place in order to improve the alliance.

The new structure aimed to reduce disparities between South African and Congolese managers and level the playing field in terms of access to key managerial positions. This sought to bring previously marginalized Congolese managers into the driving seat of the alliance. Yet, despite some of the progress towards reducing procedural inequality in the alliance, the case study analysis indicates that at low and middle management levels marginalization of Congolese managers persisted. Interviewees described the new context as a move from an explicit prejudice to a more subtle and implicit one. At the top management level, however, data analysis indicates that managers from both cultures embraced the new structure and worked well together. There are two plausible explanations for this finding. First, top managers' commitment to the alliance's success transcends individual work values differences. As a result, managers from both parties may have suppressed their differences to facilitate the effective management of the alliance. Second, this may be evidence of convergence of managerial values and practices within the professional managerial class in Africa. Further, this finding underscores the importance of focusing on line and low-level managers in addition to top managers when examining interactions in international strategic alliances. The analysis indicates that, while top management team members from both partners were willing and able to work together, at lower levels there was a high incidence of cross-cultural clashes and conflicts. There was an absence of a reserve of goodwill and trust in each other's capability, particularly from South African lower managers, who seemed to have cultural blindness. As a result, as the alliance matured over the years, mistrust intensified and detachment between managers from the two firms became more visible.

The case study shows that, while management sought to address the disproportionate allocation of power to South African managers, who occupied the most powerful positions in the alliance, it overlooked the sources and consequences of perceived interactional injustice. Interactional injustice was given less prominence, perhaps because it is harder to address than procedural injustice. Interactional injustice is often too subtle to be noticed, and not tangible enough to be easily addressed. Furthermore, addressing interactional justice issues requires careful assessment of the causes of perception of injustice, takes considerable time because it deals with changes in behaviour, and is a gradual process requiring regular enforcement to create the will and desire for individuals to adapt their deeply etched norms and value systems to the sensitivities of working in a cross-cultural alliance. In contrast, as shown in the present study, procedural injustice was attended to relatively easily by changing decision-making processes and reallocating some of key management position within the alliance.

Importantly, however, the results show that the effectiveness of actions taken to address procedural injustice was circumscribed by the continued presence of perceived interactional injustice. The reshuffle of management position did not facilitate integration between the two groupings, nor did it lessen the sense of unfairness, especially at middle and lower management levels. The case study shows that, with the exception of top management teams, South African managers did not surrender their decision-making powers to local line managers. Rather, South African managers remained trapped in their own mindset, holding on to their ways of doing things, and lacked confidence in local managers' ability to manage the alliance. Therefore, we suggest that perceptions of injustices in strategic alliances cannot be dealt with in a piecemeal fashion. The different types of (un)justice in strategic alliance are interrelated and no single component can be dealt with in isolation. This underscores the importance of appreciating the interconnectedness between different types of justices in strategic alliances, an issue which has not been sufficiently highlighted in past research.

Our study is based on a single case study from two African countries. Considering the research design limitations, our findings and interpretations must be taken with caution. Further case studies from different parts of Africa are highly warranted. In addition, a survey of strategic alliances between African firms would provide a useful snapshot of the challenges facing cooperation between African firms.

References

Adams, S. J. (1965) 'Inequity in Social Change', in L. Berkowitz (Ed.) *Advances in Experimental Social Psychology* Vol. 2 (New York: Academic Press), 267–299.

Anakwe, P. U. (2002) 'Human Resource Management Practices in Nigeria: Challenges and Insights', *International Journal of Human Resource Management*, 19(4), 1042–1059.

Angwin, D. (2001) 'Mergers and Acquisitions across European Borders: National Perspectives on Preacquisition Due Diligence and the Use of Professional Advisors', *Journal of World Business*, 36(1), 32.

Ariño, A., J. de la Torre, and P. S. Ring (2001) 'Relational Quality: Managing Trust in Corporate Alliances', *California Management Review*, 44(1), 109–131.

Barret, P. (1973) *The Human Implications of Mergers and Takeovers* (London: Institute of Personnel Management).

Bies, R. J. (1986, August) 'Identifying Principles of Interactional Justice: The Case of Corporate Recruiting', in R. J. Bies (Chair) *Moving beyond Equity Theory: New Directions in Research on Justice in Organizations*. Symposium conducted at the meeting of the Academy of Management, Chicago.

Bies, R. J., and T. Tripp (1995) 'Beyond Distrust: "Getting Even" and the Need for Revenge', in R. Kramer and T. R. Tyler (Eds) *Trust in Organizations* (Newbury Park, CA: Sage), 246–260.

Blunt, P., and M. L. Jones (1992) *Managing Organisations in Africa* (New York: Walter de Gruyter).

Buono, A. F., J. L. Bowditch, and J. W. Lewis III (1985) 'When Cultures Collide: The Anatomy of a Merger', *Human Relations*, 38, 477–500.

Chang, Y. Y., K. Mellahi, and A. Wilkinson (2009) 'Control Mechanisms of HRM Practices by Taiwanese MNCs in the UK', *International Journal of Human Resource Management*, 20(1), 75–95.

Daniel, J., V. Naidoo, and S. Naidu (2003a) 'The South Africans Have Arrived: Post-Apartheid Corporate Expansion into Africa', in J. Daniel, A. Habib, and R. Southall (Eds) *State of the Nation: 2003–2004* (Cape Town: HSRC Press).

Daniel, J., V. Naidoo, and S. Naidu (2003b) 'Post-Apartheid South Africa's Corporate Expansion into Africa', *Traders: Africa Business Journal*, August-November, 15.

Danis, W., and A. Parkhe (2002) 'Hungarian-Western Partnerships: A Grounded Theoretical Model of Integration Processes and Outcomes', *Journal of International Business Studies*, 33, 423–455.

Eisenhardt, K. M., and M. E. Graebner (2007) 'Theory Building from Cases: Opportunities and Challenges', *Academy of Management Journal*, 50(1), 25–32.

Ellis, K., T. Reus, and B. Lamont (2009) 'The Effects of Procedural and Informational Justice in the Integration of Related Acquisitions', *Strategic Management Journal*, 30(2), 137–161.

Folger, R., and M. A. Konovsky (1989) 'Effects of Procedural and Distributive Justice on Reactions to Pay Raise Decisions', *Academy of Management Journal*, 32, 115–130.

Games, D. (2004) *The Experience of South African Firms Doing Business in Africa: A Preliminary Survey and Analysis*. South African Institute of International Affairs (SAIIA).

Ghebregiorgis, F., and L. Karsten (2006) 'Human Resource Management Practices in Eritrea: Challenges and Prospects', *Employee Relations*, 28, 144–163.

Goldstein, A., and W. Pritchard (2006) *South African Multinationals: South-South Co-Operation at Its Best? Doing Business in Africa* (Johannesburg: SAIIA).

Graebner, M. E., and K. M. Eisenhardt (2004) 'The Seller's Side of the Story: Acquisition as Courtship and Governance as Syndicate in Entrepreneurial Firms', *Administrative Science Quarterly*, 49(3), 366–403.

Greenberg, J. (1990) 'Organizational Justice: Yesterday, Today, Tomorrow', *Journal of Management*, 16, 399–432.

Hambrick, D. C., and A. A. Cannella (1993) 'Relative Standing: A Framework for Understanding Departures of Acquired Executives', *Academy of Management Journal*, 36, 733–762.

Heifetz, R. A., and D. L. Laurie (2001) 'The Work of Leadership', *Harvard Business Review*, 79(11), 131–141.

Horwitz, F. M., V. Browning, H. Jain, and J. N. Steenkamp (2002a) 'Human Resource Practices and Discrimination in South Africa: Overcoming the Apartheid Legacy', *International Journal of Human Resource Management*, 13(7), 1105–1118.

Horwitz, F. M., K. Kamoche, and I. K. H. Chew (2002b) 'Looking East: Diffusing High Performance Work Practices in Southern Afro-Asian Context', *International Journal of Human Resource Management*, 13(7), 1019–1041.

Johnson, J. P., M. A. Korsgaard, and H. J. Sapienza (2002) 'Perceived Fairness, Decision Control and Commitment in International Joint Venture Management Teams', *Strategic Management Journal*, 33, 1141–1160.

Kamoche, K. (1992) 'Human Resource Management: An Assessment of the Kenyan Case', *International Journal of Human Resource Management*, 3, 497–521.

Kamoche, K. (2002) 'Introduction: Human Resource Management in Africa', *International Journal of Human Resource Management*, 19(4), 993–997.

Kim, W. C., and R. Mauborgne (1993) 'Procedural Justice, Attitudes, and Subsidiary Top Management Compliance', *Academy of Management Journal*, 36, 502–526.

Kitching, J. (1967) 'Why Do Mergers Miscarry?' *Harvard Business Review*, 45(6), 84–101.

Klein, J. G., R. Ettenson, and M. D. Morris (1998) 'The Animosity Model of Foreign Product Purchase: An Empirical Test in the People's Republic of China', *Journal of Marketing*, 62, 89–100.

Konovsky, M. A. (2000) 'Understanding Procedural Justice and its Impact on Business Organizations', *Journal of Management*, 26, 489–511.

Korsgaard, A., D. M. Schweiger, and H. Sapienza (1995) 'Building Commitment, Attachment, and Trust in Strategic Decision-making Teams: The Role of Procedural Justice', *Academy of Management Journal*, 38, 60–84.

Leighton, C. M., and R. G. Tod (1969) 'After the Acquisition: Continuing Challenge', *Harvard Business Review*, 47(2), 90–102.

Leventhal, G. S., J. Karuza, and W. R. Fry (1980) 'Beyond Fairness: A Theory of Allocation Preferences', in G. Mikula (Ed.) *Justice and Social Interaction* (New York: Springer), 167–218.

Light, D. (2001) 'Who Goes, Who Stays?' *Harvard Business Review*, 1, 34–44.

Lodorfos, G., and A. Boateng (2006) 'The Role of Culture in the Merger and Acquisition Process: Evidence from the European Chemical Industry', *Management Decision*, 44(10), 1405–1421.

Luo, Y. (2005) 'How Important are Shared Perceptions of Procedural Justice in Cooperative Alliances?' *Academy of Management Journal*, 48, 695–709.

Luo, Y. (2007) 'The Independent and Interactive Roles of Procedural, Distributive and Interactional Justice in Strategic Alliances', *Academy of Management Journal*, 50(3), 644–664.

Luo, Y. (2009) 'Are We on the Same Page? Justice Disagreement in International Joint Ventures', *Journal of World Business*, 44, 383–396.

Luo, Y., and R. Tung (2007) 'International Expansion of Emerging Market Enterprises: A Springboard Perspective', *Journal of International Business Studies*, 38(4), 481–498.

Lyles, M. A., and E. J. Salk (1996) 'Knowledge Acquisition from Foreign Parents in International Joint Ventures: An Empirical Examination in the Hungarian Context', *Journal of International Business Studies*, 27(5), 877–903.

Meschi, P. (1997) 'Longevity and Cultural Differences of International Joint Ventures: Toward Time-Based Cultural Management', *Human Relations*, 50(2), 211–227.

Mikula, G., B. Petrik, and N. Tanzer (1990) 'What People Regard as Unjust: Types and Structures of Everyday Experiences of Injustice', *European Journal of Social Psychology*, 20, 133–149.

Miller, D. (2004) 'South African Multinational Corporations, NEPAD and Competing Spatial Claims on Post-Apartheid Southern Africa', *African Sociological Review*, 8(1), 176–202.

Miller, D. (2005) 'New Regional Imaginaries in Post-Apartheid Southern Africa: Retail Workers at a Shopping Mall in Zambia', *Journal of Southern African Studies*, 31(1), 117–145.

Miller, D. (2008) 'Retail Renaissance or Company Rhetoric: The Failed Partnership of a South African Corporation and Local Suppliers in Zambia', *LABOUR, Capital and Society*, 41(1), 34–55.

Mulaudzi, C. (2006) The Politics of Regionalism in Southern African, Institute for Global Dialogue. Occasional Paper No.15.

OECD. (2008) African Economic Outlook, Available at: http://www.oecd.org/dataoecd/13/39/40577125.pdf. Downloaded 20 September 2009.

Parkhe, A. (1991) 'Interfirm Diversity, Organizational Learning, and Longevity in Global Strategic Alliances', *Journal of International Business Studies*, 22(4), 579–601.

Pritchett, P., D. Robinson, and R. Clarkson (1997) *After the Merger: The Authoritative Guide for Integration Success* (Second ed.) (New York: McGraw-Hill).

Riad, S. (2007) 'Of Mergers and Cultures: What Happened to Shared Values and Joint Assumptions?' *Journal of Organizational Change Management*, 20(1), 26–43.

Schuler, R., S. Jackson, and Y. Luo (2003) *Managing Human Resources in Cross-Border Alliances* (London: Routledge).

Schweiger, D. M., N. C. Ernst, and N. K. Napier (1993) 'Implementing International Mergers and Acquisitions', *Human Resource Planning*, 16(1), 53–70.

Schweiger, D. M., and Y. Weber (1989) 'Strategies for Managing Human Resources during Mergers and Acquisitions: An Empirical Investigation', *Human Resource Planning*, 12(2), 69–86.

Sheppard, B. H., R. J. Lewicki, and J. W. Minton (1992) *Organizational Justice: The Search for Fairness in the Workplace* (New York: Lexington Books).

Thibaut, J., and L. Walker (1975) *Procedural Justice: A Psychological Analysis* (Hillsdale, NJ: Erlbaum).

Thomas, A., and M. Bendixen (2000) 'The Management Implications of Ethnicity in South Africa', *Journal of International Business Studies*, 31, 507–519.

Vale, P., and S. Maseko (1998) 'South Africa and African Renaissance', *International Affairs*, 72(4), 279.

Vermeulen, F., and H. Barkema (2001) 'Learning through Acquisitions', *Academy of Management Journal*, 44(3), 457–476.

Vodacom Interim Results (2006) www.vodacom.com accessed 6 March 2009.

Vogel, A. J., J. J. Van Vuuren, and S. M. Millard (2008) 'Preparation, Support and Training Requirements of South African Expatriates', *South African Journal of Business Management*, 39(3), 33–40.

Weber, Y. (1996) 'Corporate Cultural Fit and Performance in Mergers and Acquisitions', *Human Relations*, 49(9), 1181–1203.

Weber, Y., and O. Shenkar (1996) 'National and Corporate Cultural Fit in Mergers/Acquisitions: An Exploratory Study', *Management Science*, 42(8), 1215–1227.

Webster, E., and G. Wood (2005) 'Human Resource Management Practice and Institutional Constraints: The Case of Mozambique', *Employee Relations*, 27(4), 369–385.

Wöcke, A., M. Bendixen, and R. Rijamampianina (2007) 'Building Flexibility into Multi-National Human Resource Strategy: A Study of Four South African Multi-National Enterprises', *International Journal of Human Resource Management*, 18, 829–844.

Wöcke, A., and M. Sutherland (2008) 'The Impact of Employment Equity Regulations on Psychological Contracts in South Africa', *International Journal of Human Resource Management*, 19(4), 528–542.

Wood, G., and K. Mellahi (2001) 'HRM in South Africa', in P. Bhudwar and Y. Debrah (Eds) *HRM in Developing Countries* (New York: Routledge), 222–237.

Yin, R. (1993) *Applications of Case Study Research* (Thousand Oaks, CA: Sage).

8
Human Resource Strategies for Managing Back-Office Employees in Subsidiary Operations: The Case of Two Investment Multinational Banks in Tanzania

Aloysius Newenham-Kahindi

Introduction

For the last three decades, research in the area of international business studies has continued to examine the extent of management and organizational influences within multinational companies (MNCs) abroad.

Discussions have ranged from the effects of organizational 'convergence' and 'divergence' systems to 'isomorphism' in managing human resources (HR) (Powell and DiMaggio, 1991; McGaughey and DeCieri, 1999). More recently, the relevance of cross-cultural management interface in international business systems has been widely discussed in an effort to understand the nature of the relationship between MNCs and their local responsiveness towards their own subsidiaries (Horwitz et al., 2002; Kamoche et al., 2004; Bartlett and Beamish, 2011).

In response to this discussion, more emphasis continues to be placed on the importance of a sector in determining the nature of organizational capabilities for coordinating HR activities internationally, at either a convergent or a divergent level, or both (Dore, 2000; Rajan and Zingales, 2003; Evanoff et al., 2007; O'Sullivan, 2007). The banking sector, in particular, has been identified as representing high levels of internal coordination of network systems, knowledge transfer, standardized training and work practices, as well as greater interdependence and tight organizational structures in business operations (Weeks, 2004; Aran and Patel, 2006). According to Pond (2007), because the banking sector deals with customers' and shareholders' investment funds, it demands a careful process of organizing, regulating and monitoring its activities.

Banking is a complex and dynamic sector that emphasizes effectiveness, efficiency and calculability with flexibility and speed (Abolafia, 1996; Dore, 2000). With increased global business competitiveness and technological growth, banks with international business orientations are under pressure to carefully organize coordination and consolidate supervision of their worldwide operations by designing specific HRM strategies and organizational systems that have an international flavour in order to meet their clients' demands and enhance competitiveness (Volmer et al., 2007). Rugman and Verbeke (2003) explain how MNCs carefully coordinate the transfer of firm specific advantages (FSAs) between parent and affiliate. The relationship between the two entities determines the degree of the MNC's influence over its subsidiaries. The banking sector reflects the nature of an institutional and cultural influence in relation to subsidiary operations, as described by Harzing (2004). Essentially, the transfer of foreign management practices, through the deployment of a head office's expatriates, to a subsidiary operation may not necessarily line up with local cultural and institutional requirements during the transfer and implementation process (Dessler, 2001; Kamoche et al., 2004). This relationship is further influenced by the sector itself, which has highly regulated organizational and operational business systems that ultimately limit the capacity of a subsidiary to influence the corporate business strategies of its parent MNC (Ferner et al., 2001; Rugman and Verbeke, 2003).

Information and communication technology (ICT) is arguably the most powerful source of global convergence in organizational business operations (Drummond, 2002). ICT speaks a universal language that is capable of influencing internal organizational systems, standardizing activities, coordinating business operations efficiently and influencing the behaviour of those who perform the activities (Kunda, 1992). The application of technology has created a structural convergence in banking whereby work systems can be easily organized, systematically standardized and constantly monitored. Technology has placed new demands on organizational configurational systems, including the normalization of activities in organizations, instituting the power of regulation, coordination and discipline between front-office and back-office workers (see Wickham, 1997; Zuurmond, 2005), and the ability to integrate work systems into delivery operational systems (Sewell, 1998; Callaghan and Thompson, 2001).

Literature

In their study of the impact of technology on banking, Zuurmond (2005) and Evanoff et al. (2007) identified the nature of the business regulation systems within the sector, and the way that global MNC banks create an organizational configuration that categorizes two types of employees: front-office employees (or floor-broker investors) and back-office employees. This labour division represents a convergence of organizational structures with highly developed levels of functional networks (Kunda, 1992; Zuurmond, 2005). In each unit or section within an organizational structure, there would be various types of workers, from those who design and define work functions (i.e. front-office) to those who have little or no input into the designing role in the overall decision-making processes (i.e. back-office) (Drummond, 2002). Most banks with international business operations have front-office investors who handle the role of regional or international supervision, representing professionals with highly specialized skills (Drummond, 2002; Zuurmond, 2005). These individuals are often located at head offices and country head offices, and their role is to align service strategies that provide guidance and coordinate and monitor the activities performed by the subsidiaries' back-office employees. Often, back-office workers are located in subsidiary/affiliate offices, such as branch centres, and have only a limited role in the overall managerial decisions of their organizations. The use of various new forms of technology within the sector establishes the back-office employees as a group of workers who fulfil the 'standardization of functionality' within a highly functional hierarchy (Zuurmond, 2005). They represent an internal labour market relationship that helps to maintain an organizational coordination and efficiency system within the head office of an MNC (Weeks, 2004).

A study of Barings Bank in Singapore in 1995 illustrates the nature and behaviour of front-office employees. At the time of the study, Barings Bank represented a group of investment managers who were regarded as 'groupthink' (Drummond, 2002). The role of such a group is to coerce back-office employees to follow their 'intellectual judgements' on financial service activities (Zuurmond, 2005). Such a rationalized nature of the internal division of labour may significantly inhibit back-office employees from having access to necessary information from front-office investors. For instance, if there are malfeasance or financial irregularities and risk or fraud, back-office employees would have limited or no influence on the financial solutions to these issues.

Internationally, the banking sector has become subject to similar global financial regulation systems (Evanoff et al., 2007). Most international accounting reporting systems, as well as currency exchange controls, stock-market forces, the International Standards on Auditing (ISA), the International Chamber of Commerce and the World Trade Organization, show tendencies towards international convergence systems (Braithwaite and Drahos, 2000). Volmer et al. (2007) illustrate how Germany and the Eurozone in particular continue to be regulated by the International Financial Reporting Standards (IFRS). The regulation also includes the US–German Generally Accepted Accounting Principles (GAAP) that follow US financial business models. Traditionally, the US financial model tends to emphasize a dispersed network of shareholding, a high degree of institutional share ownership and tightly controlled stock-market systems, and many other international banks in developed and emerging markets have been inspired (Wickham, 1997; O'Sullivan, 2007) to follow this particular institutional system. National-institutional systems of banking in different countries have fallen under the dictates of corporate regulations and the guidance of the New York Stock Exchange (NYSE) and Wall Street – the largest financial regulators in the world (Braithwaite and Drahos, 2000) – and, to some extent, the London Stock Exchange (LSE) (Evanoff et al., 2007). The NYSE and Wall Street both have significant influence in the regulation of major foreign financial corporations (Dore, 2000; *Financial Times*, 29 January 2004, pp. 21–24). As such, countries are expected to provide financial disclosure to the NYSE and to Wall Street, and to the ISA, mainly because these institutions demand such disclosure and corporations must comply. The information above shows how the function and regulatory systems of global financial services exert an extensive effect on the internationalization of rules and compliance in the financial market system (Aran and Patel, 2006). They also have implications with respect to the standardization of business activities within MNC banks, the training of employees and the handling of HR tasks.

The specific purpose of this chapter is to examine how the two subject MNC banks carried out their international business strategies in order to effectively manage their organizational systems and relationship-building through the use of HRM strategies in the developing country of Tanzania. We examine the implications of these changes for the host nation and its people and for the investors (i.e. the two MNCs and their customers). Through this study, we gain an understanding of MNCs' HR strategies and the host nation's institutional ability to influence global banks with respect to employee relations issues in this particular sector.

HRM is specifically about gaining the employees' commitment and adaptability, and about standardizing employee contracts and wages (Storey et al., 1991). It involves selecting the best ways to manage people, their skills and knowledge through established rules, regulations, procedures and techniques (Kunda, 1992). From a Parsonian structural functionalist view of social systems, HRM is a movement in management practices and studies that attempts to impose control systems through supervision in order to achieve its functional goals of strategic integration, commitment, 'flexibility' or adaptability, and quality (Guest, 1991; Kunda, 1992). In order to explore these employee relations issues further, we examine the subject of HRM and its use within organizations as a tool for planning, designing and executing the daily management of people and work.

Flexibility is one of the most often applied facets of HRM practices in contemporary organizations. Flexibility is understood to involve numerical flexibility, implying achievement through the use of short-term or part-time workers; functional flexibility, implying achievement through the training of employees and the use of teamwork; and financial flexibility, such as that which has already been achieved through pay variation and individualized contracts (Atkinson, 1984). More specifically, numerical flexibility refers to a situation in which employees can be called in or let go, as dictated by the workload. This may mean hiring employees on flexible contracts, the most extreme form of which is the zero-hour contract, or the use of part-time work or outsourcing. Functional or task-oriented flexibility refers to a situation where employees are skilled enough to be able to switch jobs or move from task to task as required. For the employees, this may mean teamwork, ongoing training or a willingness to change work situations and skills on a periodic basis. Financial flexibility underpins the other two aspects of flexibility. For the employees, this may mean that the company practises a variety of payment methods, from non-standard or skills-based wages to individually negotiated salaries. The three aspects of flexibility may be seen in this way as being mutually supportive (Wickham, 1997).

With increasing internationalization of businesses, and particularly in MNCs, HRM has emphasized the importance of a firm's strategy, structure and choices. Some researchers have suggested the importance of balancing the economic need for integration with the pressure for local responses (Harzing, 2004). Scullen (2001) and Collings (2003) have argued for the importance of a 'fit' between corporate strategy, HR policies and the overall corporate culture. While global strategy is a significant determinant of an MNC's success, the role of HRM remains a challenge for firms operating abroad (Dicken, 2002). For example, training and developing HRM managers and expatriates for overseas responsibilities and developing truly transnational companies seem to be a challenge for many MNCs (Harzing, 2004). In their studies of MNCs and HRM in Africa, Kamoche et al. (2004) noted that there is a need for further research in order to strengthen the theoretical underpinning of HRM. They also identified a need to bring about more effective 'cross-cultural management' practices across nations. In studies of global MNCs in Africa and Asia, Horwitz (2000) and Horwitz et al. (2002) identified the importance of 'cross-vergence' in managing HRM practices. Despite the literature addressed above, HRM remains a critical area for empirical research on the international business strategies of MNCs.

An MNC's ability to transfer organizational systems and HRM strategies tends to be influenced by the 'bargaining power' of its headquarters and subsidiaries and by the institutional establishment of the host nations (Kostova and Roth, 2002). As far as the banking sector is concerned, MNCs have a strong influence on the transfer of headquarters' organizational practices since they use expatriates, who bring knowledge and HRM innovation systems of headquarters' practices to a given subsidiary (Harzing, 2004). The use of HRM functions, for example, in the areas of training systems and socialization in the workplace could be seen as the appropriate means by which to skilfully influence the transfer process and outcomes of an MNC's organizational and management practices, through either adaptability or persuasion. Expatriates can be regarded as 'human knowledge resources' (Kamoche, 2002) that use corporate socialization mechanisms to influence employee behaviour in the workplace. These are examples of multifarious transfer agents of isomorphism, and a source of direct behavioural control that is representative of the headquarters' interests (McGaughey and DeCieri, 1999).

Cultural and institutional perspectives can be considered as alternative ways of conceptualizing and capturing national-level characteristics of the host nation's environment (Kostova and Roth, 2002). Institutional perspectives often capture the extent of local influences on the organizational practices and the implementation of an MNC's HRM strategies. For example, local institutions may facilitate or constrain the MNC's influence. According to Ferner et al. (2001), strong local institutional effects may work as a counterforce against an MNC's transfer of organizational practices and HRM strategies, thus inhibiting subsidiaries from emulating their headquarters' effects. Weak subsidiary institutions may actually enhance the transfer and implementation of an MNC's behaviour into their workplace. When US MNCs go abroad, for example, they attempt to universalize many of their employment styles in other countries by concentrating on an employment system of non-union HRM, participative management, quality circles, worker innovation and organizational efficiency, thereby making unions unnecessary. They formalize and standardize work systems wherein relationships between workers and employers tend to focus on regular evaluation analysis, centralized reporting and flexible practices (Ferner et al., 2001, 2005). In the international banking sector, however, with its highly globalized systems and technology application, the institutional culture of a host nation may have little influence on management behaviour when it comes to the HR strategies exercised by MNCs.

As a developing country that is currently modernizing its economic and institutional systems following the collapse of African socialism (which, in Swahili, is called *Ujamaa*, meaning 'collectiveness') in the 1990s (Mapolu, 2000), Tanzania is an example of a local context under the influence of MNCs. Like most developing countries, the host nation suffers from many social issues, ranging from high unemployment and poverty to institutional weaknesses. Since 1995, the country has abandoned its command economic system, attempting instead to attract foreign direct investment (FDI) to create new opportunities for economic growth and employment. Investment in a variety of private sectors such as mining, tourism, fishing, banking and agriculture is seen as an alternative means by which to create employment and improve the welfare of Tanzania's citizens.

The rationale of the study

In the context of foreign subsidiaries, the banking sector has been selected as a case study for three very specific reasons. First, both the MNC banks in our study came to the country to provide financial services to a small niche of their foreign clients, that is, their original intention had nothing to do with offering financial services to the local public. The country is passing through a pattern of economic development that provides an interesting setting for exploring the way the organizational systems of MNC banks interact with and influence the host nation's context in order to mould HRM strategies in the MNCs' subsidiary business operations. Second, the sector appears to be a highly globalized industry. According to the academic literature reviewed, the sector uses highly standardized and compliance organizational systems across its range of operations. Compliance is a useful tool by which to understand the impact of the globalization process of a given MNC's HRM strategies and how back-office employees might, in turn, be influenced to adapt new values of work and learning in the host nation (Braithwaite and Drahos, 2000), thus offering them more opportunities. Third, in terms of social connectivity, the banking industry uses ICT and a highly digitized market system to handle large volumes of information and financial transactions across countries (Weeks, 2004). As such, we examine the way that ICT shapes work organizations and employee–employer relationships (Burawoy, 1979; Kunda, 1992) and the overall implications of ICT in a developing society. We focus here on the two MNC banks to see how they have systematically rationalized and internationalized their organizational systems (Zuurmond, 2005). We also examine their use of specific forms of technology to perform tasks, and their management of so-called HR best practices on to back-office employees to meet their potential customers.

Methods

The primary methods of data collection and analysis used in this chapter are qualitative. Observation, documents and semi-structured interviews with bank and branch representatives (such as front-office managers), expatriates from the two MNC banks and local employees contributed to the research material. Fieldwork and data collection were carried out between 2001 and 2002, and a subsequent follow-up was conducted in 2004 and 2006 on the three commercial cities of Arusha, Dar Es Salaam and Mwanza, and later in Mbeya, all in Tanzania (see Table 8.1). A total of 30 interviews with 47 subjects were collected: 22 from the American bank and 25 from the South African bank. The interviews took place at the country head offices in Dar Es Salaam and in the banks' branches, and lasted between 30 and 45 minutes. Our questions focused on issues pertaining to organizational structures, the functions of HRM strategies, the role of expatriates, branches and head offices, business strategies, and the corporate management systems in general.

To some degree, this chapter derives some of its inspiration from the proposal of grounded theory approach (Glaser and Strauss, 1967), in that the data are analysed in order to construct a social reality – in this case, from the participants' perspective – and generate ideas for future theoretical implications. The goal here is to provide an exploratory approach to the collection and analysis of qualitative data that aims to 'generate theory out of research data' (Strauss and Corbin, 1998). It follows the interests, leads and hunches that were uncovered during

Table 8.1   Case study subjects and their banking activities in Tanzania

Company	Business activity	Country of origin	Region of operation (branches)
American bank	Offshore mutual fund services: fund management, investment advice, credit cards, money transfer and foreign-currency trading	USA	Johannesburg (regional head office) Dar Es Salaam (country head office) Dar Es Salaam **Mwanza **Arusha
South African Bank	Offshore banking services: fund administration, corporate finance, asset management and custodial services/fund accounting	South Africa	Dar Es Salaam (country head office) Dar Es Salaam Mwanza *Mbeya Arusha

At the time of research: March 2002–2004. Since 2003, the American bank has closed two branches (**), and Standard bank has opened another branch (*).

the data collection process to determine the extent of convergences and divergences in the management of HRM strategies and internal organizational structures in the two MNC banks.

Observation was used to gain a real-life understanding of the interrelationships between action and social structure in the workplace (Glaser and Strauss, 1967). Interviews were conducted in English and those that were conducted in Swahili (a local language) were translated into English. Details of the interviews were recorded, either on tape or in the form of notes, and, like the observation notes, could be further reviewed for analysis. Recording data was based on those materials that were representative of and pertinent to the respondents' daily activities, place of work, and topics of concern. In the South African bank, some of the older employees felt uncomfortable about being interviewed by someone who was much younger than they were. Blunt (1990) and Kamoche (2002) note that in an African context respondents may feel uncomfortable with an overly formal approach, particularly when questioned by someone younger than themselves. Whenever a situation like this was encountered, a 'friendly approach' was developed in order to sustain a more flexible and relaxed conversation, thus allowing interviewees the freedom to provide data that might not otherwise have emerged.

We obtained secondary data from company websites and brochures that detailed the nature and business activities of the banks' investment in the country and provided excerpts, quotations and information about the two companies. The banks' literature helped the researcher to become aware of certain similarities and differences and also served to improve the quality of the research method, design and objectives by pointing the researcher in a specific direction. In analysing our data, a checking system was used to measure the consistency and validity of the research (Bryman, 2004), a technique that was intended to reduce the likelihood of the researcher being deceived by a respondent. The process involved cross-checking statements of fact against their context.

The two MNC banks

The American MNC is a global bank with a significant degree of internationalization. Our fieldwork data revealed that the bank was driven by global market demands from its potential customers, who operated MNCs in the mining and tourism sectors in Tanzania. The bank responded to the growing and various demands of its customers (see Table 8.1) who had invested in the newly liberalized country. At the time of our fieldwork, the American bank's customers were neither locals nor Tanzanian institutions, but, rather, a small niche of clients who had business relationships with the bank. Its customers came mainly from the US and other western countries, and the bank employed over 200 back-office workers across its three branches (see Table 8.2). However, since 2005, the bank has allowed a handful of local customers to hold accounts that contain a balance of over 10 million Tanzanian shillings (~US$850).

According to our interviews with the country head office in Dar Es Salaam, the bank's head office in Johannesburg deployed eight expatriates to engage in the overall training and auditing activities (see Table 8.2). The American bank's services were located in three main commercial cities (see Table 8.1). It employed hundreds of locals in all three cities, and it offered a variety of specialized financial services and products. As shown in Table 8.1, the bank was involved in electronic banking, as well as in the selling and purchasing of foreign exchange and the issuing and monitoring of credit card systems.

The bank's headquarters organized and managed its strategic business activities across nations (Rugman and Verbeke, 2003), including

Table 8.2 The two MNCs in Tanzania

Bank	Origin of the bank	Number of expatriates	Nationality of bank representatives and expatriates	Number of employees
American bank	USA	8	USA	250
South African bank	South Africa	15	South Africa and Namibia	450

Current at the time of research, March 2002–2004.

Tanzania. Core decision-making took place at the head office and was subsequently transferred across the bank's range of business operations. Management's mission statements clearly outlined the company's international role in providing top organizational and management strategies to its customers. The bank's strategic management policies also ensured that all HRM practices, culture and values corresponded with its overall corporate strategy of best practices (Scullen, 2001; Collings, 2003). The purpose of the headquarters' role in this sector was reported during interviews with bank representatives as being 'to maintain consistency, efficiency and institutional coercive influence of an MNC over its subsidiary activities'.

The South African bank is a regional bank found mainly in Africa and other emerging economies in Asia and Eastern Europe. It is one of the leading financial institutions in South Africa and in Africa as a whole, serving larger companies and investors in its home country and beyond. The bank came to invest in Tanzania in 1995. At the time of our fieldwork, the bank's entry was intended to provide financial services to a small niche of MNC customers in the mining, tourism and construction sectors, all from South Africa. Since 2005, however, tens of thousands of local middle-class customers with solid earning capabilities have also been allowed to hold accounts.

According to interviews with the country head office in Dar Es Salaam, the bank's head office deployed eight expatriates (see Table 8.2) to engage in the overall training and auditing activities. One bank representative put it this way:

> Due to the competitive nature of the banking industry, the role of expatriates from the head office is crucial for our business success and development. They have the necessary skills and know-how to run businesses.

Since 2002, the bank has provided retail banking and other electronic banking services to local customers and government institutions, and its operations in Tanzania have expanded from five branches to nine, employing hundreds of local workers in the process. The bank's long-term objective is to provide the best banking services in Tanzania and in Africa in general (see *Financial Times*, 5 December, 2003). Headquarters' influences were exerted in Tanzania in order to ensure that the corporate business focus at the branch level met the needs and interests of the bank's clients (Scullen, 2001; Collings, 2003).

Evidence of convergence

Interview reports by front-office managers in both banks suggested that headquarters played a key role in the implementation of HRM strategies and organizational systems. The country head office in Dar Es Salaam was largely responsible for implementing key decisions already made by the head office, such as those related to technological organizational systems, financial services and the hiring of management personnel. One representative put it in this way:

> The Regional Head Office has monthly global and regional [within Southern Africa] conference calls, referred to as human resource conferences, to facilitate greater flow of communication across the bank's country head office operations in Tanzania.

The idea of 'thrive for efficiency' was the main function of the headquarters–subsidiary relations (Kunda, 1992). A significant attempt was made by both banks to narrow the functionality of most jobs through rules, procedures and written regulations from the headquarters (Wickham, 1997). An organizational and convergence process in this sector showed the nature and effects of the financial services that the bank provided to its customers (see Table 8.1). The nested structures with interconnected operations reflected the organizational structure of the banks, conveying a social system in which work procedures and organizational processes were carefully organized in an interconnected structure (Powell and DiMaggio, 1991; McGaughey and DeCieri, 1999). The resulting power relations invoked an interrelationship network between headquarters and the subsidiary units in Tanzania (Braithwaite and Drahos, 2000).

The use of technological databases, communication between front-office investors and their headquarters, the transmission of financial information to customers, and changes in institutional financial structures were the major determinants of this sector's success in managing its work systems and HRM practices (Weeks, 2004). Our field study found that the work performed by back-office workers was highly standardized, automated and predictable because of technology (Kunda, 1992). Back-office workers had to follow a set of decision-making rules to ensure consistency with the directives of the front-office investors and corporate headquarters. As most local employees revealed during interviews:

> It has been clear to us that every single day of work, we regularly observe and perform routine tasks. We, as professional accountants, have our own accounting package where we have to meet the so-called 'delivery strategies' at different business hours. Since all of our routine accounting services use computers and other financial instruments, branch representatives are able to use their computers to monitor our activities. We are constantly damn well monitored because we have our secret passwords that we can't pass to anyone.

This phenomenon placed employees in a technology network system.

The application of ICT in both banks was socially constructed and shaped according to the 'dictates of the headquarters' (Evanoff et al., 2007). Interviews revealed evidence of the social construction system through the use of electronic monitoring in officiating 'passwords'. Passwords for back-office employees were officiated and monitored from headquarters and, to some extent, at the country head offices. Technology acted as a mechanism of observation, surveying and reporting that enabled the two banks to gain business efficiencies and the ability to guide their management practices and organizational behaviour (see Burawoy, 1979; Kunda, 1992; Zuurmond, 2005). Front-office managers in both banks reported:

> New technology had been put in place to provide institutional trades with automatic execution service for sales and buying of stocks from major financial centres, enabling them to quickly respond to any major financial fluctuations and ensure that their clients' investments were safe.

There was an emphasis on deploying expatriates from headquarters to perform local training, indicative of a deeper motivation to transmit international best practices (Collings, 2003). Expatriates brought with

Table 8.3 Similarities in organizational systems

Technology	Organizational systems
Application of technology in communication: i.e. use of Reuters and Bloomberg	Centralized system from the headquarters
Interconnected organizational system	Systematically organized work system, i.e. standardized work system, sitting arrangement and interconnected communication system
Application of modern electronic system	Introducing 'best practices' of HRM policies, i.e. to meet customers' and shareholders' interests
Technical use of expatriates in key areas, i.e. training, work socialization	Expatriates used to transfer corporate culture from the headquarters
Use of electronic database and passwords to monitor financial activities	Regular survey and report system to the head offices, i.e. use of passwords

them an array of cultural values and practices that would serve to integrate these best practices into the culture of the host society within the bank's subsidiary branches. Back-office employees were trained to ensure that headquarters' regulations were abreast of the industry's best practice norms (see Table 8.3).

Despite the power that automated machine procedures exerted over those who performed the daily tasks, there were also social structures in place for training purposes. A 'social demarcation' existed between front-office employees and back-office workers (Burawoy, 1979). The training opportunities that were provided to bank representatives and back-office employees were markedly different, however, mainly in terms of skill and responsibility. Those working in front-office jobs were perceived by local employees as 'actors'; they were specialized in their work, had a broader understanding of various tasks in the banks, and had more control over the work and various tasks performed by operational employees. Unlike back-office workers, front-office workers did not perform routine tasks (Zuurmond, 2005).

Since 2004, the deployment of expatriates has naturally declined. The roles of expatriates have gradually been taken on by local, experienced employees who have worked with the banks for long periods and who have adapted their workplace practices and attitudes from those of the

MNCs. Their roles and responsibilities, however, still represent those of back-office employees. While training guidelines are still controlled and monitored from headquarters, localization in this sector is nonetheless limited.

When it came to HR functions, both banks' business activities were driven by their clients' demands. Recruitment of back-office employees in both banks was done at the country head offices, not by the branches. Training then brought about the integration and value consensus that lead to employee work commitment (Zuurmond, 2005). ICT was found to systematically coordinate work systems across branches, which had significant influence on employees' work behaviour, especially when it came to tasks, meeting deadlines and delivering accuracy of information. As two employees revealed their experience:

> The work is interesting and we are learning lots of interesting stuff. Em, the nature of our work in the bank means that what we do is constantly checked. There is so-called surveillance software that monitors every activity we do. Even when we have our lunch or tea break in the canteen we are monitored. There is no escape from these surveillance machines.

> At the beginning we seemed not to care much about the presence of all these electronic cameras at work. The foreign managers kept saying they needed to protect their property from forgery, terrorism and crime. We never knew where the boundaries were. It came to our attention only when the bank representatives gave our first performance appraisal feedback at the end of the year. In the appraisal, each one of us came out expressing shock... It seemed they were monitoring our work and movements every day. They knew [the bank representatives] how often we came late to work, who was not working properly, who deserved disciplinary action, and who spent more time in the canteen watching CNN television programmes!

Both banks had resorted to mobile HRM training, whereby expatriates visited branches frequently to impart on-site organizational training (see Table 8.3). Since all customers were from either Europe and North America or South Africa, training in communication skills was essential. For instance, the American bank emphasized the importance of communicating with its customers in Tanzania and abroad using an American accent, which was perceived as the best practice by which to communicate efficiently with customers who might not understand local employees' accents. As two employees said in the interview:

I am a graduate of journalism and communication studies. Right from the day I started learning English, locals or foreign teachers taught me. But here, the foreign expatriates teach us to speak with an American accent. We are constantly told that when you have to deal with customer 'X' in Europe or America you need appropriate customer relations... [meaning an American accent], otherwise customers won't understand what you are talking about. It is absolutely ridiculous to have to adjust your voice when you enter the building.

I have just got married, and the manager told me that smiling at customers is the best gesture... he is a complete nutter... you wouldn't believe what they are imposing over here... how can I keep smiling at customers? People [reflecting] will think I am enticing men around me, something that goes completely against my culture.

Employees in the South African bank were not subject to such rules.

Within the banking sector, the host nation's influence on MNC banks was significantly limited, especially when it came to influencing the transfer of corporate business practices in branches. The host nation's institutional and social conditions and the demands of the customers in the mining, tourism and construction sectors enabled the banks to maintain consistency within their organizational structures and management strategies. The banks were governed by the global institutionalization of various stock exchanges and capital markets as 'dictated by international financial institutions' (Aran and Patel, 2006; Evanoff et al., 2007). This was necessary in order to 'consolidate financial practices' that followed international standards (Dore, 2000; O'Sullivan, 2007). Since both banks provided financial services to only a small niche of foreign customers, it was possible for them to remain confined within the same jurisdiction of international best standards, rather than being regulated by the host nation's institutional supervision.

Evidence of divergence

Both banks structured and centralized their organizational systems in order to transfer HRM and organizational strategies smoothly from their headquarters to the host nation. Strategies handed down in this way seemed to be the most powerful means of developing the competitive advantages needed to compete globally and to offer the best customer service to potential clients in Tanzania. Significant differences, however, in the HRM practices of the two banks occurred mainly in the area of social relations, as defined by the dynamic 'levels of cultural

Table 8.4   Differences in management practices

South African bank	American bank
Recruitment and selection	
Internal referral	No referrals
Experienced employees recruited	No experience needed (only recent graduates)
A mix of age and gender-specific	Age-specific: younger employees over 18 years old
Training	
Infrequent emphasis on training	Frequent training essential
English as a medium of workplace communication, and sometimes Swahili	Communication specific: with an American accent and flavour
Performance appraisal and rewards	
Team/group-based	Individual-based
Bonus made known to all	Privacy and individual bonus rewards
Promotion: age and gender-specific	Promotion: individual merit, competency
Trade unions	
Unions allowed in the workplace and in the membership	Non-union working environment and no membership outside work allowed
Team/group representative management system	Individualized HRM approach
Standard employment and more security	Unstable, flexible contracts, less job security

management practices' (Horwitz, 2000; Horwitz et al., 2002; Kamoche, 2002; Kamoche et al., 2004). In particular, differences emerged regarding the level of cultural influence systems in managing HRM and within the systematic practices of HRM functions, such as implemented by both banks (see Table 8.4).

The South African bank's employees would have had work experience before joining the bank. Their mindset and attitude towards corporate cultures of the bank would have been influenced to some degree by their previous employment. New recruits had to be over the age of 35 years old. As part of its recruitment and selection practices, the bank seemed fixed on recruiting through referral, which was illustrative of the overarching power of the organization. Due to the nature of new employees, training was reported as infrequent. In contrast, the American Bank's HR functions and practices sought to recruit recent graduates between

18 and 35 years old (see Table 8.4). The application of this policy was 'intended to *mould* new employees to the bank's ways and to build a labour force that was effectively at the bank's disposal' (see Kunda, 1992). This is illustrative of the bank's desire within the host nation to mould either inexperienced young graduates or experienced locals into its own 'art of discipline' (Burawoy, 1979).

Despite the fact that both banks claimed to be global and similar, they responded differently within the local context of Tanzania (Pugh and Hickson, 2002; Harzing, 2004). When it came to managing employees, each bank seemed to be more influenced by its deeply rooted beliefs in motivating employees. The American bank performance appraisal and incentives as perceived by local employees were more indicative of its management influences than simply of its managerial efficiency, as the bank claimed. The South African bank structured its HR practices according to the characteristics of a traditional system of patriarchy found in Tanzania, which is a common practice in many southern African societies (see Table 8.4). As some interviewees revealed:

> It is increasingly becoming the norm [though not exactly certain], that if you are in your late thirties and forties you stand in a far more suitable position for managers to promote you. No matter how skilful you are, it is not easy for those of us in our twenty-something to get promoted. When we meet the bank representatives individually for assessment, they say things like: 'well, we have to wait to see what the head office has to say about it'. We feel left out.

Promotion was another aspect of management practices that differed between the two banks. The American bank promoted its employees based on individual merit, experience and competence (see Table 8.4). This reflects the internationalization nature of contemporary western management practices (Kamoche et al., 2004) and the desire of the bank to recruit young employees from within a specific age category. As one bank representative in Arusha said:

> If you think how you are going to transform a society to innovation and enterprise mindset, these young men and women will tell you something special. They learn with great enthusiasm, and put everything they learn into practice. They are the future of this country. The best skills and knowledge we offer will be important for this society.

The South African bank, on the other hand, had a mixed age group of employees; however, age was certainly a determining factor when it came to promotion. In order to create positive social relations in the workplace, the older employees were promoted to team leadership positions. Other human relations differences in management practices relied on the ambience of working conditions and work flexibility (Atkinson, 1984; Scullen, 2001; Dicken, 2002). For example, the American bank promoted an individualistic working environment, and the resulting workplace atmosphere was decidedly tense.

On the issue of trade unions (TUs), the Tanzanian Ministry of Labour and Employment legislated the use of TUs only where a branch had a minimum number of employees (Mapolu, 2000). As such, the American bank followed Tanzanian employment laws in the workplace. The bank's business practices on TUs, however, led some local employees to perceive that the bank was not supportive of unions in branches. The South African bank did allow union membership among its employees in the workplace. The changes in TUs and labour movements in Tanzania, however, made it harder for locals to become TU members. The government did not allow TUs in a workplace where there were fewer than 100 employees, and it even deregistered unions that were smaller than this. Any form of collective bargaining was to be submitted to the Industrial Court System (ICS) for approval, with the ICS holding the power to overturn any form of collective agreement (Mapolu, 2000; Newenham-Kahindi, 2007). As such, the two banks had little difficulty in implementing their distinctive management models in order to run non-union workplaces. The American bank, for example, paid its employees particularly well, and the South African bank was able to institute a form of cooperation with its employees by creating standard employment conditions and a form of collective representation.

Our interviews with local employees found no trace of outright rejection of employers' demands by local employees. The locals accepted the nature of the MNC's HRM strategies, although certain elements of social relations did give them some discomfort. Given the nature of frequent training at the American bank, the young employees were pleased to be exposed to new forms of work and variable payment practices. Employees acknowledged the fact that the nature of their daily work was repetitious but also interesting.

Given the difficult conditions in the country's labour market, the employees greatly appreciated the level of wages and salaries they were receiving in the bank.

When it came to managing HRM practices, a cultural function (Atkinson, 1984; Collings, 2003) was found to exist in the South African bank's system of career development, that is, traditional social structures in Tanzania dictated that elders were considered for leadership roles over the younger workers. While they respected the cultural determinants of their society in theory, the young men and women who worked in the South African bank expressed negative responses towards the operation of these ideologies in practice.

Employees acknowledged the reality of technology in their daily work, with individuals expressing a degree of discomfort regarding the extent to which their work was affected by technology (Kunda, 1992). On the one hand, employees acknowledged that their exposure to new technology facilitated efficiency and learning opportunities within their working environment. On the other hand, the employees also felt that the same workplace technology significantly intruded upon their private lives, such as frequent surveillance at workplaces. Thus, both banks seemed to have the upper hand through the control functions of their organizational and work systems. Responses from back-office employees on a variety of issues (such as their work being repetitious and boring, or the fact that they were constantly monitored through electronic surveillance (Sewell, 1998; Drummond, 2002; Heiskanen and Hearn, 2004), or the fact that the organizational systems were systematically coordinated) show that these aspects were all broadly accepted as part of everyday life in such a working environment.

Conclusion

This chapter has examined the internal organizational systems and the practice of managing human resource strategies in multinational corporations in subsidiary operations in Tanzania. The aim of this chapter was to explore the way the organizational systems of MNC banks interacted with and influenced the host nation's environment in order to implement specific HRM strategies in the MNCs' subsidiary business operations. Also, the chapter set out to examine the extent of ICT influences on the design of work and employees' compliance behaviour in the workplace.

The research conducted in both banks revealed how the two MNCs transferred their head office organizational systems and HRM strategies into their subsidiary operations in Tanzania. Our data revealed the extent to which the banking sector was significantly influenced by the mix of global market forces, which drove the need for cross-border integration and coordination of activities. Another driver was found in the nature of the local customers and the host nation's efforts to influence their behaviour in managing human resource strategies.

Technology was found to have a significant influence on work coordination and the behaviour of front-office and back-office employees. In this regard, our research showed that both banks managed to highly centralize their organizational system through the use of ICT. Such a networked organizational structure enabled the convergence of organizational systems and the monitoring of financial activities and employees from the head offices. However, the divergences in both banks (with respect to the socialization processes and cultural functions with respect to HRM practices) revealed the limitation of the convergence view within the banking sector. Thus, the concept of the two MNCs representing international HRM and organizational best practices within the same sector seemed unachievable.

Future implications

The similarities and differences that we uncovered in both banks do have policy implications for Tanzania's institutions and its people. The country and its people have been forced to navigate through the challenges and opportunities of the globalization practices of the MNCs. The continuous presence of the two MNC banks in the country, and the presence of other MNCs in the country as well, is an indication that Tanzania should continue to attract MNCs and collaborate with them as key business partners to address its institutional problems of poverty, mismanagement, corruption and unemployment in order to rejuvenate the prospects of building a knowledge-based society and competent institutions in the midst of globalization. In doing so, Tanzania would stimulate innovative education and experience within its labour force (HR) and would be able to generate cross-cultural, interface-based ideas congruent with its local institutional environment.

Kamoche et al. (2004) pointed out that the African continent is increasingly becoming a new frontier of economic opportunities for investment. The new millennium has seen many African countries embarking on ambitious programs to attract FDI by liberalizing their institutional and business regulations, improving their investment climates and legal capacities, and providing a raft of incentives. MNCs have been quick to capitalize on improved infrastructure, free market conditions, democratic governance systems, and large availability of low-cost HR across the host nations in Africa (Horwitz, 2000). As these new opportunities arise, MNCs with business interests in Tanzania, in conjunction with several African countries, should embark on proactive initiatives and identification of potential resources, thereby advancing new ways of doing business with African institutions and their people.

Embracing elements of social local values along cross-cultural lines would transform mere collaboration between MNCs and African institutions into a substantive responsive and transformational engagement process (Newenham-Kahindi, 2007). Rather than persistently deploying international best practices, engagement of a cross-cultural nature would be needed in order to draw the MNCs into the local environmental context to address chronic social issues such as poverty and unemployment. These kinds of social challenges should not be allowed to continue, given the availability of resources, the untapped local HR, local entrepreneurial skills and innovation, and the capital that exists in many African countries. The New Partnership for Africa's Development (NEPAD), which was adopted in 2001, the economic regionalization of African countries (i.e. Southern African Development Community (SADC)), and the UN Global Compact (1999) that promotes sustainable business partnerships as development frameworks for the continent should all be seen as opportunities to promote business and technology investment in Africa.

References

Abolafia, M. T. (1996) *Making Markets: Opportunism and Restraint on Wall Street* (Boston, MA: Cambridge University Press).

Aran, H. and A. B. Patel (2006) 'Global Financial Market Revolution', in *The Future of Exchanges and Global Capital Markets* (New York: Palgrave Macmillan).

Atkinson, J. (1984) 'Manpower Strategies for Flexible Organizations', *Personnel Management*, 16 (8), 28–31.

Bartlett, C. and P. Beamish (2011) *Transnational Management: Text, Reading and Cases in Cross Border Management* (6th ed.) (London: McGraw-Hill).

Blunt, P. (1990) 'Recent Developments in Human Resource Management: The Good the Bad and the Ugly', *International Journal of Human Resource Management*, 1, 45–59.

Braithwaite, J. and P. Drahos (2000) *Global Business Regulations* (Boston, MA: Cambridge University Press).

Bryman, A. (2004) *Social Research Methods* (London: Oxford).

Burawoy, M. (1979) *Manufacturing Consent: Changes in the Labour Process under Monopoly Capitalism* (Chicago, IL: The University of Chicago Press).

Callaghan, G. and P. Thompson (2001) 'Edwards Revisited: Technical Control and Call-Centres', *Economic and Industrial Democracy*, 22 (1), 13–37.

Collings, D. (2003) 'Human Resource Development and Labour Market Practices in a US Multinational Subsidiary: The Impact of Global and Local Influence', *Journal of European Industrial Training*, 27 (2), 188–200.

Dessler, G. (2001) *A Framework for Human Resource Management* (2nd ed.) (New Jersey, PA: Prentice Hall).

Dicken, P. (2002) *Global Shift* (4th ed.) (London: Paul Chapman).

Dore, R. (2000) *Stock-market Capitalism: Welfare Capitalism, Japan and Germany versus Anglo-Saxons* (London: Oxford).

Drummond, H. (2002) 'Living in a Fool's Paradise: The Collapse of Barings' Bank', *Management Decision*, 40 (3), 232–238.

Evanoff, D., G. G. Kaufman, and J. R. LaBrosse (2007) *International Financial Instability: Global Banking and National Regulation* (New Jersey, PA: World Scientific).

Ferner, A., J. Quintanilla, and M. Varul (2001) 'Country-of-Origin Effects, Host-Country Effects, and the Management of HR in Multinationals: German Companies in Britain and Spain', *World of Business Journal*, 36 (3), 107–127.

Ferner, A., P. Almond, and T. Colling (2005) 'Institutional Theory and the Cross-National Transfer of Employment Policy: The Case of Workforce Diversity in the US Multinationals', *Journal of International Business Studies*, 36, 304–321.

Financial Times, 5 December 2003.

Financial Times, 29 January 2004.

Glaser, B. and A. Strauss (1967) *The Grounded Theory* (Chicago, IL: Aldine).

Guest, D. (1991) 'Personnel Management: The End of Orthodoxy?' *British Journal of Industrial Relations*, 29 (2), 149–175.

Harzing, A. (2004) 'Composing an International Staff', in J. Van Ruysseveldt, J. Van and A. Harzing (eds.) *International Human Resource Management* (London: Sage), 251–282.

Heiskanen, T. and J. Hearn (2004) *Information Society and the Workplace: Spaces, Boundaries and Agency* (London: Routledge).

Horwitz, F. (2000) '*Management in South Africa*', in M. Warner (ed.) *Management in Emergent Countries* (London: Thomson Learning), 214–227.

Horwitz, F., K. Kamoche, and I. K. H. Chew (2002) 'Human Resource Management in Africa', *International Journal of Human Resource Management*, 13 (7), 1019–1041.

Kamoche, K. (2002) 'Human Resource Management in Africa: Introduction', *International Journal of Human Resource Management*, 13 (7), 993–997.

Kamoche, K., Y. Debrah, F. Horwitz, and G. N. Muuka (2004) *Managing Human Resources in Africa* (London: Routledge).

Kostova, T. and K. Roth (2002) 'Adoption of an Organizational Practice by Subsidiaries of Multinational Corporations: Institutional and Relations Effects', *Academy of Management Journal*, 45 (1), 215–233.

Kunda, G. (1992) *Engineering Culture: Control and Commitment in a High-Tech Corporation* (New Jersey, PA: Temple University Press).

Mapolu, R. (2000) *Poverty and Economy in Tanzania*. Institute of development studies paper series. UDSM, Dar Es Salaam: University of Dar Es Salaam.

McGaughey, S. L. and H. DeCieri (1999) 'Reassessment of Convergence and Divergence Dynamics: Implications for International Human Resource Management', *International Journal of Human Resource Management*, 10 (2), 235–250.

Newenham-Kahindi, A. (2007) 'The Impact of Global Business Models in a Developing Country: The Case of Human Resource Management in Two Multinational Banks Operating in Tanzania', Unpublished PhD Dissertation. TCD, Dublin: University of Dublin, Ireland.

O'Sullivan, M. (2007) 'Acting out Institutional Change: Understanding the Recent Transformation of the French Financial System', *Socio-Economic Review*, 5 (3), 398–436.

Pond, K. (2007) *Retail Banking* (London: Fitzroy House).

Powell, W. W. and P. J. DiMaggio (1991) *The New Institutionalism within Organizational Analysis* (Chicago, IL: University of Chicago Press).

Pugh, D. S. and D. J. Hickson (2002) *Managing across Cultures: Issues and Perspectives* (London: Sage).

Rajan, R. G. and L. Zingales (2003) 'The Great Reversals: The Politics of Financial Development in the Twentieth Century', *Journal of Financial Econometrics*, 69, 5–45.

Rugman, A. M. and A. Verbeke (2003) 'Extending the Theory of the Multinational Enterprises: Internationalization and Strategic Management Perspectives', *Journal of International Business Studies*, 34, 125–137.

Scullen, H. (2001) 'International Human Resource Management', in J. Storey (ed.) *Human Resource Management* (London: International Thompson).

Sewell, G. (1998) 'The Discipline of Teams: The Control of Team-Based Industrial Work through Electronic and Peer Surveillance', *Administrative Science Quarterly*, 43, 397–428.

Storey, J., L. Okazaki-Ward, and I. Gow (1991) 'Managerial Careers and Management Development: A Comparative Analysis of Britain and Japan', *Human Resource Management Journal*, 1 (3), 33–58.

Strauss, A. and J. M. Corbin (1998) *Basics of Qualitative Research: Techniques and Procedures for Developing Grounded Theory* (Thousand Oaks, CA: Sage).

UN Global Compact (1999). http://www.oecd.org/daf/inv/mne/34873731.pdf, accessed 7 February 2008.

Volmer, B. P., J. R. Werner, and J. Zimmermann (2007) 'New Governance Modes for Germany's Financial Reporting System: Another Retreat of the Host State?' *Socio-Economic Review*, 5 (3), 437–465.

Weeks, J. (2004) *Unpopular Culture: The Rituals of Complaint in a British Bank* (Chicago, IL: The University of Chicago Press).

Wickham, J. (1997) 'The Search for Competitiveness and its Implications for Employment', *Fifth IIRA European Regional Industrial Relations Congress*, Ireland: Dublin, 26–29 August (Dublin: Oak Tree Press).

Zuurmond, A. (2005) 'Organizational Transformation through the Internet', *Journal of Public Policy*, 25 (1), 133–148.

Index

Note: Page references to figures are indicated by an "*f*"; to tables by a "*t*".

Access Bank, 25, 27, 38–9
  merger, 38–9
African humanism, 11, 131, 139
Afro-Asian nexus
  contingency approach, 130,
    147–8
  cross-cultural diffusion, 130
  cultural context and HR practice,
    132–5
  diffusion patterns, 140–6
  diversity, 140–6
  emerging market MNCs, 126–7
  HRM framework, 129–30
  HRM process implementation,
    139–40
  indigenous thought, 130–2
  qualitative approach, 129
  six-factor typology, 129, 131*t*–2*t*
  socio-economic development,
    127–9
  talent management, 140–6
  typology, 147–9
American bank, 11, 209–12, 216–20
  customers, 211
  HR functions and practices, 218
  management practices, 218*t*
  monitoring of credit card systems,
    211
  performance appraisal and rewards,
    218*t*, 219
  promotion, 219
  recruitment and selection, 218*t*
  services, 211
  strategic management policies, 212
  trade unions, 218*t*
  training, 218*t*
American values, 117–18
Angola
  Chinese investment, 133, 137
  mining MNEs, 160

policy-level talks, 128
rapid economic growth, 127
antiretroviral therapy, 55
apartheid era, 181, 185, 195
appraisal and reward systems, 102,
  218*t*, 219
appropriation regime, 97–100, 114,
  118–19, 121
ART, *see* antiretroviral therapy
automated machine procedures,
  215
axial coding, 78

back-office employees, 202–23
  activities performed by, 204
  behaviour of, 222
  financial irregularities and, 204
  HRM strategies, 209
  internal labor division, 204
  passwords for, 214
  recruitment of, 216
  roles and responsibilities, 216
  training, 215
Bamboo Network, 156
banking regulation, nature of, 204
bargaining power, 207
bargaining rights, 83, 86
Barings Bank, 204
Bell Equipment, 137
Black Economic Empowerment (BEE),
  134
boundary-spanning activities, 67
Brazil, Russia, India, China and South
  Africa, 126–7, 141, 158
bribery, 2
BRICS, *see* Brazil, Russia, India, China
  and South Africa
budgetary cutbacks, 87
bureaucratic systems, 102
Bureau of Standards, 81

business competitiveness, 158, 203
business sustainability, hybrid model,
    175

capital utilization, 87
case study methodology, 160–1
CBN, *see* Central Bank of Nigeria
CCTV surveillance, 112
Celtel, 187
Central Bank of Nigeria, 18, 22, 27,
    31, 45
China
    debt forgiveness, 128
    exploration of energy development,
        128
    FDI, 128
    interest in Africa's raw materials,
        128
    investment, 3, 127, 137
    managerial practices, 138
    merit-based recruitment, 138
Chinese Quanxi, 139
Citibank, 11, 104–20
    Americanization of workplace,
        105–7
    appraisal system, 110
    bonuses, 106
    career development, 118
    compliance, 115
    dress code, 105
    employees evaluation, 110
    focus on American culture, 115
    hierarchical structure, 107
    HR practices, 116
    identity, 105–7
    implications of work specialization,
        113
    inculcation of fitness consciousness,
        120
    knowledge appropriation, 108, 119
    organizational setting, 105–7
    over-specialization, 113
    promotion and training., 116
    recreational activities, 106
    reliance on individual performance,
        110
    resource centres, 106
    security checks, 105
    structural rigidity, 110

    training, 118
    workplace environment, 105
CIVET, *see* Colombia, Indonesia,
    Vietnam, Egypt, Turkey
civil war, 73, 75–6, 185
class mobility, 147
collaboration techniques, 161
collective effort of creating productive
    knowledge, 99
collective solidarity, 130–1
Colombia, Indonesia, Vietnam, Egypt,
    Turkey, 126, 141, 146
colonial agricultural companies, 79
colonial rule, 73, 75, 85
communication theory, 45
community-based volunteer activities,
    166
community development projects,
    171
community workshops, 173
competitive strategies, 100, 160
conflict resolution strategies, 10
Confucianism, 130–2, 139
Congo Chine, 187
Congolese Company Act, 186
Congolese Wireless Networks, 186–7,
    189–90, 192–3, 195
contingency approach, 147–8
    class mobility, 147
    cross-cultural and contingency
        features, 147
    racial and ethnic disparities, 147
convergence, 1, 6, 11, 46, 48, 129,
    132–3, 135, 137, 139, 147, 156,
    176, 196, 202–5, 213, 222
    –divergence debate, 6
    evidence of, 213–17
    of organizational systems, 222
    thesis, 132
corporate business practices, 217
corporate culture, 11, 33, 36, 38,
    97–100, 106, 108–9, 119, 139,
    175, 206, 215, 218
corporate governance, 4, 5, 18, 156,
    164, 188
    Africa–Europe model, 5
    in banking industry, 18
    industrial relations and, 5
    restructurings in, 156

corporate social responsibility, 4, 61,
    152–7, 160–8, 172–7
  challenges, 154
  convergence of global best practices,
    176
  formulation and implementation,
    161
  giving back ideology, 153
  global convergence model, 156
  global practices, 175
  implementation process, 161, 176
  importance of localizing initiatives,
    154
  initiatives, 154, 160–1, 163, 176
  initiative strategies, 156
  mobilize activities, 167
  nature of implementation, 161
  partnership approach, 154
  policies, 166
  relevance of, 153
  sectoral interaction, 167
  sense-making initiatives, 176
  stakeholder legitimacy, 176
  stakeholders engagement, 157
  standard practices, 175
  sustainable partnership, 155
  taken-for-granted standards of
    conduct, 155
corporate socialization mechanisms,
    207
corporate strategy, 100, 206, 212
corruption, 2–3, 128, 173, 188, 222
cross-case comparisons, 26
cross-convergence, 87
cross-cultural alliance, working
    sensitivities, 196
cross-cultural analysis, 132
cross-cultural interactions, 180, 182
cross-cultural management, 100, 174,
    177, 184, 207
cross-cultural management interface,
    202
cross-cultural misunderstanding, 181
cross-cultural strife, 181
cross-cultural variation in the labour
    market, 146
cross-culture management, 177
cross-relationship approach, 9
cross-sector partnerships, 171

crossvergence
  importance of, 101, 207
  notion of, 3, 7
CSR, *see* corporate social responsibility
cultural conflict, 115–18
  American values, 117–18
  inappropriate values, 115–16
cultural differences
  handling, 43
  quality of management, 45
cultural distance, 45, 135
cultural homogeneity, 115, 184
cultural sensitivity, 100, 138, 183
currency exchange controls, 205
CWN, *see* Congolese Wireless
    Networks

data analysis, 59, 78, 163, 196
data collection, 188–9
  case study, 188
  convergences and divergences, 210
  documents, 209
  face-to-face interview, 189
  fieldwork and, 209
  interviews, 210
  observation, 209–10
  primary methods of, 209
  semi-structured interview, 189, 209
decent work, notion of, 138
delivery strategies, 214
democratic governance, 222
Democratic Republic of Congo (DRC),
    80, 181
Diamond Bank, 25, 27, 38, 44
  merger, 27, 38
direct worker control, 76
dispute resolution, 149
distribution of power, 192*f*, 192
divergence, evidence of, 217–21
diversity management, 85, 134
drop-in centres, 166
due diligence, 10, 18–20, 28–9, 34, 43,
    47, 189, 195
  consequences for, 28
  cultural, 10, 18
  financial, 20
  formalized process, 29
  HRM, 20, 28–9, 43, 47
  importance of, 43

legal, 189
pre-acquisition, 34
pre-merger, 28, 43
quality, 43

Econlit (online database), 26
economic reforms, 138
economic uncertainty, 187
The Economist, 3, 127, 140, 150
efficient rationalism, 58
Egon Zehnder International, 20
electronic cameras, 102, 112, 216
electronic control system, 101–2
electronic monitoring, 109, 112, 214
electronic panopticism, 108
electronic surveillance, 101–3
  electronic control system, 102
  electronic monitoring, 102
  hierarchical surveillance, 102
employee rights, 103
employer federation, 77
employment equity, 86–7, 134, 136,
  146
Employment Equity Act, 55
employment equity legislation, 134
employment level, rise in, 74
employment relations
  central feature of, 73
  equity issue, 73
  insecure, 74
  recruitment, 73
  reduction in employees, 75
  remuneration, 73
  retention, 73
  short-term, 74
  study, 73
entrepreneurial development, 148
environmental degradation, 153, 168,
  171
Equal Employment Opportunity, 53
Equatorial Trust Bank, 28
ETB, *see* Equatorial Trust Bank
ethnic disparities, 133, 147
ethnocentricity, 98, 101, 119, 122
Exarro Resources, 126
exploratory research approach, 104

FCMB, *see* First City Monument Bank
FDI, *see* foreign direct investment

Fidelity Bank, 29–30, 40, 44
Fidelity Bank, merger, 29, 40
financial and motivational
  techniques, 115
financial flexibility, 206
financial irregularities, 204
FinBank, 26–7, 29, 31–4, 43–5
FinBank, communication, 31
First Bank, 26, 30, 32
First City Monument Bank, 28, 39
foreign direct investment, 3–7, 85, 99,
  126, 159, 208
  ambitious programs, 222
  benefits of, 6
  employment generation, 6
  influx of, 103
  resource-seeking investment, 5
foreign management practices,
  transfer of, 203
Foucauldian normalization, 101–3
Foucauldian subjection, 99, 118
Foucault's social theory, 121
Foundation of Civil Society, 173
free market, 159, 222
front-office employees, 204, 215
functional flexibility, 206
functional hierarchy, 204
functionality, standardization of, 204

giving back philanthropy, 153
glasnost effect, 147
global competitiveness, 128, 148
global financial regulation, 205
Global Fund to Fight AIDS, 55
global mining MNEs, 160, 170, 177
global network of subsidiaries, 7
Global System for Mobile
  Communications, 187
governance, hybrid form of, 154
gross national product (GNP), 126
groupthink, 204
GSM, *see* Global System for Mobile
  Communications
GTBank, *see* Guaranty Trust Bank Plc
guanxi networks, 130, 137
Guaranty Trust Bank Plc, 27

Habib Bank, 27, 33
Habitat for Humanity, 167

Haier, 126
hegemonic organization of work, 102
hierarchical coding, 78
hierarchical power relation, 102
hierarchical surveillance, 102
HIV/AIDS at workplace
  advocacy skills, 68
  antiretroviral therapy (ART), 55
  company-sponsored AIDS
    education, 69
  conflict management, 68
  data analysis, 59–60
  descriptive statistics, 63t
  economic impact, 54
  external factors, 56
  formal policies, 60
  hindering factors, 62–5
  HIV education programmes, 54
  HR/OHS participation, 62, 65
  impact at, 54
  incidence of, 53
  institutional frameworks, 55, 57
  internal perspectives, 57–9
  legislations, 55
  Malawi Business Coalition against
    AIDS, 54
  managers and HR practitioners,
    68–9
  multiple regression analysis, 64t
  National AIDS Commission (NAC),
    55
  non-adoption of policy, 65–7
  organizational response, 54–5
  practical implications of
    campaigning, 68
  regression analysis, 66
  resource-based theory, 57–8
  resource dependence, 57–8
  risk profiles of employees, 69
  social skills, 68
  target populations, 61t
  technical issues, 68
  theoretical perspectives, 56
  top management role, 67
HR practices, 132–5
  adoption of best global practice,
    133, 137
  class mobility, 133
  conflict resolution, 134

  cross-cultural convergence, 133, 137
  cultural ethnocentrism, 134
  diffusion pattern, 140–6
  diversity, 140–6
  diversity management, 134
  ethnic disparity, 133
  generic, 47
  historical disparity, 133
  hybrid forms of, 133
  managerial styles, 134
  merit promotion, 132, 136
  and national culture, 133
  organizational culture, 133
  performance-related pay, 132, 136
  post-instrumental model, 133
  process implementation, 139–40
  racial disparity, 133
  standardization of, 104
  talent management, 140–6
human capital, 132, 137
human knowledge resources, 207
human relations, idea of, 8
hybridization, 1, 87
Hyundai, 126, 139

IBTC, *see* Investment Bank Trust and
  Company
ICS, *see* Industrial Court System
ICT, *see* Information and
  communication technology
identity creation, forms of, 106
IFRS, *see* International Financial
  Reporting Standards
IMF, *see* International Monetary Fund
impact assessment, 170
inclusive engagement platform,
  9, 153
Indaba, 109, 115–16, 133–4, 156–68,
  173–4
India
  import–export businesses, 79
  investment by, 3, 5, 127
  managerial practices, 138
indigenous governance, 87
indigenous workers, 83, 85
Industrial Court System, 220
industrialized North, 149

Information and communication
technology
  application of, 214
  attributes of, 102
  complexity of, 102
  global convergence, 203
  implications of, 209
  key posts, 106
  operation and power of, 111
  source of global convergence, 203
  use of, 101–2, 122, 222
Infosys, 126
institutional complexities, 157, 159
institutional dependency, 160
institutional framework for
  employment relations, 132
institutionalization systems, key
  features of, 165*t*
institutional regulatory, 158
institutional theory, 7, 56–8, 152, 155,
  158, 176
institutional transformation, 156, 159
integration approaches, 32–40
integrative corporate partnership, 169
intellectual judgements on financial
  service, 204
interactional injustice
  case analysis, 195
  perceptions of, 193–4
    cross-cultural clashes, 193–4
    cultural incompatibility, 193
interactional justice, 180, 183–5, 196
  antecedents and determinants of,
    181
  conflict and misunderstanding, 184
  cross-cultural training, 184
interactive communication, 30
intercultural communication, 9
intercultural values, 165
internal labour market, 101
international accounting reporting,
  205
International Chamber of Commerce,
  205
International Financial Reporting
  Standards, 205
International Labor Organization, 138
International Monetary Fund, 2, 72,
  75–6, 78, 81, 86, 103, 149

International Standards on Auditing,
  205
international strategic alliances, 182–3
  actual (in)justices, 182
  cross-cultural clashes, 182
  distributive (in)justice, 182
  distributive justice, 182–3
  interactional (in)justice, 182
  interactional justice, 183
  procedural (in)justice, 182
  procedural justice, 183
interpersonal conflicts, 181, 185
interview methodology, 161–3
Investment Act, 159
Investment Bank Trust and Company,
  32–4, 41, 45
ISA, *see* International Standards on
  Auditing
isolation mechanism, 112
isomorphism, 202

job evaluation, 137
job security, 83–4
joint venture partners, 137–8
Jugaard, 156
just-in-time methods, 137

Khumba Resources, 128, 139
knowledge appropriation, 11, 97–101,
  104–6, 108, 111, 118–22
  design of, 121
  employment relation, 99
  extent of, 111–15
  impact of, 111–15
  institutional configurations,
    101
  strengthening of banks, 122
  through HR functions, 108–11
knowledge creation, 99
knowledge protection, 112
knowledge spillover, 6–7
knowledge transfer, 7, 21, 99, 118,
  120, 202
  importance of, 98
knowledge utilization, 99

labour legislation, 121, 184
Labour Relations Act, 55

Lake Victoria Zone, 11, 160–1, 164,
      166, 168, 170, 173
   social and ecological problems,
      173
   stakeholders demands, 173
language, 9–10
leadership, 8
learning curve, 46
Liberia, 88
Likert scale, 59
Lion Bank, 27, 38
local cultures, erosion of, 122
local-for-local innovation, 164
local legitimacy, 177
London Stock Exchange (LSE),
   205

M&A, *see* mergers and acquisition
Malawi Business Coalition against
   AIDS (MBCA), 54–5, 60
Malawi Confederation of Chambers of
   Commerce and Industry
   (MCCCI), 54
managerial implications, 121
marginalization of identity, 122
market complexity, 137–8
market economy, 103, 159
market reforms, 75
measure of resilience, 127
Medical Schemes Act, 55
mergers and acquisition, 10, 17–22,
      26–9, 40, 43, 45–8
   assimilation, 21
   challenges from, 17
   consolidated banks and acquisition,
      23t–4t
   cross-border, 149
   cross-sectional approach, 22
   employee uncertainty, 20
   financial due diligence, 20
   HRM issues, 19–20, 22
   HRM practices, 41t, 42t
   integration approaches, 21, 32–40
   leadership styles, 20
   learning theory, 46
   merger rationale, 27
   Nigerian banking industry, 18
   novation, 21
   operational alignment, 45

phases identification, 19
post-acquisition phase, 18–22, 47
post-merger phase, 32–40
   assimilation, 36
   cultural differences, 33, 35
   HRM practices and policies, 39
   IBTC–Chartered merger, 34
   novation, 35
   regional difference, 34
   soft landing, 38
   structural integration, 33
pre-deal stage, 18
pre-merger phase, 19–20, 27–32
   communication management,
      29–32
   cultural differences, 29
   HRM due diligence, 28–9
   partner selection, 27–8
regional differences, 47
research on, 17
resource redeployment, 27
role of external influencers, 46
structural integration, 21
time horizons, 20
migrancy, 146
mining company, 161, 167–8
   stakeholder interaction, 168
mismanagement, 79, 173, 188, 222
Mittal Steel, 138
MNC best practices, critique of, 118
MNC management, centralized, 118
Mobile Telephone Networks, 135,
   186
mobile telephony, 3
Mozambique
   challenges, 76
   collapse of industry, 76
   currency devaluation, 78
   democratic elections, 76
   economic growth, 76
   employment conditions, 77–9
   employment equity, 84–7
   employment relations, 86t
   export earnings, 76
   HIV population, 76
   job security, 83–4
   loan reliant, 77
   non-compliance with employment
      law, 82

ports and railways company, 80
poverty, 76
price liberalization, 78
privatization impacts, 77–9
public sector employment, 81–7
remuneration, 84
socialist economy, 76
sugar and textile industries, 79
tourism, 76
unionization, 81–3
MTN, *see* Mobile Telephone Networks
multinationals, 5–7
multiple regression analysis, 64*t*
Murray and Roberts, 128, 139

NAC, *see* National AIDS Commission
Nampak Management Services, 137
Nando's International, 135
Naspers, 126, 128, 139, 149
National AIDS Commission, 55
National Civil Service Union, 82
National HIV/AIDS Strategic
    Framework, 55
National Investment Centre, 163
neo-liberal market system, 104
nepotism, 2, 188
New Partnership for Africa's
    Development (NEPAD), 223
New York Stock Exchange, 205
Nigerian banking consolidation, *see*
    mergers and acquisition
Nigerian banks
  good-quality communication, 44
  performance appraisal system, 40
  retirement policy, 40
  staff handling, 40
non-probability sampling method,
    24
normalization, manifestation of,
    101
normalizing gaze, power of, 120
novation, 21, 32, 35–6
NVivo, 78
NYSE, *see* New York Stock Exchange

Occupational, Health and Safety
    (OHS), 58
online databases, 26
on-site organizational training, 216

open system school, 56
organisational capacity for change,
    138
organizational and cultural alignment,
    195
organizational capabilities, 169, 202
organizational commitment, 174
organizational configurational
    systems, 203, 204
organizational strategies, 8, 153, 217
organizational values, form of, 174

panoptic institutions, 102–3, 110
Parsonian structural functionalist
    view, 206
patriarchal system, 116
performance improvement, 136
performance literacy, 136, 148
performance management, 136–7, 147
Petrobas, 126
PHB, *see* Platinum Habib Bank
Platinum Habib Bank, 27
policy implications, 121, 222
Portuguese colonialism, 80
post-acquisition integration, 44, 46–7
post-agreement implementation, 195
post-apartheid labour legislations, 184
post-colonial theory, 98, 101, 119
poverty, 3, 12, 73, 75–6, 84, 103, 128,
    153, 161, 167, 171, 208, 222–3
  highest levels, 73, 75, 159
  reduction, 3, 76, 84, 167
  unemployment and, 103, 161, 223
pre-merger communication, 30
Prescribed Minimum Benefit
    Amendment, 55
prison institutions, 102
privatization
  aspects of, 88
  associated changes, 75
  changes in governance, 80
  criticisms, 79
  currency devaluation, 78
  effects, 87
  employment conditions, 74–5
  employment equity, 84–7
  employment level, rise in, 74
  future trajectory of, 81
  impact of, 72

privatization – *continued*
  impact on employment, 73, 78–81
  job security, 83–4
  jobs loss, 74
  outsourcing, 74, 81
  part-ownership or leasing, 74
  price liberalization, 78
  reduction in employment rights, 75
  remuneration, 84
  sale of state owned enterprises, 74
  socialist to capitalist economy,
    transition, 73
  standardized pay systems, 81
  of state assets, 72
  state owned companies, 78
  sugar and textile industries, 79
  tariff barriers, 79
  transport sector, 80
  unionization, 81–3
  wages and working conditions,
    improvements, 79
procedural injustice, 12, 185, 190–3,
  195–6
  decision-making structure, 191
  effectiveness of actions, 197
  feeling of unfairness, 191
  negotiation process, 191
  pre-agreement evaluation, 191
procedural justice, 180, 183–5
  antecedents and determinants of,
    181
  conflict and misunderstanding, 184
  cross-cultural training, 184
Protea Groups, 137
public sector employment, 81–7
  additional benefits, 84
  bargaining rights, 82, 83
  casual workers, 82
  employment equity, 84–7
  employment relations, 86*t*
  essential services, 82
  fixed salary for life, 84
  further advantage, 84
  health insurance, 84
  job security, 83–4
  promotion prospects, 84
  remuneration, 84
  retirement pensions, 84

  sugar cane and cashew nut
    industries, 83
  unionization, 81–3
public services, marketization of, 74
purposive and snowball techniques,
  24

qualitative approach, 129, 139, 160
Quanxi, 156

racial disparities, 147
racial divisions, 85
racism, 85, 188
rebel movement, 76
regression analysis tests, 66
regulatory environment, 137–8
relationship-building, 9–10, 156–7,
  165, 176, 205
remuneration, 18, 28, 73, 141, 146
renaissance element, 141
replication logic, 22
resource-based theory, 58
resource dependency, 152, 155, 158,
  160, 176
Return on Investment (ROI), 190

SABMiller, 126, 128, 135, 137, 139,
  149
SADC, *see* Southern African
    Development Community
SAP, *see* structural adjustment
    programme
Sappi, 126
Sasol, 126, 135
scholarship funding, 166
Science direct (online database), 26
Sectoral interaction, 167
sexually transmitted infections, 60–1
shareholder orientation, 4, 104
Sierra Leone, 88
skill development, 119, 172
  market-driven approach, 141
skills formation, 148
Skye Bank, 29, 35–6, 45
  merger, 36
snowball sampling, 77
social benefits, 169
social capital, 130
social connectivity, 209

social construction system, 214
social injustices, 171
social investment projects, 166
socialist command policy, *see* Ujamaa
social licence model, 177
social local values, elements of, 223
social organizational systems, 156
social organizations, nature of, 8, 156
social transformations, 102
socio-economic development, 127–9
socio-economic reforms, 156
solidarity, 130, 157, 180, 183
South African bank, 11, 209–10, 212,
    217–21
  auditing activities, 212
  corporate culture, 218
  customers, 212
  electronic banking services, 213
  employees age, 219
  intention, 212
  investors, 212
  management practices, 218*t*
  objective, 213
  performance appraisal, 218*t*
  promotion, 219
  recruitment and selection, 218*t*
  retail banking, 213
  rewards, 218*t*
  standard employment conditions,
    220
  trade unions, 218*t*
  training, 212, 218*t*
  union membership, 220
South Africanisation of the African
    economy, 181
Southern African Development
    Community, 223
Spring Bank merger, 35–6
stakeholder orientation, 8, 152, 156
stakeholder partnerships, 154–5, 168
stakeholder relationships, 9–10
Standard Bank, 11, 104, 107–10,
    113–19
  African values, 115
  appraisal system, 110
  career development, 114
  compliance, 115
  employees evaluation, 110
  group appraisal, 110

HR functions, 118
HR policies application, 116
HR policies via group initiatives, 119
HR recruitment, 114
key decisions implementation, 108
knowledge appropriation, 108
multi-skilling, 113–14
organizational setting, 107–8
reporting systems, 107
security checks, 107
strategic management, 107
structural rigidity, 110
team appraisal, 110
vision of *Indaba* and *Ubuntu*, 115
Sterling Bank, 29, 35–6, 43–4
  communication at, 29
  merger, 29, 36
  novation integration, 36
STI, *see* sexually transmitted infections
stock exchanges, institutionalization
    of, 217
stock market ethos, 104
strategic alliances, 186
strategic mix, 166
structural adjustment policies, 72
structural adjustment programme, 12,
    72, 149
structural convergence, 203
subsidiary operations, 161, 170, 203,
    221
subsidiary relations, 98–9, 213
Sun International, 137
super-panopticon, 108, 115
surveillance at workplaces, 221
surveillance of HR in the workplace,
    97
surveillance software, 216
sustainability behaviour, 154
sustainability framework, 171
sustainability practices, responsive
    behaviour, 154
sustainable development, 11, 152–8,
    164, 168–70, 175–6
  global transition of, 168
  home-based, 154
  implementation of, 152, 176
  local communities, 153
  of mineral resources, 170
  mining MNEs, 152

sustainable development – *continued*
    stakeholders' orientation, 155
    western best practices, 175
sustainable management, 7–9

talent management, 12, 129, 140–6
    retention of needed talent, 146
    skills requirement, 141
    in transitional economy, 141*t*
    uncertainty environment, 140
task-oriented flexibility, 206
Tata, 126, 132, 138
technological growth, 203
technological surveillance, 98
Telkom (Pty) Ltd, 186
temporary shelters, 166
thrive for efficiency, 213
The Times, 127
total quality management, 133
tourism growth, 128
trade liberalization, 159
trade unions, 57, 59, 62, 66, 81, 132,
    149, 220
traditionalism, element of, 103
transformational engagement process,
    223
transitional business behaviour, 9
transitional economy, 100, 140–1
transnational organization, 101
triangulation, 162
tribalism, 188
trust erosion, 122
t-test, 67

UBA, *see* United Bank for Africa
Ubuntu, 109, 115–16, 138, 156–9,
    161–2, 164–6, 173–4
Ujamaa (socialist command system),
    103, 159, 208
unemployment, 12, 80, 85, 103, 161,
    173, 188, 208, 222–3

UN Global Compact, 153, 156, 175,
    223
unionization, 73–4, 78, 81–3, 87
union strength, 73
United Bank for Africa, 28
United States Agency for International
    Development, 55, 77
Unity Bank
    communication, 31
    merger, 35
UN report of looting mineral
    resources, 185
US financial business models, 205
US–German Generally Accepted
    Accounting Principles (GAAP),
    205

VCT programmes, *see* Voluntary
    counselling and testing
VILLAGE SQUARE, 30
vocational training, 84, 87
Vodacom, 186–95
Voluntary counselling and testing,
    60–1

Wall Street, 205
Wema Bank, 24, 26, 28, 30
western instrumentalism, 131, 139
western management theories, 130
western managerial practices, 137
Winecon (online database), 26
Wipro, 126
workplace inequalities, 148
work standardization, 119
World Bank, 2, 54–5, 72, 75, 77–9, 81,
    103, 140, 149
World Trade Organization (WTO), 2,
    205

zero-hour contract, 206

Printed and bound in Great Britain by
CPI Group (UK) Ltd, Croydon, CR0 4YY